FOOD AND AGRICULTURAL POLICY

With a foreword by Don Paarlberg

American Enterprise Institute for Public Policy Research
Washington, D.C.

Library of Congress Cataloging in Publication Data

Conference on Food and Agricultural Policy, Washington,
    D.C., 1977.
    Food and agricultural policy.

    (AEI symposia ; 77C)
    Papers presented at the Conference on Food and
Agricultural Policy held in Washington, D.C.,
March 10-11, 1977.
        1. Agriculture and state—United States—Congresses.
2. Food supply—Congresses. I. Title. II. Series:
American Enterprise Institute for Public Policy Research.
AEI symposia ; 77C.
HD1761.C64   1977   338.1′873   77-27937
ISBN 0-8447-2109-3
ISBN 0-8447-2108-5 pbk.

Printed in the United States of America

MAJOR CONTRIBUTORS

Martin E. Abel
Professor of Agricultural Economics
University of Minnesota

J. Dawson Ahalt
Staff Economist
U.S. Department of Agriculture

Julia C. Bloch
Professional Staff Member
Senate Select Committee on Nutrition and Human Needs

George E. Brandow
Professor Emeritus
Pennsylvania State University

Willard W. Cochrane
Professor of Agricultural Economics
University of Minnesota

Kenneth J. Fedor
Vice President, Economics and Planning
Quaker Oats Company

Richard L. Feltner
President, Federal Intermediate Credit Bank (Louisville)

Paul Findley
United States Congressman, Illinois

Thomas S. Foley
United States Congressman, Washington

Bruce L. Gardner
Professor of Economics
Texas A & M University

W. E. Hamilton
Chief Economist
American Farm Bureau Federation

CONTENTS

FOREWORD

Don Paarlberg

The Conference on Food and Agricultural Policy brought together people of diverse backgrounds, from various parts of the country. Most of them were agricultural economists from the universities. But also present were people from the Congress, the Department of Agriculture, the White House, the farm organizations, agribusiness, consumer groups, and from the press. Though most of the people were professional economists, some were politically oriented; both major political parties were represented. A fairly wide band of the ideological spectrum was in evidence.

The full range of farm and food policy was brought up for examination, but the sharpest focus was price and production policy for the major farm commodities. This was to be expected, since the conference was held while the executive branch of the government was shaping up its position on a new farm bill, and the agricultural committees of the Congress were already deeply involved in legislative deliberations.

I

For forty years there have been two fundamental farm policy positions. One favored a powerful role for government in the pricing and production of farm commodities. The other favored a strong role for the individual.

The major development in this conference was growing evidence that these two positions are converging. The old advocates of a strong government role in agriculture have lost some of their ardor and some of their clout. The old free market forces are now willing to accept a greater degree of government intervention than they were in former times. The old farm policy issue has been "de-escalated." Perhaps the statute of limitations is operating. Some of the most zealous protagonists have disappeared from the scene, and their places have been taken by younger, less indoctrinated people.

Speakers at the conference, both during the daytime sessions and the evening Round Table, were chosen so as to provide a clash between opposing points of view. To the astonishment of many, these sessions produced much agreement.

1

Several of those in attendance pointed out that the convergence on farm policy issues was not limited to the participants in this conference, but that the farm organizations were also moving perceptibly toward one another. So are the political parties. In earlier presidential campaigns, farm policy matters had been an important issue, but such was not the case in 1976.

The respective roles of the individual and of the government in the production and pricing of farm products remain important public issues. But the degree of confrontation has perceptibly abated.

The cause of this de-escalation was considered but not agreed upon. Perhaps the generally good experience with individual decision making during 1973–1976 served to weaken the belief that free markets meant disaster. Perhaps the volatility of prices in recent years and the concern about the permanence of the newfound markets has led free-market advocates to accept some degree of federal intervention, at least as a standby provision. In any case, it appears that an opportunity has been provided to move this old issue away from the center of the stage and off toward the wings, where it can more easily be resolved.

Fortunately, the conference lifted up the fact that there is an area within which accommodation can be found. Agricultural prospects appear to be such that the protagonists can, in some measure, retreat with honor from their former rigid ideological positions. The mood of the conference was that any such move should be welcomed.

II

On a number of points there was general agreement, not as expressed by vote but rather as a "sense of the meeting."

There was considerable discussion of the structure of agriculture as this relates to commodity legislation. It quickly appeared that the facts are at variance with the political stereotype. There was agreement with Gale Johnson's point that "at the present time half or more of the incomes of farm people come from nonfarm jobs." Bruce Gardner observed that "the mainstream commercial producers of farm products are no longer poor people." This view was corroborated by George Brandow and went unchallenged. Likewise unchallenged was a set of data supplied by Luther Tweeten which showed "that there is a redistribution of income from lower-income people, in general—not just farm people, but throughout society—to high-income farmers through commodity programs." There was general agreement on the existence of a low income problem in agriculture and on the inability of commodity programs to cope with it. Hendrik Houthakker underscored this point.

There was agreement that production control programs have

limited effect on total output of farm products, though no single estimate of this effect was agreed to. Johnson said "by the early 1970s, agricultural output was not significantly different as a result of the various government programs and subsidies from what it would have been in their absence." Tweeten estimated that diverting 15 percent of our cropland may have reduced agricultural output by 5 percent. He also commented on the poor cost effectiveness record of the feed grain program. Some studies showed, he said, that it cost a dollar to remove a dollar's worth of production, "which is about as bad as you can get."

There was some discussion of how we got where we are in our agricultural policies. Tweeten observed that changes in farm policy resulted more from economic crises than from changes in ideology, and that farm policy for commodities was a collection of piecemeal programs. This view was supported by several people and was challenged by none.

One speaker after another referred to difficulties caused by the wide fluctuations in price and income during recent years. The volatility of price and income, rather than a low average level thereof, was seen as the problem. There was general agreement that this volatility would be reduced by carrying larger stocks than were held during recent years. Some government role with respect to the carryover was accepted, but no program specifics won general approval.

Several people stated that loan levels should not be so high as to price us out of world markets. There was no dissent from this proposition. John Schnittker emphasized that such income transfers as were desired should be accomplished through payments rather than by setting loan rates high. This view was generally accepted.

There was agreement that agriculture's economic condition had slipped as compared with a year ago, particularly for wheat. Cattle have been in trouble for some time. Dry weather in the west and in parts of the Great Plains were considered a problem. There was, of course, the continuing low income problem on farms too small to be efficient. But overall, commercial agriculture was not thought to be in distress.

In the evaluation of standards by which loan and target levels should be set, parity had no defenders. The cost of production fared little better. Particularly troublesome was the charge for land. Several people pointed out that inclusion of a charge for land would set the stage for a spiral of production costs and price supports. Gene Hamilton of the Farm Bureau had particular concern about this problem.

III

On a number of subjects there was disagreement, varied in degree and in the vigor with which the differences were expressed. On world food prospects, Ed Schuh discounted the Malthusian specter, at least in the next decade or so. Most other speakers declined to take positions on this subject, which was conceded to be enormously important with regard to American farm policy.

An issue that came up repeatedly was whether the rate of growth in the efficiency of agricultural production had slowed. If it had, the effect on price, production, and policy could be profound. Johnson said that agricultural efficiency continues to advance. Schuh had his doubts about this as far as the United States was concerned but was hopeful regarding increased productivity in the developing countries. World expenditures on agricultural research, he said, had tripled in real terms from 1959 to 1974, leading to the view that efficiency may increase. Jim Hildreth expressed concern whether the productivity of American agriculture was slacking off.

Foreign trade prospects, which can also be expected to have strong influence on American farm policy, were perhaps more a subject of uncertainty than of disagreement. Few firm assessments were offered. As regards further trade liberalization, there was full agreement with Clayton Yeutter's view that the quest of liberal trade should be vigorously pursued. But there was disagreement over the prospects for success.

Several issues, frequently debated among agricultural economists, came up for discussion, without being moved toward resolution. A disagreement arose between Schuh and Trezise over the effect of flexible exchange rates on agricultural trade. Likewise, there was a disagreement whether the labor supply in agriculture was excessive; Tweeten said it was, but Johnson had doubts.

A spirited debate arose as to the boom in farm land values and the possible effect on farm policy. Yeutter expressed concern whether recent buyers with limited equity could meet the cash flow problem. This concern was shared, as was the concern that efforts to help these people with higher loans and targets might price us out of the world market. On the other hand, some of the group thought the rising tide of inflation would justify the advance of farmland prices. Howard Hjort raised a question that went unanswered: Are high farm real estate values making it too difficult for a young man to get started in farming? Do we want to have a system where ownership and operation are separated?

There was a spirited debate on the quality of the food supply. Julia Bloch of the Senate Select Committee on Nutrition was critical both of the quality of the diet and of problems in distribution. Ellen Haas of the Community Nutrition Institute supported Bloch in this view. The agricultural economists were unconvinced. The central issue, on which no agreement was reached, was the degree to which education on the one hand and government coercion on the other should be used in efforts to improve the diet.

Another dispute arose as to the role of the agribusiness in the distribution and pricing of food. Dawson Ahalt, Joel Popkin, and Ken Fedor supplied data on the performance of the food business, which generally gave the industry passing marks. But consumer-oriented members of the conference appeared unconvinced. The entire group seemed to agree that the consumer is not the adversary.

To those who work closely with farm policy, the disagreements were predictable and were less vociferous than usual. The agreements, on the other hand, were somewhat of a surprise and were closer than anticipated.

IV

The final session of the conference was intended to provide a confrontation of rival views. Hence it offered papers by Don Paarlberg, Republican, and John Schnittker, Democrat, both former officials of the Department of Agriculture. Discussants were Willard Cochrane, economic adviser to a Democratic secretary of agriculture, and Hyde Murray, Republican counsel to the House Agriculture Committee.

Surprisingly, Paarlberg and Schnittker expressed views more notable for their similarities than for their differences. Both advocated a market-oriented approach, with competitive pricing. Both were ready to accept some degree of government intervention in production and pricing if supplies became excessive. Schnittker was somewhat more ready to transfer income into agriculture, to set aside acreage, to operate a grain reserve program, and to enter into agreements of various kinds with other countries.

Cochrane observed that "there's a hell of a big rapprochement going on here," and associated himself with it. He said that "the market is an efficient allocator of productive resources, and should be relied upon, wherever possible, to allocate those resources; but, too, the market can produce some highly inequitable situations."

Murray made what was undoubtedly the liveliest presentation of the conference. He stated that market orientation was dead, that it had died on November 3, 1976—election day. He reported that members of the House Agricultural Committee were ready to vote for high loans and high targets, bringing the cost of farm programs to fantastically high levels. He said that an informal alliance had been worked out between farm and nonfarm groups, associating a generous food stamp program with high farm price supports in a log-rolling operation.

Schnittker warned that loan levels should not be linked to production costs. "They should follow a different drummer," he said. This drummer he identified as world market prices. The group appeared to agree.

The meeting drifted into speculations as to what kind of commodity legislation would be forthcoming. Murray feared the worst, that is, costly farm programs that price commodities out of markets. The short-run attractiveness of high price supports would take precedence over the long-run adverse consequences thereof. Paarlberg was more hopeful, counting on the executive branch to hold the line. Schnittker said that those who believed in economically sound farm legislation would have to fight hard to keep the Congress from enacting a bad law. Most people offered no prognosis.

The conference accomplished at least one significant result: it defined the protagonists involved in the debate on commodity programs. It is not the Democrats versus the Republicans, as once was the case. It is not the farmers versus the consumers, as some say it now is. The real issue is between the White House, which has concern for the entire economy, and the Congress, where the special interests are strongly entrenched.

Bruce Gardner probably best summed up the situation. He commented that we economists often seek an economic rationale for farm programs. But, he observed, "the purpose of legislation is better described in political terms. And the purpose is to take from those who have less political clout and give to those who have more." Thus has the farm policy issue evolved—or degenerated—in recent years.

PART ONE

BACKGROUND AND STATUS

FOOD PRODUCTION AND MARKETING: A REVIEW OF ECONOMIC DEVELOPMENTS IN AGRICULTURE

D. Gale Johnson

It is not an easy task to present a review of economic developments in U.S. agriculture within the confines of a single paper. Obviously one must be selective and matters that I consider to be of major significance may well exclude some that others believe to be important. What I shall try to do is to highlight several significant developments affecting American agriculture during the past quarter century—roughly the period since 1950—and to indicate the major responses to those developments.

The most fundamental and pervasive development affecting American agriculture during the past quarter century has been economic growth. The characteristics of income elasticities of demand and resource substitutions and augmentations are such that agriculture's share of the nation's employment of labor and capital and its share of gross national product decline as per capita incomes increase.[1] Agriculture cannot escape this consequence of economic growth, no matter whether one defines *agriculture* as "the traditional land, labor, and capital employed on farms"; or as "all resources used on farms"; or as "all activities involved in the production, processing, transportation, and marketing of food and fiber products."[2]

---

[1] For further discussion, see D. Gale Johnson, *World Agriculture in Disarray* (New York: Franklin Watts, 1973), chap. 5.

[2] Data are available on the total value of food and fiber output of the United States for 1958–1974 in 1967 dollars. This includes consumer expenditures on food, agricultural exports, and manufactured products utilizing agricultural products (such as cotton) as input. If these values are divided by the gross national product in 1958 dollars, the percentages are as follows: 1958, 20.1 percent; 1970, 16.7 percent; 1974, 15.6 percent. Consumer expenditures on food accounted for 72 to 78 percent of the total value of food and fiber output. In current dollars, the percentages of disposable income spent on food have been: 1960, 20.0 percent; 1970, 16.2 percent; 1974, 16.8 percent. Sources: Donald D. Durost and James E. Kirkley, "Productivity Changes in the Food and Fiber System, 1958–74," *Agricultural Economics Research*, vol. 28, no. 4 (October 1976), p. 131, and U.S. Department of Agriculture, *Food Consumption, Prices and Expenditures*, Supplement for 1974 to Agricultural Economic Report no. 138, p. 77.

Since the activities of food and fiber production are space related and widely dispersed, the relative decline of agriculture and its slow absolute growth present adjustment problems. Fortunately, the degree to which agricultural resources are bound by space changes with economic growth. When nonfarm-produced inputs account for an increasing share of farm output, the importance of land as a factor of production declines. Similarly the relative importance of labor that must perform its services in a particular location has declined. Thus one would expect that as agriculture becomes a progressively smaller component of national income, adjustment to changing conditions becomes less difficult.

Other features of economic growth may be equally important in easing agriculture's adjustment to changing conditions. The great expansion of communication media available to farm people has been important. Thanks to rural free delivery of mail and to radio and television, farm people have basically the same access to ideas and knowledge as city dwellers. Their access to education has also improved with economic growth. And cheaper and more rapid forms of transportation have helped integrate rural and urban communities. Many of these trends were well underway before World War II, but the changes since the war have been considerable, too.

Because of these changes farm people now have more options and more flexible margins available to them. For example, proper investments in land can increase its productivity substantially. And varying combinations of inputs can be used to bring about the same output from a given piece of land. While the most flexible margins probably apply to annually purchased inputs, relatively long-lived assets, such as tractors and combines, can also be effectively depreciated at different rates. Perhaps most important in terms of personal welfare, farm families now have a wide variety of employment alternatives, in addition to farm labor and management.

Although some consequences of economic growth have required significant adjustments on the part of farm people, other consequences have increased their capacity to adjust and have lowered the costs of adjustment. Put another way, it is now less difficult and painful for farm people to share in rising real per capita incomes than it was twenty-five years ago.

This paper will cover seven major economic developments affecting American agriculture since 1950. Each has implications for the future directions of appropriate farm policies and the welfare of farm people, though this paper will not address food and agricultural policies. The essential point to recognize about the developments is that they are ongoing. They must, therefore, be taken as underlying assumptions in the formulation of future agricultural policies.

Increased Importance of Nonfarm Incomes

In most recent years approximately half of the income of farm families has derived from nonfarm sources.[3] In 1975 agriculture, as a business, generated a gross income of $100 billion, but in the same year rural families earned another $100 billion by other means. Since 1967 half or more of the income of the farm population has come from nonfarm sources.[5] The only exception was 1973, when net farm operator income was nearly 80 percent above the previous year. In 1950 only 31 percent of the income of the farm population came from nonfarm sources; in 1960, 39 percent.[6] Continuous data on the off-farm income of farm operators have been available only since 1960. In 1960 off-farm income accounted for 43 percent of the total income of farm operators; in 1970, 57 percent; and in 1975, 56 percent.[7]

The estimates of the income of farm operators from farm operations and off-farm sources can be broken down according to sales classes. In 1975 only farms with sales of more than $20,000 took in more income from their farming operations than from other sources. The number of such farms was 1,014,000 (36 percent of all farms). For farm operator families in the $40,000-to-$99,999 range, off-farm income accounted for only 27 percent of total family income. Eighty-nine percent of total cash receipts from farming is on farms with sales in excess of $20,000. For the average farm family with cash receipts of $20,000 or more, off-farm income accounted for 26.5 percent of net family income. In 1960 the largest 38 percent of the farms (representing 87 percent of the total sales) obtained only 20 percent of their incomes from off-farm sources. We may conclude from these data that, in general, off-farm income has steadily become a larger portion of overall income for farmers, regardless of the size of their operation.[8] Even farm

---

[3] All of the data in this section may be found in Department of Agriculture, *Farm Income Statistics*, Statistical Bulletin no. 557, July 1976.

[4] Ibid., p. 40.

[5] The Economic Research Service (U.S. Department of Agriculture) provides two different estimates of farm and nonfarm income of farm people. The one above refers to the income (by sources) of all persons living on farms. It therefore includes hired farm workers and farm operators who live on their own farms, but it excludes a substantial number of farm operators who live in nonfarm areas. The series on incomes of farm operator families estimates incomes by source for all farm operators, excluding hired farm workers and their family members, and including those farm operators who do not live on the farms operated.

[6] Ibid.

[7] Off-farm incomes include income from all sources other than the farm operated and thus include some income from farm sources, such as rent or wages from work on other farms.

[8] Ibid., pp. 58–63. Income of farm families is the sum of off-farm income and the net income from farm operations (sales of farm products minus farm expenses).

families with the largest farm operations get much of their income from off-farm sources.

But the most striking income development for farm families since 1960 has been the remarkable increase in both the relative and the real incomes of families operating small farms. In 1960 families with farm sales of less than $5,000 had incomes of less than two-fifths that of families in the $20,000-to-$39,999 bracket. In 1975 families with sales of less than $10,000 had incomes three-fifths as large as those of families with sales of $40,000 to $99,999.[9] This reduction in income disparity came about primarily because families on the smaller farms had found alternative uses for their labor.[10]

During the 1960s the per capita disposable income of the farm population compared with that of the nonfarm population rose from less than 54 percent (the average for 1959–1961) to more than 74 percent (the average of 1969–1971). In 1975 the percentage was almost 90. Of the total increase in the incomes of the farm population from 1960 to 1970, 62 percent derived from nonfarm sources.[11] Much of the improvement in the relative income of farm families during the 1960s resulted from increased nonfarm earnings rather than from increased agricultural earnings. Furthermore, a large part of the increase in the marginal productivity of farm labor resulted from changing factor proportions. The changing factor proportions were themselves a result of a migration of persons from farms and the diversion of farm labor into nonagricultural employment. (This aspect of the resource adjustment process will be discussed more in detail in the next part.)

In the formulation of farm commodity policies, the government should bear in mind that only 36 percent of farms are operated by families receiving more than half of their income directly from the farm. These families would be the only ones to realize substantial benefit from the subsidies government programs might involve.

The Labor Market

There has been a striking change in the integration of the farm and nonfarm labor markets during the past quarter century. This integration has taken two forms. One has been the growing tendency of the farm people to work at nonfarm jobs. The other has been the growing portion of those who work at farm jobs not to reside on farms. These two changes

[9] Ibid., p. 62. In deflated dollars $10,000 in 1975 was approximately the same as $5,000 in 1960.

[10] We do not know how many of the 1,468,000 families on farms with less than $10,000 sales were among the 2,465,000 families on farms with less than $5,000 in sales in 1960.

[11] Ibid., p. 42.

coincided with a high migration rate from farm to nonfarm residences during the 1950s and the 1960s. During those decades the annual migration rate from farms exceeded 5 percent. Interestingly enough, the migration rates were actually slightly higher during the 1960s than in the 1950s even though the relative income position of farm people had improved during the 1960s.

In 1960 the percentage of the employed farm population working in nonagricultural industries was 33; in 1970, 44; and 1975, 47. Thus by 1975 almost half of all employed farm residents worked at other than farm occupations.[12]

Looking at the reverse side of the coin, more farm jobs are today being held by nonfarm residents than ever before. In 1960 a quarter of those employed in agriculture were nonfarm residents; in 1970, 38 percent; and in 1975, 42 percent.[13] Nearly one out of six farm operators have nonfarm residences. In 1975 these people earned approximately a sixth of total net farm income.[14]

If we jointly consider the distribution of employment of farm residents by farm and nonfarm occupations and the distribution of the residences of those who do farm work, it is obvious that the labor markets for farm people and for farm workers can no longer be described accurately apart from the rest of the economy. Considering that about half of the labor force living on farms have nonfarm jobs and that more than two fifths of farm workers are nonfarm residents, elasticity of supply of labor to agriculture has obviously increased since the end of World War II. For all practical purposes the economic fate of persons living on farms is no longer so closely tied to events affecting agriculture as it used to be.

Elimination of Excess Resources in Agriculture

My third major conclusion is that most, if not all, of what were thought to be excess farm resources had, by 1972, been put back to use.[15] Land

---

[12] U.S. Department of Commerce and U.S. Department of Agriculture, *Farm Population*, Series Census-ERS, P-27, no. 41 (June 1971) and no. 47 (September 1976). Comparable data are not available for 1950 due to the change in the census definition of a farm in 1960. On the basis of a comparable definition of a farm in 1950 and 1960, the portion of the employed workers living on farms in nonagricultural jobs increased from 30 percent in 1950 to 42.5 percent in 1960 (P-27, nos. 24 and 28).

[13] *Farm Population*, P-27, nos. 21 and 47.

[14] Department of Agriculture, *Farm Income Statistics*, p. 40.

[15] The term *excess resources* is defined as "resources that are not fully employed because, at politically acceptable price levels, output would exceed the quantity demanded." A similar term is *excess productive capacity* which could be defined as "the difference between the potential supply and the amount demanded at the politically determined prices and incomes."

had been diverted from current production during 1972 and many previous years. In fact, 1972 was nearly a record year for land diversion—almost 62 million acres. But, according to my estimates, by 1973 the acreage diversion programs had reduced the area devoted to the major crops by less than 25 million acres, and possibly by less than 20 million acres. The return of this land to production, accompanied by other necessary inputs, should have increased gross farm production by about 2 percent as of the early 1970s.[16] (This estimate assumes that real prices for crops remained more or less unchanged.) Obviously with the significant increase in real crop prices in 1973, 1974, and 1975, the actual increase in acreage was expected to exceed 20–25 million acres. In fact, the increase in cropland harvested between 1972 and 1975 was 41 million acres.[17] But this figure does not approach the 62 million acres diverted in 1972. (Crop failure was essentially the same in the two years—in 1975 it was a million acres less than in 1972.) Thus farmers responded to the expected price rises in 1975 by expanding cultivated acreage. If my estimates are correct, the acreage expansion for that year was approximately 20 million acres. This is about 7 percent of the cropland I estimated would have been harvested in 1972 without the acreage diversion programs, assuming the real crop prices of the early 1970s.

Even if my estimate of the effects of acreage diversion programs on the value of crop output is somewhat high or low, it is much closer to the mark than estimates of the effect of acreage diversion on farm output of nearly 7 percent in the late 1960s.[18]

Despite the expectation of higher real crop prices, total crop production went up by only 8 percent between 1972 and 1975. Obviously weather could have affected these crop yields, but the fact remains that crop production *per acre of cropland* (including crop failure and summer fallow) was essentially the same in 1972 as in 1975.[19]

---

[16] D. Gale Johnson, *Farm Commodity Programs: An Opportunity for Change* (Washington, D.C.: American Enterprise Institute, 1973), pp. 33–42.

[17] Economic Research Service, U.S. Department of Agriculture, *Changes in Farm Production and Efficiency*, Statistical Bulletin no. 561 (September 1976), p. 17.

[18] Leroy Quance and Luther Tweeten, "Excess Capacity and Adjustment Potentials in U.S. Agriculture," *Agricultural Economics Research*, vol. 24, no. 3 (July 1972), p. 60. In testimony before the Senate Committee on Agriculture and Forestry in July 1976, Tweeten said, "In short, 1972 acreage diversion reduced total farm output between 2 percent and 10 percent. The best estimate is perhaps 5 percent."

[19] If the change in acreage between 1972 and 1975 is measured by cropland used for crops (cropland harvested, crop failure, and cultivated summer fallow) rather than for harvested cropland alone, the increase in cropland was only 33 million acres. The area of summer fallow declined by 7 million acres. A large part of the land classified as diverted in 1972 was cultivated summer fallow which farmers had no intention of seeding that year. For change in cropland used for crops, see U.S. Department of Agriculture, *Changes in Farm Production and Efficiency*, p. 17.

Besides land diversion, other government farm policies could reasonably be said to have brought about an absorption of excess production capacity. Price support activities of the Commodity Credit Corporation had resulted in inventory accumulations; export programs had required subsidies of various sizes. But during 1970, 1971, and 1972, inventories held by the CCC were actually reduced, thus adding supplies to the market, not taking them away.[20] Experience since 1972 indicates that not all transactions under Public Law 480 (food aid) should be regarded solely as outlets for unwanted agricultural products. In recent years the quantities of agricultural products shipped under P.L. 480 have been only about half of the level of the early 1970s. It is reasonable to assume that the reduction of CCC inventories in the period 1970–1971 represented an offsetting reaction to increased demand. Similarly, there were some export subsidies paid in 1970 and 1971, but by June of 1972 these were minimal.[21]

Nevertheless, direct governmental payments to farmers exceeded $3 billion annually in 1970, 1971, and 1972. If there were few excess resources in agriculture, why were payments equal to 25 to 30 percent of net farm operator income necessary? Three observations may help explain the situation. First, the payments did not represent an equal addition to net farm operator incomes. In other words, farmers had incurred a loss of income because of acreage diversion, which was required for receipt of most of the payments. I have estimated that the increase in net farm income resulting from this type of payment was approximately $1.5 billion annually during the early 1970s, or sometihng less than half of the payments made.[22] Admittedly, this is a crude estimate, but unquestionably some real diversion had occurred. And farmers who participated in the voluntary programs were induced to increase yields on the land actually cropped. Some amount went directly to landlords and was not retained by farm operators.[23]

Second, a large part of the increase in net income represented added income or rent to land and not to mobile factors such as labor, current inputs, and capital equipment. Thus the payments did not go

---

[20] For data on government farm program operations, see F. J. Nelson and Willard W. Cochrane, "Economic Consequences of Federal Farm Commodity Programs, 1953–72," *Agricultural Economics Research*, vol. 28, no. 2 (April 1976), pp. 54–55.

[21] In 1971–1972 total agricultural exports were $8.0 billion; export subsidies cost $237 million (primarily for wheat, rice, peanuts, and tobacco). Source: U.S. Department of Agriculture, *FATUS*, May 1975, p. 74.

[22] U.S. Department of Agriculture, *Farm Commodity Programs*, pp. 45–49.

[23] Out of total government payments to farmers in 1972 of $3,961 million, $507 million went directly to landlords. See U.S. Department of Agriculture, *Farm Income Statistics*, pp. 50, 63.

primarily to hold resources in agriculture but to enhance the returns to those who held land.

Third, it is significant that the size of the payments was roughly equal to the loss of income of American crop producers because of the over-valuation of the dollar during the first part of the 1970s. Crop products account for approximately 90 percent of U.S. agricultural exports. In 1970 and 1971 the value of production of crops for which exports were an important factor in the price of output was approximately $20 billion. If the U.S. dollar was overvalued by 12 to 15 percent during those years, the dollar price of American crops was about 10 percent of what it should have been had the exchange rate been stable.[24] Thus it is not altogether unreasonable to argue that the government payments, after taking into account the real costs imposed upon farmers, were of approximately the same order as the income loss imposed on crop producers by the overvaluation of the dollar. This income loss was probably about $2 billion, roughly equal to the increase in net farm operator income plus the increased income of nonfarm landlords resulting from the payments. Such rough equality, if it did exist, suggests that net farm income might have remained about the same if there had been no over-valuation of the dollar and no farm programs or payments. The one factor that has not been taken into account in this approximation is the effect on farm prices of the increase in farm output due to the return of the diverted acreage to use. As I have argued above, the increase in farm output due to the return of the diverted acreage was probably about 2 percent.

Changes in Comparative Advantage

In most years between 1925 and 1943 the United States was a net importer of agricultural products. In the late 1930s, partly as a result of climatic factors and partly as a result of governmental programs, the value of agricultural imports was almost twice that of exports; during most of the 1950s agricultural imports again exceeded agricultural exports. In fact, not until 1960 did our exports regularly exceed our imports. In 1974, 1975, and 1976 the value of farm exports was roughly double the value of farm imports.[25]

---

[24] To my knowledge, G. Edward Schuh was the first to point out the implications of the overvaluation of the dollar to American agriculture during the 1960s and early 1970s ("The Exchange Rate and U.S. Agriculture," *American Journal of Agricultural Economics*, vol. 56, no. 1 [February 1974], pp. 1–13). Obviously both supply and demand effects need to be considered in estimating the effect of currency overvaluation on the dollar prices of agricultural products.

[25] Historical data on agricultural trade from U.S. Department of Agriculture, *Agricultural Statistics, 1972*, p. 698. Recent years from *FATUS*.

The value of U.S. agricultural exports has increased substantially in recent years. Some have interpreted this to mean that the comparative advantage of agriculture in the United States has improved. It is not immediately obvious that this is the case. The share of agricultural exports of total U.S. exports has increased since the late 1960s—from a low of 16 percent in 1969 to 21 percent in 1975—but agriculture's share of total U.S. exports during 1971–1975 was slightly below any five-year period since 1950.[26]

It is remarkable that the share of agricultural exports in total exports has remained so great since World War II. It is almost double the similar share for Canada. It is also remarkable that the U.S. share in world agricultural trade has increased since 1950—from 12.3 percent in 1951–1955 to 16.3 percent in 1971–1975. While the share of farm exports in total U.S. exports has remained about the same since 1950, the U.S. share in total world exports has declined. In fact, the U.S. share in world agricultural exports has actually risen. The U.S. share of world nonagricultural exports was 20.5 percent in 1951–1955; in 1971–1975, 11.2 percent.[27] Thus given the changes in the world market in terms of the opportunities for exporting agricultural and nonagricultural products, it is probably correct to say that the comparative advantage of U.S. agriculture has improved significantly since World War II.

There has been a major change in the composition of U.S. agricultural exports since 1950. In 1950 cotton and tobacco together accounted for 44 percent of the value of agricultural exports, grains for 29 percent, and oilseeds (including products) 6 percent. By 1960 cotton and tobacco accounted for only 18 percent of agricultural exports and in 1975 only 8 percent. By 1975 grains accounted for 53 percent and oilseeds 20 percent of agricultural exports.[28] Livestock products, including dairy and poultry, have accounted for slightly less than a tenth of agricultural exports for the past two decades. Grains and oilseeds—primarily soybeans—are the critical factors in the export performance of U.S. agriculture.

While there is no simple and accurate measure of the importance of agricultural exports to U.S. agriculture, even rough indicators are valuable. In 1975 exports provided an outlet for 100 million acres (that is, 30 percent of all cropland harvested in the United States).[29] Except for a dip in the 1960s, the percentage of crop output exported has been

[26] Ibid.

[27] U.S. Department of Agriculture, *FATUS*, December 1976, p. 12.

[28] U.S. Department of Agriculture, *U.S. Foreign Agricultural Trade Statistical Report*, annual supplement to *FATUS*, fiscal years 1974 and 1975.

[29] U.S. Department of Agriculture, *Changes in Farm Production and Efficiency*, p. 16.

increasing steadily since 1950 when the percentage was about 15. If the values of agricultural exports are compared with cash receipts from marketings less farm purchases of feed and livestocks, the percentage has increased from 12 percent in 1950 to 30 percent in 1975.[30] Another rough measure of the importance of agricultural exports is the percentage of the output of various crops that were exported from the 1975 crop—feed grains, 25; wheat and flour, 55; soybeans, 50; tobacco, 30; and cotton, 40.[31]

This rather detailed depiction of the importance of agricultural exports should serve to emphasize one extremely important point: U.S. agriculture, particularly in the Corn Belt and the Great Plains, has now become quite dependent upon international trade for its economic well-being. One can only hope that this heavy regional dependence is recognized as farm commodity policies evolve in the years ahead.

Marketing

Because of an oversight on my part, I permitted the title assigned to me to include the word *marketing*. About all I know about marketing is that after landlords and money lenders, the next most maligned group in any society comprises those involved in buying and selling—trafficking in the product of others—the marketing agencies. The processors and marketers of farm products are always considered fair game by Congress and the secretary of agriculture. When food prices increase, or do not fall as fast as farm prices decline, the scapegoat is usually the packers, canners, wholesalers, and retailers.

There do not appear to have been many striking changes in the marketing of farm products in the past twenty years. But there does seem to be more marketing. If the marketing bill for food products is deflated by the implicit price deflator for the gross national product, the 1974 marketing bill is about 37 percent greater than in 1958 while the quantity of food consumed increased by 30 percent.[32] Naturally, we assume that the factor prices in marketing increased at the same rate as factor prices generally. Casual observation suggests that the marketing activity has expanded more rapidly than consumer expenditures for

---

[30] U.S. Department of Agriculture, *Farm Income Statistics*, pp. 44, 48 for net cash receipts.

[31] U.S. Department of Agriculture, *FATUS*, October 1976, pp. 5–6.

[32] U.S. Department of Agriculture, *1975 Handbook of Agricultural Charts*, Agricultural Handbook no. 491, p. 27 for marketing bill and p. 36 for food consumption. Change in food consumption from 1958 to 1960 estimated by author to be 5 percent.

food. A larger percentage of meals today are eaten away from home; foods sold in retail stores are often more processed now than they would have been twenty years ago; and the chances of their being packaged are greater, too. In 1974 the costs of packaging materials were 12 percent of the total food marketing bill and were 50 percent greater than the cost of transporting the food; they were more than four times the expenditures on advertising, and nearly four times the after-tax corporate profits of the food marketing sector.[33]

Recently the Council on Wage and Price Stability published a report on the responsiveness of wholesale and retail food prices to changes in farm prices and other costs. The report concluded that responses to changing costs at either the wholesale or the retail level are probably not symmetrical. In other words, cost decreases at, say, the farm level are reflected just as quickly and fully as cost increases.[34] Neither response is immediate.

A study was made of the impact of changes in farm value on the retail price of twenty-two products, such as choice beef, butter, apples, and lettuce. The data indicated that half of the total impact of changes in farm value on retail prices occurred in as little as 0.8 month (lettuce) and as long as 4.6 months (long grain rice). The median period was 2.4 months.

There is little agreement about the efficiency and competitiveness of the food and agricultural marketing sector. Most of the disagreement, in my opinion, results from prejudice and misinformation rather than careful analysis. There is no evidence of excessive profits; in fact, the profit data make one wonder how the sector is able to attract adequate capital.

Some changes in recent years indicate a high degree of competition. The largest slaughterers of beef no longer include the names of the former Big Four. Within the last two years, an important Chicago local grocery chain went out of business, and a large regional grocery chain closed all of its operations in the city. Numerous other instances could be noted.

---

[33] Ibid., pp. 27, 30.

[34] For the twenty-two commodities there were twelve cases in which there was no significant difference in the response to increased and decreased farm prices; in two cases the response to falling farm prices was greater than to increases and in eight cases there was a significant difference in the response to increased farm prices compared to decreased farm prices. The study covered the period from 1960 through 1970. Council on Wage and Price Stability, "The Responsiveness of Wholesale and Retail Prices to Changes in the Costs of Food Production and Distribution," Staff Report, November 1976. The analysis was undertaken by Dale Heien, "A Study of the Relationship between Farm-Level Prices and Retail Food Prices," September 1976.

Has Productivity Growth Slowed Down?

In 1975 a committee of the National Academy of Sciences issued a report, *Agricultural Production Efficiency*. This report is often interpreted as concluding that agricultural productivity growth has slowed during the past decade. While it may, in fact, be true that growth has slowed, that was not the conclusion of the report. The most frequently quoted paragraph is the following:[35]

> Clouds on the horizon do indeed cast doubt upon our national ability to produce all the food we and the world market require, especially if food prices are to remain at approximately their present portion of the citizen's pay checks. The clouds are yet small; we cannot be sure how significant they may turn out to be. . . . The public must realize that new conditions, such as the supply and cost of energy and the rate of production of new knowledge and technology, are challenging our access to the plentiful supply of low-cost food that has dominated our attitudes towards agriculture over the past quarter century.

The report does present evidence to suggest diminishing marginal and average returns to single variables, such as crop yields per acre as a function of fertilizer used or egg production per hen. But these relationships do not "prove" that total factor productivity has declined. If output per unit of fertilizer declines as more fertilizer is used, there may still be sufficient savings of other inputs as yield per acre increases to offset the cost of the diminishing return on fertilizer. This may not be the case, but average or marginal productivities of single inputs are insufficient to explain changes in total factor productivity.

I have seen no references to chapter 2 of the committee's report, a circumstance that I find troubling since I wrote most of that chapter. The basic thrust of the chapter is that we know far less than we think we know about past changes in factor productivity in agriculture. The series that we all seem to depend on, the U.S. Department of Agriculture's factor productivity index, has many weaknesses, as Griliches and others have mentioned.[36] Another measure of factor productivity, Denison's, shows almost no decline in productivity growth in 1960–1969 compared

---

[35] Committee on Agricultural Production Efficiency, National Academy of Sciences, *Agricultural Production Efficiency* (Washington, D.C.: National Academy of Sciences, 1975), p. 19.

[36] Z. Griliches, "The Sources of Measured Productivity Growth, U.S. Agriculture, 1940–60," *Journal of Political Economy*, vol. 71 (1963), pp. 331–46.

with 1950–1960, while the USDA index shows growth in the 1960s to be less than half what it was in the 1950s.[37]

My own calculations lead me to doubt that factor productivity declined during the 1960s compared with the 1950s. I took the change in real income of farm operators plus nonoperator landlords per unit of nonpurchased inputs and compared it with the change in the adjusted parity ratio, which included governmental payments in the prices-received index. The increase in purchased inputs was nearly the same for the two decades—22 percent during the 1950s and 24 percent during the 1960s. During the 1950s real income per unit of nonpurchased inputs (owned land, capital, management, and family labor) declined 9 percent while the adjusted parity ratio declined almost 20 percent. During the 1960s, however, the real income per unit of nonpurchased inputs increased 19 percent while the adjusted parity ratio declined by 6 percent. This calculation is consistent with a greater increase in total factor productivity during the 1960s than during the 1950s.[38] My calculation may not necessarily prove that total factor productivity increased, but the result is the same as one would get if the growth of total factor productivity had increased.

My main point is that we really do not know what has happened to the growth of total factor productivity in recent years. Quite frankly, we may be using a data series in which too little time and effort have been invested to justify drawing ironclad conclusions. Input quality adjustments, such as labor quality, have not been taken into account even when it has been easy to do so. Thus we do not know how much increase in total factor productivity is due to qualitative improvements of input that affect the quantity of services.[39]

Farm Land Prices—Reversal of a Trend?

In articles published during the 1950s my colleague Theodore W. Schultz discussed the role of land in agricultural production. In the first of these

---

[37] Edward F. Denison, *Accounting for United States Economic Growth 1929–1969* (Washington, D.C.: Brookings Institution, 1974), p. 288, and U.S. Department of Agriculture, *Changes in Farm Production and Efficiency*, p. 68.

[38] For data on nonpurchased and purchased inputs, see U.S. Department of Agriculture, *Changes in Farm Production and Efficiency*, p. 56, and on income, see U.S. Department of Agriculture, *Farm Income Statistics*, pp. 37, 49.

[39] There is another important consideration that should be included in productivity measurements in agriculture: namely, the effects of climatic conditions. We now know enough about the effects of weather and climate on crop output to improve considerably our measurement of short-term changes in factor productivity.

articles, "The Declining Economic Importance of Agricultural Land,"[40] he developed two propositions:

(1) the aggregate inputs of a community required to produce farm products are declining, and

(2) of the inputs used the proportion represented by land does not increase even as the relative input of human labor declines.

The first proposition was clearly substantiated. In his analysis of the second proposition he found that farmland (excluding buildings) had probably suffered a relative decline in importance in agricultural production between 1910–1914 and the late 1940s.

In his article "Land in Economic Growth" he noted that both the price and the rent rate of land during the period 1910–1956 had declined relative to the prices of farm products and to the prices of all other inputs (except fertilizer).[41] Professor Schultz's data are presented in the first two columns of Table 1; the third and fourth columns present the same data for 1974. The price and income data are annual averages; the land price represents the average of the beginning and end of the year, and buildings are excluded from land value.

As noted above the price of land declined relative to prices received from 1910–1914 to 1956 and also compared with all inputs except fertilizer. The situation in 1974 was significantly different. Compared with either 1910–1914 or 1956 the land price had risen sharply relative to prices received. In fact, the price of land relative to prices received more than doubled between 1956 and 1974. The index of land prices relative to input prices in 1974 was approximately the same for building and fencing, farm machinery, and motor vehicles compared with 1910–1914 and was higher relative to farm supplies and fertilizer. Wages, relative to 1910–1914, were approximately double the land price.

The increase in the ratio of the farmland price to prices received started immediately after World War II. Using the 1910–1914 period as a base, the 1950 index of the land price was almost exactly half the index of prices received. As shown in table 1, the land price index by 1956 had increased to 77 percent of the prices-received index; in 1960 the land price index had moved slightly ahead of the prices-received index. By 1970 the land price index was 1.6 times the prices-received index—almost identical to the relationship in 1974.

While farm product prices fell between 1974 and 1975, the price of farmland continued to increase. At the beginning of 1976 the land

---

[40] Theodore W. Schultz, "The Declining Economic Importance of Agricultural Land," *The Economic Journal*, vol. 61, no. 244 (December 1951), p. 727.

[41] Theodore W. Schultz, "Land in Economic Growth," in Harold G. Halcrow, ed., *Modern Land Policy* (Urbana: University of Illinois Press, 1959), p. 30.

Table 1

U.S. FARM OUTPUT AND INPUT PRICE INDEXES, 1910–1914, 1956, AND 1974

	Increase 1910–1914 to 1956	Relative to Prices Received 1956	Increase 1910–1914 to 1974	1974 Relative to Prices Received
Prices[a] received	235	100	467	100
Prices[a] of inputs				
Farm wages	543	231	1506	322
Building and fencing	374	149	778	167
Farm machinery	329	140	769	165
Farm supplies	279	119	409	88
Fertilizer	150	64	299	64
Motor vehicles	367	156	758	162
Land price per acre[b]	181[c]	77	762[c]	163
Net agricultural income[d]	288	122	759	163

Note: 1974 data used since prices-paid indexes were revised for 1975 and later years and categories for 1975 were not comparable to those used by Mr. Schultz.
[a] The price and income data are annual averages.
[b] Excludes value of buildings.
[c] Average of land prices at beginning and end of calendar year.
[d] Includes net operator income, wages, interest on mortgage debt and rent to nonoperator landlords.
Sources: Theodore W. Schultz, *Economic Growth and Agriculture* (New York: McGraw-Hill, 1968), for first two columns, except net farm income and U.S. Department of Agriculture sources. The third and fourth columns present the same data for 1974.

price index was almost exactly double the prices-received index. One other comparison may be of interest. Between 1970 and 1975 farm wage rates increased by 50 percent; land prices doubled.

The deflated value of farmland and buildings per acre has increased steadily for three decades. During the 1950s the annual rate of increase was 3.2 percent; during the 1960s, 4.3 percent; and from 1970 to 1976, 2.8 percent.[42] Thus the rising real price of farm real estate has not been a recent phenomenon.

Why have land prices increased so significantly since 1950? I do

---

[42] The deflator was the index of prices paid for family living and production. Over the period the relative importance of buildings in the value of farm real estate declined from 28 percent to approximately 15 percent.

not have what I consider to be a satisfactory explanation, but I think the following considerations may be relevant:

(1) Farmland prices were below long-run equilibrium levels in 1950 because of expectation of a severe downturn in farm prices and incomes; in other words, land was undervalued in the short term.

(2) The large increase in land prices during the 1950s represented, therefore, the return of normal expectations for the capitalization of return to land.

(3) During the 1960s two related factors were at work—net agricultural income increased while, at the same time, the share of that income deriving from land or rent increased, too.

(4) The greater value of farm real estate since 1970 is consistent with the increases in net agricultural income, in the share of income going to rent, and in the capitalization rate.

Admittedly these considerations involve a considerable amount of what one might call casual empiricism. But not entirely.

The first observation is not new: I made essentially the same point in an article nearly thirty years ago.[43] At that time there was concern that the land price increases in the early postwar period might create a serious problem: in view of the high rates of return on rented land through 1947 (10 percent or more) it seemed that agricultural income might decline sharply while land prices would remain constant or go up.

The second point may be somewhat less compelling. The current return on land was approximately 4.8 percent in 1950; it appears to have fallen to as low as 2.5 percent in 1960. The share of net rent in net agricultural income was approximately the same in 1950 and 1960 (net agricultural income in absolute dollars in 1960 being some 6 percent below the 1950 level).[44]

The third point reflects, in my opinion, a speedup in reducing

---

[43] D. Gale Johnson, "Allocation of Agricultural Income," *Journal of Farm Economics*, vol. 30, no. 4 (November 1948), pp. 733–34.

[44] The estimates of the current rate of return on land and the share of net agricultural income attributed to land presented in this section have been derived by relating net rent paid to nonoperator landlords to the current market value of land owned by the landlords and by estimating the total rent on all farmland by assuming that the rate of return on all land was the same as on rented land. This approach is described in my article "Allocation of Agricultural Income" referred to above. The data on which these estimates are based have many limitations, and the estimates of the current rate of return may not be accurate. The sources of data are U.S. Department of Agriculture, Statistical Bulletin no. 557, *Farm Income Statistics*, and two other publications of the Economic Research Service (USDA): *Balance Sheet of the Farming Sector*, 1976, Agriculture Information Bulletin no. 403, September 1976; and *Balance Sheet of the Farming Sector*, Supplement no. 1, Agriculture Information Bulletin no. 389, April 1976.

excess farm resources. This brought about an increase in net agricultural income during the 1960s and a larger per capita disposable income for farm people relative to the nonfarm population. In addition, government payments to farmers more than quadrupled in the early 1960s—rising from $700 million in 1960 to over $3 billion by 1966. A large fraction of the payments accrued to land. In fact, the estimated share of land rent in net agricultural income stood at about 20 percent in 1960, 30 percent in 1965, and 29 percent in 1969. The current rate of return on land moved up from about 2.5 percent in 1960 to approximately 3.5 percent in the latter half of the 1960s.

Why has the share of rent in net agricultural income increased between 1970 and 1975 by 5 percentage points?[45] The increase could be due to a change in the agricultural production function, but the more likely explanation has been the shift in the relative importance of land-intensive output (crops) relative to more labor-intensive output (livestock products) and the shift in relative prices favoring crops. Between 1970 and 1975 the output of livestock products declined by 7 percent while crop output rose by more than 20 percent. The increase in livestock prices was 45 percent; the increase in crop prices was 100 percent.

Are current land prices too high? Should we expect a fall in prices in the years ahead? While instinctively I feel that the answer to the question should be in the affirmative, an examination of the factors affecting land prices during the past three decades leads to the conclusion that the current prices will be sustained and, in fact, may well increase further.

If net farm operator income remains at approximately $24 billion and net agricultural income at approximately $40 billion (the levels of 1975 and 1976 and the projection for 1977), land prices are likely to increase in the years ahead. If net rents paid in 1976 were at the 1975 level of $4.8 billion, the net current return on the farm real estate value of $422 billion at the beginning of 1976 was 3.6 to 3.9 percent. From 1960 through 1974 the average current return was 3.8 percent; but from 1960 through 1971 (before the major increase in farm product prices)

---

[45] A critical variable in the estimate of the share of net agricultural income attributed to rent is the percentage of the value of farm real estate owned by nonoperator landlords. The most recent series, contained in Supplement no. 1 to Agriculture Information Bulletin no. 389, appears to have a significant discontinuity between 1969 and 1970 (see table 14). For 1969 it is estimated that 33.1 percent of all farm real estate is owned by nonoperator landlords; for 1970 the percentage given is 28.4. Such a large change could not have occurred in a single year. The series seems to be consistent from 1960 to 1969 and from 1970 to 1975 although one must remain somewhat suspicious about the data when such a large change occurs in one year. The increase in the percentage of net agricultural income attributed to rent between 1970 and 1975 assumes that there was no change in the importance of rented land in the total.

the current return averaged 3.3 percent. If farm and agricultural incomes remain at recent levels and if the current rate of return required to induce the ownership of land returns to the rate of the 1960s, further increases in land values are probable. Obviously other factors, such as the anticipated rate of inflation, will affect land prices. I am not predicting that within the next three or four years the value of farm real estate will approach $500 billion, though it could do so if the above assumptions turn out to be correct. The most critical assumption is the future level of net income of agriculture. For the years ahead, we cannot rule out a decline in net agricultural income of 10 percent and a decline of farm operator income of somewhat more. If this should occur there would probably be some downward pressure on farm real estate values, unless the income decline were thought to be temporary. In that case the effects would be modest—perhaps nothing more than a leveling off in the absolute value of farm real estate for a year or two before the general upward trend resumed.

Concluding Comments

In this paper I have stressed relatively long-term developments that have affected American agriculture. I deliberately did not dwell on the events of the past five years except as those years represented an extension of the two previous decades.

In the months ahead there will almost certainly be modifications of our farm commodity policies. One can only hope that the striking changes that have occurred in American agriculture since 1950 and 1960 (and even since 1970) will be fully recognized before major alterations are made in the existing legislation and programs. In the interests of farmers, consumers, and taxpayers, we should be careful to avoid policy mistakes like those made after World War II. The policies and programs of the 1950s were primarily concerned with attempting to protect agriculture from the need to adjust to changing conditions. The policies and programs adopted were successful, if at all, only in delaying the time when the adjustments had to be made. The policies of the 1960s were reasonably effective in aiding agriculture to adjust to the inevitable resource transfers and the relative contraction of the farm sector. But much of the need for the farm commodity programs of the 1960s resulted from policy errors made in the late 1940s and early 1950s.

If my analysis of the flexibility of resource allocation in agriculture is approximately correct, small errors in program formulation will very soon result in substantial costs to taxpayers, and possibly in difficulties in maintaining our preeminent position as a great agricultural exporter.

It will, in other words, be relatively easy to create significant excess capacity in agriculture by providing incentives, through prices or payments, that are inconsistent with the underlying demand and supply situation. Experience has shown clearly that when agricultural output is greater than the demand at politically acceptable levels of prices, a long time and large income transfers are required to eliminate the excess productive capacity.

AGRICULTURAL POLICY: A REVIEW OF LEGISLATION, PROGRAMS, AND POLICY

Luther G. Tweeten

With farm policy again at the crossroads in 1977, the assigned topic is timely, challenging, and broad. If we fail to learn from history, we are condemned to repeat its mistakes—and surely there is much to learn from past farm legislation, programs, and policy. The objectives of this paper are twofold: (1) to review the past, and (2) to analyze what we have learned. The two main sections of the paper deal with each of these objectives. The paper addresses only the major farm commodity programs. Space limitations preclude evaluation of programs for wool, sugar, tobacco, rice, and peanuts.

Government Commodity Programs in Brief

The struggle to find an acceptable compromise of farm, consumer, and taxpayer interests in formulating farm policy has been long and dramatic. That struggle is by no means over. The drama is largely sacrificed for brevity in the sometimes pedantic presentation below.[1] The cause of brevity might be served by omitting programs proposed but never enacted into law. But some of these programs such as the McNary-Haugen, the Brannan, and the Cochrane proposals are deemed too important in understanding the mainstream of policy to be relegated to the sidelines. They are included.

---

[1] Additional detail is provided in Luther Tweeten, *Foundations of Farm Policy* (Lincoln, Nebr.: University of Nebraska Press, 1970), chapter 10; Irving Dubov and E. L. Rawls, "American Farm Price and Income Policies: Main Lines of Development, 1920–73," Tennessee Agricultural Experiment Station Bulletin 939 (Knoxville, Tenn.: University of Tennessee, 1974); Wayne Rasmussen, Gladys Baker, and James Ward, "A Short History of Agricultural Adjustments, 1933–75," Agriculture Information Bulletin no. 391 (Washington, D.C.: Economic Research Service, USDA, 1976); and Willard Cochrane and Mary Ryan, *American Farm Policy, 1948–1973* (Minneapolis: University of Minnesota Press, 1976).

The McNary-Haugen Plan. The McNary-Haugen Plan originated with George Peek and Hugh Johnson of the Moline Plow Company. The first McNary-Haugen bill was introduced in 1924. Three versions of the bill were defeated in Congress. The fourth and fifth versions were passed by Congress but vetoed by President Calvin Coolidge, the latter in 1928.

Despite defeat of the plan, the proposal established two principal features that appeared in subsequent farm legislation.

(1) The plan originated the concept of parity prices under the term "fair exchange value." This was defined as the same current ratio of farm prices received to the general price index as the ratio that prevailed in the 1905–1914 period. If the ten-year prewar base period (1905–1914) is cut to a five-year base (1910–1914), and if the general price index is replaced by the index of prices paid by farmers, the "fair exchange value" becomes the "parity price" of the 1933 Agricultural Adjustment Act.[2]

(2) The plan inserted the concept of the two-price scheme into agricultural policy. The scheme was simple in concept. A government export corporation would issue debentures to pay for farm commodities that would not sell in the inelastic domestic market at the "fair exchange value." The government corporation would dispose of excess supplies in the elastic foreign market at the world price. Tariffs would keep the commodities from being imported into the United States at the higher domestic price. The farmer would receive an average price made up of the parity price for the domestic portion and the world price for the excess.

The Federal Farm Board. President Calvin Coolidge vetoed the last two McNary-Haugen proposals on the advice of his secretary of commerce, Herbert Hoover. When Hoover himself became President in 1929, economic conditions in agriculture were sufficiently critical to acquire attention. The Agricultural Marketing Act of 1929 was passed accordingly and provided for a Federal Farm Board with a $500 million revolving fund. "Orderly marketing" was to be obtained through vigorously encouraged formation of large farm cooperative marketing associations, financed through low interest loans. The highly centralized commodity organizations were to exercise a degree of bargaining power through monopoly over the sales of farm products. The Federal Farm Board purchased supplies of wheat and cotton to stabilize prices and belatedly turned to land use planning to control production. But by the early 1930s, it was apparent that the Federal Farm Board was unsuccessful in securing bargaining power for farmers, that improved marketing through

---

[2] Dubov and Rawls, "American Farm Price and Income Policies," p. 5.

cooperatives was not a solution to serious farm price and income problems, and that board funding was inadequate to support farm prices through purchasing commodities or controlling production. In May 1933, President Franklin Roosevelt abolished the board by presidential order.

The Agricultural Adjustment Act of 1933. The Agricultural Adjustment Act as approved in May of 1933 began massive federal intervention in the farm economy. Farm purchasing power was to be restored to its fair exchange value in the 1909–1914 base period through several devices: (1) voluntary controls on the acreage of basic crops, using direct payments to induce participation in the program; (2) taxes on processors of agricultural commodities, with the proceeds to be used to fund the cost of adjustment operations, expansion of markets, and removal of agricultural surpluses; and (3) regulated marketing of farm commodities through voluntary agreements among processors and distributors to eliminate "unfair" practices. The licensing and regulating features were the early origins of marketing orders.[3] The first marketing order agreement became effective in the Chicago fluid milk market in August 1933.

"Nonrecourse" loans[4] were made by the federal government to farmers on corn at 60 percent of parity and on cotton at 69 percent of parity in 1933.

Marketing quotas were introduced by the Bankhead Cotton Control Act and by the Kerr-Smith Tobacco Control Act, both passed in 1934. Two-thirds of the producers of cotton and three-fourths of the tobacco producers voting in referendum had to approve allotments before they would go into effect. As an emergency measure in 1933, programs were undertaken for plowing under portions of planted cotton and tobacco crops. Pork, butter, cheese, and flour were purchased for surplus removal and distributed in relief channels under commodity distribution programs.

With the basic machinery for controlling production and raising farm prices now operating and abetted by droughts in 1934 and 1936,

---

[3] Congress saw fit to reaffirm certain portions of the Agricultural Adjustment Act of 1933 by passing the Agricultural Marketing Agreement Act of 1937. Under the 1937 act, regulations can be established to classify milk according to use and fix minimum prices that handlers must pay to producers in the various uses of milk. Furthermore, other commodities could be regulated according to quality, quantity, and rate of shipment to market. Prices received by producers are indirectly affected.

[4] If the market price was above the loan price, the farmer could sell on the open market and repay the loan. If the loan rate was above the market price the farmer could turn in the commodity as full payment of the loan to the Commodity Credit Corporation, a government financed corporation created by executive order in October 1933.

farm economic conditions improved. However, the *Hoosac Mills* decision of the U. S. Supreme Court in 1936 declared unconstitutional the production control and processing tax features of the program.

Soil Conservation and Domestic Allotment Act of 1936. The mission of the 1933 act was to bring prices to parity levels, an ambitious goal, which—to no one's surprise—it failed to reach. The 1936 act introduced the concept of parity income aimed at maintaining the same relationship between purchasing power of farm and nonfarm per capita incomes as existed in the 1909–1914 period.

The three objectives of the 1936 act were to (1) promote soil conservation and profitable use of agricultural resources, (2) maintain farm income at fair levels, and (3) protect consumers by assuring adequate supplies of food and fiber.[5] The basic features of the 1933 act were unchanged in the 1936 act, but the latter, appealing to public concern over soil conservation, paid farmers for voluntarily shifting acreage from soil-depleting crops to soil-conserving legumes and grasses. The soil-depleting crops, of course, were those for which lawmakers wished to support the price.

Agricultural Adjustment Act of 1938. The Agricultural Adjustment Act of 1938 became a pattern for subsequent farm commodity programs. New features included (1) mandatory nonrecourse loans at flexible support rates for cooperating producers of corn, wheat, and cotton under specified supply and demand conditions if marketing quotas were approved in referendum; (2) crop insurance for wheat; (3) payments, if funds were available, to producers of corn, cotton, rice, tobacco, and wheat in amounts that would provide a return as close as possible to parity prices and parity income; and (4) protection of consumers by the maintenance of adequate reserves of food, feed, and fiber, with systematic storage made possible by nonrecourse loans for the "ever normal granary" plan.[6]

In addition to acreage allotments, a notable feature was flexible nonrecourse loan support rates for cotton, wheat, and corn. Loan rates were inversely related to available supplies.

Allotments reduced acreages of the major crops. Overall crop output was not markedly reduced because of higher yields of allotment

---

[5] Rasmussen et al., "A Short History of Agricultural Adjustments, 1933–75," p. 5.
[6] Other farm policies were contained in the 1938 act. In addition to the direct distribution of surplus commodities begun under the act of 1933, the 1938 act provided for a nationwide school lunch program, a low cost milk program, and a food stamp program that reached almost 4 million people in 1942, then was discontinued. Federal all-risk crop insurance was introduced in Title 5 of the Agricultural Adjustment Act of 1938.

crops and additional production of substitute crops on acres taken out of allotment crops. Although major provisions of subsequent legislation were in place, it was apparent in the rising surpluses that the programs had not come to grips with the required production control. These surpluses proved beneficial in World War II.

Agriculture in a War Economy. With the onset of World War II in 1941, emphasis changed from restraining production to encouraging production with high price guarantees that were to dominate farm legislation until the 1950s. Steps in the creation and retention of high fixed price supports were as follows:

(1) Congress passed legislation in May 1941 to raise the loan rates to 85 percent of parity on the 1941 crops of cotton, corn, wheat, rice, and tobacco if producers approved marketing quotas.

(2) The May 1941 legislation was amended in December 1941 to add peanuts to the list of commodities and to extend the high loan rates on basic commodities to subsequent years.[7]

(3) The rate of support was raised to not less than 90 percent of parity for corn, cotton, peanuts, rice, tobacco, and wheat and for the "Steagall" nonbasic commodities by the Stabilization Act, approved in October 1942. Section 8 of the 1942 legislation provided that the prices of basic commodities would be supported at 90 percent of parity for two years immediately succeeding the first day of January following a presidential or congressional declaration that hostilities had ceased. This condition in essence provided for termination of the Stabilization Act as of December 31, 1948. Price supports for basic commodities would then drop back to 52 to 75 percent of parity as provided by the Agricultural Adjustment Act of 1938.

(4) The price support rate for cotton was raised to 92.5 percent of parity and for corn, rice, and wheat to 90 percent of parity by a law approved in June 1944.

(5) The Surplus Property Act of October 1944 raised the price support rate for cotton to 95 percent of parity with respect to crops harvested after December 31, 1943, and those planted in 1944.

(6) The Agricultural Adjustment Act of 1948 established mandatory price supports at 90 percent of parity for 1949 crops of wheat, corn, rice, peanuts, cotton, and tobacco if producers had not disapproved marketing quotas. The 1948 legislation contained provisions for a new parity formula to account for changes in demand

---

[7] Rasmussen et al., "A Short History of Agricultural Adjustments, 1933–75," p. 8.

and supply since the 1910–1914 period and a sliding scale of price supports between 60 and 90 percent of parity to begin in 1950.

(7) The Agricultural Act of 1949 superseded the 1948 act and provided support for basic commodities at 90 percent of parity for 1950 and from 80 to 90 percent of parity for the 1951 crops. Co-operating producers were to receive price supports at 75 to 90 percent of parity depending on supply for 1952 and succeeding years if producers approved marketing quotas.

(8) Secretary of Agriculture Charles Brannan used the national security provisions of the Agricultural Act of 1949 to keep price supports at 90 percent of parity for all the basic commodities except peanuts for 1951 and 1952.

(9) Legislation in June 1952 amended and extended the Defense Production Act of 1950 to provide price support loans for basic crops to cooperators at the rate of 90 percent of parity through April 1953 unless producers disapproved marketing quotas.

(10) Legislation approved in July 1952 provided mandatory price supports at 90 percent of parity for basic commodities for the 1953 and 1954 crops if producers approved marketing quotas.

(11) The Agricultural Act of 1954, approved in August, established flexible price supports for basic commodities at a range of 82.5 to 90 percent of parity for 1955 and 75 to 90 percent of parity thereafter. Flexible price supports had finally arrived but the battle against surplus production was by no means over.

The Brannan Plan. The farm program advocated by Secretary of Agriculture Charles Brannan in 1949 was a substantial departure from the past programs. Although income parity had been introduced as a concept in the Agricultural Act of 1936, it had never been implemented. A key feature of the Brannan Plan was an income standard based on a moving average of income in the ten most recent past years. In practice, price support standards would be employed with the level of prices for individual commodities selected to raise farm income to that of the base period. All commodities would be sold at prices that would clear the market and the difference between the market price and the support price would be made up by compensatory, direct payments to farmers.

Another important feature was that supports would be limited to a fixed number of units of corn, wheat, cotton, or other commodities. Because marginal output would receive the market price rather than the higher supported price, an incentive would be provided for farmers to restrain production.

Congress was concerned with a potentially high Treasury cost of direct payments and discarding of the "comfortable" parity standard used in previous programs. The Brannan Plan was not enacted, although the direct, compensatory payment feature was contained in subsequent programs.

Korea and Beyond. Following the end of the Korean War in 1953, surpluses began to mount and were first dealt with by expanding demand, then by reducing supply. The Agricultural Trade Development and Assistance Act (Public Law 480) in July 1954 disposed of surplus agricultural commodities mainly by export sales for soft foreign currencies. The Agricultural Act of 1956 established the Soil Bank, the first real effort to control production since the programs of the 1930s. It contained two portions, one an Acreage Reserve to reduce acreage planted to allotment crops of wheat, cotton, corn, tobacco, peanuts, and rice, but like previous controls paid little attention to cross compliance features. The second part was the Conservation Reserve, a long-term general land retirement program which idled as many as 29 million acres in 1960 under contracts up to ten years.

Under the Agricultural Act of August 1958, corn producers were given two options and they chose to discontinue acreage allotments for 1959 and subsequent crops and to receive supports at 90 percent of average farm price for the preceding three years but not less than 65 percent of parity.

Two types of programs are workable: high price supports and effective production controls or low price supports and no production controls. The option farmers selected contained comparatively high price supports and no production controls except for the small scale Soil Bank program. The result was massive stocks of wheat, 1.4 billion bushels, in July 1960, and of corn, 2.0 billion bushels, in October 1961. A major policy shift was clearly overdue.

Commodity Programs in the 1960s. The emergency Feed Grain Act was passed in March 1961 and was designed to divert corn and sorghum acreage to soil-conserving uses. Producers were eligible for price supports at 74 percent of parity if in 1961 they diverted to soil-conserving uses 20 percent of the average acreage they had devoted to corn and sorghum in 1959 and 1960. These years became the allotment standard for subsequent feed grain programs. Payments for reducing the minimum acreage were equal to 50 percent of the support rate times the normal yield. Additional reductions of 20 to 40 percent of the base were paid at 60 percent of the county support rate. The programs were voluntary, but the payments were sufficiently generous and the release of surplus stocks on the market to reduce prices was sufficiently ominous that participation was widespread. Production was reduced and the burdensome carryover reduced. The 1961 experience demonstrated that production could be controlled by voluntary programs (though at great Treasury cost), a demonstration that silenced critics who had contended this could not be done.

An omnibus farm bill was sent to Congress by the John Kennedy administration in late 1961 and contained a number of ideas promulgated by the director of agricultural economics, Willard Cochrane. Under the bill Congress would establish broad guidelines for programs, but the decisions regarding allotment levels and price supports would be made by the secretary of agriculture with the opportunity for a congressional veto sixty days after it was submitted. Like the defunct omnibus farm bill proposed in 1961, the original version of the Food and Agriculture Act of 1962 was introduced to establish a comprehensive supply control program for major farm commodities, including grains and dairy products. The secretary of agriculture would establish quotas with producers deciding in a national referendum whether to approve mandatory quotas and price supports. If no more than one third disapproved, the quotas would become mandatory, and violating producers would be penalized. The administration saw the Cochrane mandatory program as the only way at once to maintain farm income, to stop the growth of stocks, and to hold down government costs. The proposal passed the Senate but was narrowly defeated in the House.

A 1963 wheat referendum further tested the acceptability of mandatory controls to farmers. Like the previous two efforts at mandatory controls, it failed to win approval, this time by farmers rather than lawmakers. The Food and Agriculture Act of 1962 as finally enacted contained an extension of the 1961 feed grain program and provided supports for the 1963 wheat crop at $1.82 per bushel for farmers who complied with allotments. A 55 million acre minimum national allotment of wheat acreage had been in effect for some years and provided more wheat than would move in commercial channels at the support rate. Consequently, substantial export subsidies were required to avoid large surpluses. Under the new law beginning in 1964 the 55 million acre minimum national wheat allotment was abolished, and the secretary of agriculture could set allotments as necessary to limit production.

The Cotton-Wheat Act was approved in April 1964 and authorized the secretary of agriculture to pay subsidies to domestic handlers or textile mills in order to bring the price of cotton consumed in the United States down to the export price. Farmers who stayed within "regular allotments" had cotton supported at 30 cents per pound. A farmer planting only his domestic allotment, which was smaller than his regular allotment, received a support price of 33.5 cents per pound.

Under the Cotton-Wheat Act of 1964 a voluntary wheat marketing certificate scheme was established for 1964 and 1965. Farmers who complied with acreage allotments and agreed to participate in land diversion programs received price supports, marketing certificates, and land diversion payments. Complying farmers received $2 per bushel for 45 percent of their normal production, $.70 of which was from purchase of certificates by processors (note the return of the processor tax). Another 45 percent was supported at a price of $1.55 per bushel (the export portion). The remaining portion was supported at $1.30 per bushel. In subsequent years the domestic portion (40 to 45 percent) was supported at parity and the remainder at $1.25 per bushel. Processors paid $.75 per bushel on the domestic or certificate portion.

Food and Agriculture Act of 1965. The Food and Agriculture Act approved in November 1965 extended the wheat and grain programs to 1969. The 1965 act was later extended to 1970 by legislation enacted in 1968.

Cotton surpluses continued to mount under the 1964 act, calling for a new policy. Under the 1965 act the market price of cotton was supported at no more than 90 percent of the world price, thereby eliminating a necessity to subsidize cotton use and domestic mills and exports. Participation in the program was voluntary, although the monetary incentives of the programs made participation overwhelmingly attractive. A minimum acreage diversion of 12.5 percent of affected allotment was necessary for farmers to be eligible for support. Provision was also made for participation at higher levels. The program was effective in reducing cotton production and carryover.

The 1965 act also set up a long-term general land retirement program called the Cropland Adjustment Program. The secretary of agriculture could enter into five- to ten-year contracts to retire cropland to conservation uses. Payments were to be not more than 40 percent of the value of possible crop production on the land, and funding authorization was set so low the effort was no more than a pilot program.

The Agricultural Act of 1970. The Agricultural Act of 1970 was an act that no group advocated, no group supported, and no one greeted with enthusiasm. The act was opposed by all major farm organizations, although for widely different reasons. Neither Congress nor the secretary of agriculture had sufficient strength to enact a partisan bill, and the result was a compromise that ultimately became more widely accepted than any previous major program. The new three-year program eschewed allotments, acreage restriction, and marketing quotas for specific crops of wheat, upland cotton, and feed grains and substituted instead a short-term partial land retirement program. That is, to qualify for price support, the farmer was required to set aside a specific percentage of his land to soil conserving practices. He could grow whatever he wished on remaining land, except for selected crops that remained under control. Payment limitations were established at $55,000 per crop (excluding commodity loans) for producers of upland cotton, wheat, and feed grains. Wheat loans were made available to participants at not less than $1.25 per bushel for 1971 through 1973, and domestic marketing certificates covering a total of not less than 535 million bushels were established. The value of certificates was the difference between the wheat parity price and the average price received by farmers during the first five months of the marketing year.

To qualify for price supports, cotton planters were required to set aside an amount not to exceed 25 percent of the cotton allotment to soil conserving uses. Loans were set at 90 percent of the average world price for the two previous years. Deficiency payments were set equal to the difference between 65 percent of parity or 35 cents per pound, whichever was higher, and the average market price for the first five months of the marketing year. Deficiency payments, however, were not to be less than 15 cents per pound. Because obtaining enough production in cotton, rather than too much, was beginning to be a problem, the justification for restricting production by diverting acres became unclear.

Producers of wheat, feed grains, and upland cotton who failed to plant that commodity or an eligible substitute crop would incur a reduction of 20 percent in allotment the following year. If the allotment or substitute crop was not planted for three years, the entire allotment would be lost. This feature was widely criticized for encouraging farmers to plant their allotment when production needed to be reduced.

Price supports on corn were to be the higher of $1.35 per bushel or 70 percent of parity on October 1, and the loan not less than $1.00 nor more than 90 percent of parity, as determined by the secretary. A producer would receive a payment equal to the difference between the support price and market price in the first five months of the marketing year on half of his basic production.[8]

Authorizations were continued for long-term land retirement at a pilot level of $10 million per year for each program.

The Agriculture and Consumer Protection Act of 1973. The Agriculture and Consumer Protection Act of 1973 was legislated in an entirely different atmosphere than farm programs since the 1930s—an atmosphere of excess demand. This emboldened Secretary of Agriculture Earl Butz to proclaim that the legislation represented a historic turning point

---

[8] Ibid., p. 18.

in the philosophy of farm programs in the United States. One could question whether the statement reflected his philosophy or new circumstances. The title also served notice of an emerging element in farm commodity legislation—the consumer.

The 1973 legislation continued the set-aside short-term partial land retirement concept and introduced target prices which were to be used when market prices fell between loan rates and the target price. In another departure from previous programs, the parity formula was dropped in setting future target prices, and the 1974 and 1975 target prices were set at 38 cents per pound for upland cotton, $2.05 per bushel for wheat, and $1.38 per bushel for corn. Target prices remained at that level in 1974 and 1975, but 1976 and 1977 target prices were adjusted upward by the index of prices paid by farmers for items used in production and deflated downward by the most recent national three-year average yield for each crop. The secretary of agriculture had considerable discretion in setting loan rates and raised loan rates for wheat from $1.37 per bushel (the minimum allowable) to $2.25 per bushel and for corn from $1.10 per bushel (the minimum allowable) to $1.50 per bushel in 1976.

Total payments to any person under the wheat feed grain and upland cotton programs was limited to $20,000. This did not include loans or purchases.

Another feature of the 1973 act was disaster payments authorized for eligible producers prevented from planting any portion of allotment because of drought, flood, or natural disaster and other conditions beyond their control. Payments were made available when natural disaster prevented a farmer from harvesting two-thirds of his normal production of the crop allotment acreage.

The support price for milk was to be at a level between 75 and 90 percent of parity but as determined by the secretary of agriculture to insure an adequate supply of milk. The actual support rate was held at a level of approximately 80 percent of parity from the beginnings of the 1973 act to 1977.

Because the dairy program frequently generated costly surpluses sometimes dumped on foreign markets in violation of the General Agreement on Trade and Tariffs, and because the U. S. apparently has a comparative disadvantage due to labor intensity in the production of manufactured milk products (which can be imported from abroad at lower cost than they can be produced domestically), reforms have been called for in the program. One suggestion has been to pay the actual market price on marginal production rather than the blend price of milk going to fluid and manufactured milk markets. This action would restrain production but force marginal producers out of business. Efficiency gains should allow compensation to such producers with enough surplus gains remaining to increase the real value of goods and services available to consumers.

For cotton, the payment limitation for large producers was accompanied by provisions that cotton producers whose basis was 10 acres or less received deficiency payments at a rate 30 percent greater than other producers.

Because of large foreign demand from 1973 to 1977, the act remained largely a backstop rather than an operating program. Except for long-term land contracts which had little effect on reducing output and except for restrictions on planting of winter wheat in 1973, production controls were not imposed under the 1973 act, which expired in 1977.

Interpretation of History

Surely there is much to learn from past government commodity programs for agriculture. Emphasis below is on costs and benefits, strengths and weaknesses of programs. Before turning to these issues, however, it is useful to review the role of crises in motivating directions for farm policy.

Accounting for New Directions in Commodity Policy. If necessity is the mother of invention, crisis seems the mother of redirection in farm policy. Programs since the 1930s remained remarkably similar in structure for extended periods, though differing in style and emphasis. Substantive changes in programs come rarely—in response to crisis.

Farm prices and incomes were depressed in the 1920s, but not in crisis proportions. The result was failure to adopt the McNary-Haugen bills but success in passage of a weak marketing program in 1929, which was predicated on the erroneous assumption that improved marketing and modest Treasury outlays could solve farm economic ills.

Economic crisis reached panic proportions by 1933. The result was farm policy which differed radically from previous policies. Although the 1933 act was declared unconstitutional, the 1936 and 1938 acts which replaced it differed in wording and justification rather than in substance.

Out of the World War II crisis emerged high, rigid price supports. These were held tenaciously until crisis again returned. The Brannan Plan of 1949, although not a radical departure from past programs, failed to win legislative approval because there was no emergency that mandated abandoning the high, rigid price supports and "traditional" parity pricing which farmers strongly supported.

The Korean War gave a temporary reprieve from the inevitable confrontation between high price supports and unmanageable surpluses, but the crisis of abundance reached intolerable dimensions by 1954. Programs to export surpluses and retire marginal land under long-term contracts could not cope with the problem—high price supports generated too much surplus production to deal with by these means.

Surpluses of crisis proportions in 1961 required firm action. The result was 1961 legislation which set the pattern of farm legislation for a decade. Treasury costs were high, yet efforts to institute mandatory controls for maintaining farm income with low Treasury costs were decisively turned back in the 1961–1963 period.

The 1970 legislation under a Republican administration was more a cosmetic change than a substantive change in policy. To be sure, the set-aside program gave somewhat greater flexibility to farmers and market orientation than previous programs. Emphasis on target prices in the 1973 act again was not a radical departure. Although excess demand for farm output emboldened Secretary Butz to herald the 1973 act as a return to free markets and a radical departure from a previous program, he was speaking from the vantage point of circumstances rather than political philosophy expressed in the 1973 act itself. After all, he presided in 1972 over the most massive intervention ever of the U. S. government in the farming economy.

Current farm legislation is a remarkable potpourri of the many programs tried or proposed since the 1920s. Export subsidies used under recent programs reflect the two-price scheme contained in the McNary-Haugen bills of the 1920s. The direct payment features characterized by deficiency payments and target prices bear traces of the Brannan Plan of 1949. The set-aside program is an eclectic wedding of the short-term land diversion programs emphasized from 1961 to 1970 with the long-term general land retirement emphasized in the late 1950s. Mandatory controls, though not features of programs for major commodities, are still used for tobacco.

An important change in farm policy that has gone almost unnoticed is the rise in discretionary power of the secretary of agriculture. Under the 1973 act, the secretary had wide discretion in setting loan rates, set-aside acreages, export subsidies, and other program features. Perhaps Congress increasingly recognizes that farm policy is too complex to legislate with precise rules that cannot be tailored to circumstances in these times, which are likely to alternate between periods of excess demand and excess supply.

Widespread economic deprivation among farm people motivated programs in the 1930s. Since the 1930s, farmers as a class have not been economically deprived. The implication is that farm price and income supports would narrow from supports for a large number or commodities produced by a broad spectrum of farmers to a few programs benefitting those commodity groups having greatest political clout and making the best case that their programs hold reserve capacity, promote efficiency, and induce price stability of benefit to consumers. In general, this trend predicted by theory has held. Ever fewer commodities receive price and income supports. Equity and economic efficiency conflicts remain, however. Some contend that programs for commercial farmers should be designed to reduce price instability and provide reserves at minimum public costs without payment limitations and that a separate negative income tax or other income-conditioned welfare programs for low income farmers should be part of a nationwide income maintenance policy.

Impact of Programs on Economic Efficiency. Two possible sources of inefficiency are indicated in Figure 1. Farm commodity programs restricting land use can engender inefficient resource combinations reducing the supply curve from S to S'. The additional cost of supplying any given output is indicated by the area B. A second source of inefficiency is indicated by area A—the value of goods and services lost through production controls which reduce output below the equilibrium level.

Estimates of the aggregate farm production function have been used to compute optimal levels of nine farm resources consistent with economic equilibrium.[9] The least-cost input combination to produce the actual average 1952–1961 output would have reduced the annual input dollar volume by $1.9 billion or 5.6 percent. Actual output exceeded the equilibrium output. Adjustment of farm resources to an equilibrium input and output level, with all resources earning an opportunity cost return, would have entailed a reduction of $4.2 billion (in 1947–1949 dollars) or 12.5 percent of the actual input volume. The cost of excess capacity was approximately $2.2 billion, or 6.6 percent of the resource volume; the cost of a nonoptimal input mix was $2.0 billion, or 5.9 percent of the resource volume. Two-fifths of agricultural labor was estimated to be in excess supply in the 1952–1961 period. Capital inputs purchased by farmers needed to increase on the average by 17 percent to reach an equilibrium. These resource allocations of an efficient market can be used as a benchmark against which to measure the resource allocations encouraged by government programs.

Acreage diversion programs idled land resources which have little value in uses other than producing farm crops. More than 60 million cropland acres were diverted in some years, entailing an inefficient input-mix cost indicated by area B in Figure 1. The resource in greatest excess

[9] Fred Tyner and Luther Tweeten, "Optimum Resource Allocation in U.S. Agriculture," *American Journal of Agricultural Economics*, vol. 48 (1966), pp. 613–31.

Figure 1

SOCIAL COST OF GOVERNMENT PRODUCTION CONTROLS

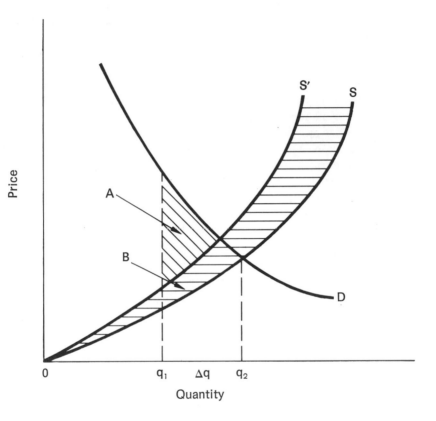

supply was farm labor during the 1950s and 1960s—the size of area *B* must consider the impact of programs on the input of labor as well as land. The operation of the farm economy has been simulated with and without commodity programs.[10] Although problems of specification and interpretation are severe in dynamic studies of this type, and no one

---

[10] Fred Tyner and Luther Tweeten, "Simulation as a Method of Appraising Farm Programs," *American Journal of Agricultural Economics*, vol. 50, no. 1 (1968), pp. 68–81; Daryll Ray and Earl Heady, "Simulated Effects of Alternative Policy and Economic Environments on U.S. Agriculture," CARD Report 46 (Ames, Iowa: Center for Agricultural and Rural Development, Iowa State University, 1974); Frederick Nelson and Willard Cochrane, "Economic Consequences of Federal Farm Commodity Programs, 1953–72," *Agricultural Economics Research*, vol. 28, no. 2 (197   52–64

study is definitive, the results are of particular significance because each study reaches the same conclusion: farm programs speeded the exodus of farm labor. There would have been more labor in agriculture with a free market than with the government programs that were in effect.

Unlike the previous two studies, the Nelson–Cochrane study made productivity endogenous to the model.[11] Their results indicated that agricultural productivity would have been somewhat higher in a free market than it actually was from 1955 to 1968. However, the longer-term effect of eliminating farm programs would have been to reduce the productivity to the level 11 percent below the historic level by 1972. Crop productivity in a free market would have fallen below actual historic levels for all years after 1958 and would have been down 19 percent by 1972. Agricultural employment under the moderately inelastic demand alternative would have been 73 percent higher in 1972 than with farm programs. Net farm income would have fallen 55 percent below the actual level by 1957, but it would have reached 58 percent above the actual level in 1971. The authors concluded that the programs apparently work to promote both long- and short-term price and income stability. In short, because of the impact of programs on labor and overall productivity, I find no substantive basis to conclude that withdrawal of land from production and other aspects of government programs shifted the supply curve from S to S' period, and hence I omit the cost designated by area B in Figure 1. Attention rather is focused on the reduced value of goods and services caused by farm programs as indicated by area A in Figure 1.

Net Social Cost of Commodity Programs. To compute net social cost A of government programs, it is useful first to estimate production diverted from markets by government programs. Estimates made several years ago and data on cropland diverted by government programs are shown in Table 1. From 1955 to 1961, excess capacity was largely in the form of P.L. 480 exports to support the domestic farm economy and net stock accumulation of the Commodity Credit Corporation. Excess capacity ranged from 4.5 percent to 11.2 percent of farm output from 1955 and 1968. More recent data used below provide additional insights into the degree of excess capacity.

The following equation was estimated by ordinary least squares for the period 1959–1975:

$$\hat{H}_t = 290 + .11\ H_{t-1} - .57\ L_t - .65\ S_t + .07\ P_t - .04\ T$$
$$\phantom{\hat{H}_t = 290 + }(1.69) (-2.63)\ (-13.04)\ (.66) (-.10)$$

---

[11] In previous analysis, I did not find productivity to be a function of the parity ratio, but the Nelson–Cochrane study found that financial variables influenced productivity.

where:

H = cropland harvested
L = acres in long-term land retirement programs
S = acres diverted by short-term acreage diversion programs
P = ratio of crop prices to prices paid by farmers
T = time (last two digits of current year)

Table 1

EXCESS CAPACITY IN U.S. AGRICULTURE, MEASURED BY PERCENTAGE OF PRODUCTION DIVERTED FROM THE MARKET AND BY CROPLAND WITHHELD FROM PRODUCTION BY GOVERNMENT PROGRAMS

Year	Total Government Diversions as Percentage of Potential Production at Current Prices	Cropland Withheld from Production (in million acres)
1955	6.4	—
1956	6.3	13.6
1957	9.1	27.8
1958	11.2	27.1
1959	9.1	22.5
1960	7.1	28.7
1961	7.4	53.7
1962	7.8	64.7
1963	6.6	56.1
1964	6.2	55.5
1965	6.5	57.4
1966	7.2	63.6
1967	4.5	40.7
1968	7.8	49.4
1969	N.A.	58.0
1970	N.A.	57.1
1971	N.A.	37.6
1972	N.A.	62.1
1973	N.A.	19.6
1974	N.A.	2.4
1975	N.A.	2.4

Note: Government diversions as a percentage of production include net Commodity Credit Corporation stock accumulation, a portion of Public Law 480 shipments, and estimated production on diverted acres.
Sources: Fred Tyner and Luther Tweeten, "Excess Capacity in U.S. Agriculture," *Agricultural Economics Research*, vol. 16, no. 1 (1964), pp. 23-31; Leroy Quance and Luther Tweeten, "Excess Capacity and Adjustment Potential in U.S. Agriculture," *Agricultural Economics Research*, vol. 24, no. 3 (1972), pp. 57-66; U.S. Department of Agriculture, *Agriculture Statistics* (Washington, D.C., 1975), p. 518.

The variables accounted for 98 percent of the annual variation in cropland harvested and t-values are shown in parenthesis. After adjusting for the impact of prices and time, the results indicate that each acre released from long-term land retirement programs L increased cropland harvested by .57 acres in the short run and .64 acres in the long run. Each acre released from short-term diversion programs is estimated to increase cropland harvested by .65 acres in the short run and by .74 acres in the long run. Based on these results, it appears that approximately two of three diverted acres would return to crop production of each acre diverted by government programs. These results are broadly consistent with numerous though somewhat dated estimates summarized by Ericksen in 1976.[12]

Diverted acres are not as productive as average land actually cropped. One study estimated that productivity of diverted acres as a proportion of productivity of acres in production averaged 90 percent for wheat, 85 percent for grain sorghum, 83 percent for barley, 82 percent for corn, and 80 percent for cotton.[13] These estimates are probably high. Assuming that diverted acres were three-fourths as productive as land actually cropped and that two-thirds of diverted acres would return to production with termination of government diversion programs, then diverted land averaging 50 million acres from 1961–1972 and comprising 15 percent of all cropland reduced crop output only 7.5 percent.

Taking first the position that all farm output including livestock production is a product of crop production and that capital and labor inputs were diverted along with land, then total farm output was reduced 7.5 percent by diversion programs. Taking an alternative position that capital and labor were shifted from diverted acres to other cropland and that land accounts for only one-fifth (elasticity of production of .2) of all farm output, then the 7.5 percent reduction in cropland reduced farm output by only $.2(7.5) = 1.5$ percent. In short, 1961–1972 acreage diversion reduced total farm output between 1.5 percent and 7.5 percent. The mid-range of these values is 4.5 percent.

Public Law 480 shipments averaged $1.33 billion annually from 1961 to 1972. Research indicates that approximately half of this amount can be imputed to foreign aid and half to domestic farm price and income supports.[14] Thus excess capacity imputed to food aid constituted

---

[12] Milton Ericksen, "Use of Land Reserves in Agricultural Production Adjustment," *Agricultural-Food Policy Review*, ERS-AFPR-1 (Washington, D.C.: Economic Research Service, USDA, 1976), pp. 76–84.

[13] P. Weisgerber, "Productivity of Diverted Cropland," ERS-398 (Washington, D.C.: Economic Research Service, USDA, 1969).

[14] Pinstrup P. Andersen, "The Role of Food, Feed and Fiber in Foreign Economic Assistance: Value, Cost and Efficiency" (Ph.D. diss., Oklahoma State University, 1969).

1.7 percent of farm output. Commodity Credit Corporation net accumulation of stocks also constituted reserve capacity, but I shall assume no net accumulation for the period. Combining production diversions with food aid gives a range of excess capacity of 3 percent to 9 percent. In the calculations below of the net social cost of government programs, I shall omit the P.L. 480 portion and use a mean estimate of 5 percent for cropland diversions only.

Net social cost C of government commodity programs expressed as a percentage of gross farm receipts is approximated by the following formula:

$$C \cong 50\left(\frac{1}{\alpha} - \frac{1}{\beta}\right)\left(\frac{\Delta Q}{Q}\right)^2$$

where α is the supply elasticity, β is the demand elasticity, and $\dfrac{\Delta Q}{Q}$ is the proportion of farm output diverted from markets by government programs. The implication is that the net social cost for diversion of 5 percent of output from price setting markets constitutes 2 percent of farm receipts. These estimates apply to the short run with a supply elasticity α of .1 and a demand elasticity β of $-.2$.

In the long run with $\alpha = 1.0$, $\beta = -.33$, the 5 percent diversion from the market implies a net social cost equal to .5 percent of gross receipts. With gross receipts averaging approximately $44 billion from 1961 to 1972, the implication is that government programs costing taxpayers approximately $4 billion annually entailed a net reduction in goods and services produced and consumed of up to $.9 billion. Estimates of net social costs of government programs for individual commodities also reveal costs in line with the above estimates.[15]

In some instances commodity programs have restricted acreages below those necessary to achieve principal economies of size. This appears to be especially true for tobacco and to a degree also for cotton farms. For grains it appears that acreage limitations have encouraged consolidation of farms and reduction in number of farms to achieve

---

[15] P. R. Johnson, "The Social Costs of the Tobacco Program," *Journal of Farm Economics*, vol. 46 (1965), pp. 242–55; Luther Tweeten and Fred Tyner, "The Utility Concept of Net Social Cost—A Criterion for Public Policy," *Agricultural Economics Research*, vol. 18, no. 2 (April 1966), pp. 33–42; Rachel Dardis and Janet Dennisson, "The Welfare Cost of Alternative Methods for Protecting Raw Wool in the United States," *American Journal of Agricultural Economics*, vol. 51 (1969), pp. 303–19; L. F. Hushak, "A Welfare Analysis of the Voluntary Corn Diversion Program, 1961–1966," *American Journal of Agricultural Economics*, vol. 53 (1971), pp. 173–81; T. D. Wallace, "Measures of Social Costs of Agricultural Programs," *Journal of Farm Economics*, vol. 44, no. 2 (1962), pp. 580–94.

economies of size in the face of allotments limiting acreages on given farms. Program provisions allowed moving allotments from one farm to another, enabling operators to use allotments on more productive land after consolidation. Allotments impaired interregional shifts in acres that would increase efficiency, but shifts among regions in production of tobacco, cotton, milk, and peanuts and provisions for sale or movement of allotments across geographic boundaries reduced the inefficiency.

Impact of Programs on Farm Income. A measure of the short-run impact on farm prices and income from release of reserve capacity on the market can be made from the price elasticity of demand for farm output β. The elasticity of prices received by farmers with respect to a 1 percent increase in output placed on the market is the price flexibility of demand $F = 1/\beta$, the elasticity of gross receipts with respect to output is $1 + F$, and the elasticity of net income with respect to output is $(1 + F)R$ where R is the ratio of gross receipts to net farm income. Given $\beta = -.2$, the implication is that 5 percent additional output placed on the market would in the short run reduce prices received by 25 percent, gross receipts by 20 percent, and net income by 60 percent.

The impact on long-term farm income is quite different. Long-term gains are eroded by (1) an increasing elasticity of supply as length of run is extended, (2) an increasing elasticity of demand as the length of run is extended, (3) capitalization of program benefits into land values, and (4) security and capital provided by farm programs encouraging additional output.

The elasticity of supply has been computed to be .1 in the short run and 1.0 in the long run. Output expands not only because of additional inputs brought into agriculture by prices supported above equilibrium levels by farm programs, but also because of the slippage element as farmers learn to avoid production controls through diversion of inferior cropland, bringing in new land, and substituting capital inputs for land. The elasticity of demand increases in the long run particularly because of the impact of price on exports. The elasticity of demand in the long run for farm commodities may be as high as -1, which implies that a change in output does not change the level of farm receipts.

Nelson and Cochrane in their simulation analysis of the farming economy estimated that in the absence of farm programs since 1953 the level of prices received by farmers would have been 28 percent higher in the 1968–1972 period and total net income 40.3 percent higher in the same period. The reason for these results is that the absence of farm programs would have reduced gains in productivity and agricultural investment, eventually driving prices and incomes to higher levels under a free market according to the Nelson-Cochrane results.

Even if the supply and demand responses do not erode gains from farm programs, capitalization of program benefits into land values means that the sellers of farmlands reap the gains and the additional income generated by programs is lost to the buyers. This impact may not have been of much consequence in the past, however. Only 2 to 3 percent of the farmland changes hands each year on the average. Furthermore, the entire benefits from farm programs are not capitalized immediately in the sales price, in part because farmers are not sure of the duration of farm programs and in part because of the inertia of the past.[16] The "free market" of the period since 1972 has raised land values far above those justified by capitalization of land values from farm programs of earlier years.

Empirical evidence of capitalization of farm program benefits into land values has been found for virtually all controlled commodities, but has been particularly pronounced for tobacco.[17] Allotment values for tobacco have been estimated to be as high as $3,000 per acre—the difference between the land value with and without tobacco allotment. After estimating capitalized benefits for numerous crops Reinsel and Krenz summarized the situation:

> The total capitalized value of farm program benefits is estimated at $16.5 billion in 1970—8 percent of the value of farm real estate. Since 1955, operators have paid about $5.9 billion to acquire program benefits. However, only about $2.7 billion of this investment remained unrecovered in 1970.[18]

In short, government programs substantially raised farm incomes in the short run and may have reduced farm incomes in the long run. In the absence of commodity programs, the period of most intense government involvement from the mid-1950s to 1972 would have been one of generally depressed farm prices, whereas the long-run impact of the programs appeared to hold down prices since 1972. It appears, therefore, that the programs dampened both short- and long-term economic instability. The unwieldy surpluses generated by programs proved of

---

[16] Luther Tweeten and Ted Nelson, "Sources and Repercussions of Changing U.S. Farm Real Estate Values," Oklahoma Agricultural Experiment Station Technical Bulletin T-120 (Stillwater, Oklahoma: Oklahoma State University, 1966).

[17] James Seagraves and Richard Manning, "Flue-Cured Tobacco Allotment Values and Uncertainty, 1934–1962," Economic Research Report, Department of Economics (Raleigh, N.C.: North Carolina State University, 1967); Garnett Bradford and James F. Thompson, "Impact of Eliminating the Tobacco Price Support, Supply Control Program," Department of Agricultural Economics Processed Series (Lexington, Kentucky: University of Kentucky, 1976).

[18] Robert Reinsel and Ronald Krenz, "Capitalization of Farm Program Benefits into Land Values," ERS-506 (Washington, D.C.: Economic Research Service, USDA, 1972).

considerable value in World War II, the Korean War, the 1966–1967 food crisis, and the 1970 corn blight and at other times. Benefits were often achieved at the considerable short-run social cost defined earlier and with large transfer payments to be discussed below.

Level and Distribution of Income Payments. Federal outlays for income stabilization total $80 billion from 1933 through 1975. Outlays reached nearly $5 billion in each of the years 1959, 1963, 1964, and 1972. Outlays for farm income stabilization totaled only $2.2 billion for the entire 1932–1939 period and did not reach over $1 billion per year until 1955, when they totaled $3.1 billion. A vast majority of the outlays have occurred since 1955.

Tables 2 and 3 provide insight into the distributive effects of government programs. Government payments as a percentage of personal taxes (primarily income taxes) paid by the farm population were considerably less than government payments to farmers from the beginning of farm programs through the year 1960 (Table 2). In the years from 1961 through 1972, government payments as a percentage of personal taxes were approximately 100 percent or higher. Payments as a percentage of net farm income also were high in those years and reached a peak of 37 percent in 1968.

While table 2 shows that in several years there was a major redistribution of income from the nonfarm to the farm population through government payments, the table does not reveal the redistribution of income among income classes. This redistribution is shown for 1968 in Table 3.[19] The estimates indicate that farms with sales of over $100,000 would have received direct payments of $8,869 per farm on the average and incurred benefit taxes of $4,953. Benefit taxes are normalized so that the total taxes just equal the total payments—highlighting the net redistribution of income. The net redistribution to the large farms averaged $3,914 per farm. At the other extreme, farms with sales of less than $2,500 a year received on the average direct payments of $231 and paid taxes of $889, leaving a net "loss" of $658 from direct payment programs.

Table 3 can be interpreted more broadly than for the farm population alone. Taxes were allocated according to national average tax rates by income group. Because the total taxes allocated thereby are close to total personal taxes paid by farmers, the tax allocation appears to be

---

[19] Other measures of the distribution of program benefits including additions to receipts on farms by economic class are found in Luther Tweeten, "Objectives of U.S. Food and Agricultural Policy and Implications for Commodity Legislation," *Farm and Food Policy 1977*, Print 75-404 0 of the Committee on Agriculture and Forestry, U.S. Senate, 94th Congress, 2d session (Washington, D.C., 1976), p. 51.

Table 2
DIRECT GOVERNMENT PAYMENTS TO FARMERS, 1934–1975

| Year | Government Payments | | |
	Total (millions)	Percentage of personal taxes	Percentage of net income
1934	446	474	18
1935	573	541	12
1936	278	228	7
1937	336	267	6
1938	446	323	11
1939	763	596	20
1940	723	613	19
1941	544	442	9
1942	650	305	7
1943	645	122	6
1944	776	78	7
1945	742	61	6
1946	772	65	5
1947	314	27	2
1948	257	17	1
1949	185	16	1
1950	283	29	2
1951	286	28	2
1952	275	20	2
1953	213	14	2
1954	257	16	2
1955	229	18	2
1956	554	45	5
1957	1,016	79	10
1958	1,089	85	9
1959	682	48	7
1960	702	51	6
1961	1,493	98	14
1962	1,747	105	17
1963	1,696	98	16
1964	2,181	129	25
1965	2,463	147	23
1966	3,277	176	30
1967	3,079	160	32
1968	3,462	161	37
1969	3,794	135	35
1970	3,717	124	34
1971	3,145	99	26
1972	3,961	115	26
1973	2,607	59	8
1974	503	10	2
1975	807	16	3

Source: U.S. Department of Agriculture, "Farm Income Statistics," Statistical Bulletin no. 557 (Washington, D.C.: Economic Research Service, USDA, July 1976 and earlier issues).

Table 3

ESTIMATED REDISTRIBUTION OF INCOME FROM DIRECT GOVERNMENT PAYMENTS TO FARMERS, BY ECONOMIC CLASS, 1968

	Economic Class of Farms, by Sales						
Item	$100,000 and over	$40,000 to 99,999	$20,000 to 39,999	$10,000 to 19,999	$5,000 to 9,999	$2,500 to 4,999	Less than $2,500
	(dollars per farm)						
Total income[a]	39,578	19,525	12,376	8,978	7,698	6,832	7,106
Direct payments	8,867	4,081	2,516	1,711	961	588	231
Taxes	4,953	2,443	1,549	1,125	963	855	889
Net redistribution	3,914	1,638	967	586	−2	−267	−658

[a] Net income of farm operator family from farm and nonfarm sources.
Sources: U.S. Department of Agriculture, "Farm Income Statistics," Statistical Bulletin no. 557 (Washington, D.C.: Economic Research Service, USDA, July 1976), pp. 62, 63; and Luther Tweeten and George Brinkman, *Micropolitan Development* (Ames: Iowa State University Press, 1976), p. 391.

appropriate for the farm as well as the nonfarm population. The implication is that substantial net transfers of income were made from lower income nonfarm households to higher income farm households in 1968 in provision of direct payments to farmers.

Imposition of the $20,000 payment limitation per recipient with passage of the Agriculture and Consumer Protection Act of 1973 potentially reduces the equity dilemma in government programs, but it also poses problems. In 1975 17 percent of farms with the largest sales per farm accounted for 70 percent of farm output. On the other hand, the smallest 50 percent of all farms produced only 5 percent of all farm output. These data highlight a dilemma in future farm programs. With no payment limitations, programs will be criticized and perhaps be judged as unacceptable to lawmakers because they inequitably redistribute income. But payment limitations of $20,000 per farm would mean that a production diversion program would have to concentrate on smaller farms. These smaller farms would receive direct payment benefits from commodity programs, but they might be required to divert substantial proportions of their cropland and would be virtually put out of the farming business with a large program. Furthermore, large farmers would still benefit from higher prices and receipts generated by reduced farm output. These considerations are not meant to imply that payment limitations are inappropriate. They do suggest that the concept of stringent payment limitation and production controls are incompatible in a sizable program. They also point to reliance on compensatory payments as opposed to production controls if farm program benefits are not to be concentrated on large farms. One argument against reliance on direct payments is that they are too costly to the Treasury. I now turn to measures of cost-effectiveness of Treasury funds in raising farm income.

Cost-Effectiveness of Commodity Programs. Policy makers appear to be much more concerned with Treasury costs than social costs of programs to support farm income. Therefore, it is well to examine cost-effectiveness of past programs, defined as the contribution to farm income per Treasury dollar spent. Mandatory controls are most cost-effective (and also entail the largest social cost), but such programs seem unacceptable for major commodities after being soundly rejected in the early 1960s. So the discussion below focuses on voluntary programs.

Programs that are most effective in removing farm production per Treasury dollar are also most cost-effective, because demand for farm output is highly inelastic in the short run. The effectiveness E in removing production per acre per program dollar is given by the following formula:

$$E = \frac{PY}{PY\text{-}C} = \frac{1}{1 - \dfrac{C}{PY}} \qquad C < PY \quad 1 < E < \infty$$

where P is product price, C is variable cost of production per acre, and Y is yield per acre. In theory, the producer is equally well-off by diverting acres or by producing a crop if the government pays rent equal to net returns $PY - C$, gross returns less variable costs of production. It is apparent for the most marginal cropland that $PY = C$ and $E = \infty$, the upper limit of effectiveness. If variable costs are zero, $E = 1$, the lower limit of effectiveness. E becomes larger, other things equal as (1) product price P is reduced, (2) yield Y is reduced, and (3) variable cost of production C is increased.

It follows in theory that effectiveness becomes large as diversion is concentrated on marginal land and whole farms under long-term contracts, so that more of the producer's costs become variable. Furthermore, E is enhanced by use of sealed bids that allow the government to discriminate among bids, paying only the amount necessary to retire land from production and selecting those bids that remove most production per program dollar. These considerations imply that long-term general land retirement programs give the highest E, a conclusion supported by empirical evidence which indicates E for the Conservation

Reserve Program was approximately 3.0.[20] But such programs have been rejected, in part because they concentrate land retirement in selected geographic areas with attendant problems for nonfarm communities.

The effectiveness of short-term diversion programs has been low in relation to reasonable estimates of potential effectiveness. Based on results from a personal interview survey of wheat producers, Carr and Tweeten found that several voluntary programs potentially could remove $2 of production per program dollar.[21]

The ratio of diversion payments per bushel to market price is an approximate measure of E. Under the 1972 corn program, producers who entered the program by diverting an initial percentage of their base could divert additional acres up to 15 percent of their base allotment for a payment rate of $.52 per bushel times normal yield. The market price was $1.57 per bushel, hence the theoretical effectiveness E of payments was $1.57/.52 = 3.0$. Under a similar arrangement for wheat producers in 1972, the payment rate for marginal diversion was $.94 per bushel times established yield. Given the market price, E was equal to 1.4. In view of these and other considerations, it is somewhat surprising to note that several estimates of actual effectiveness of programs were approximately 1.0 for feed grains[22] and even lower for other commodities.

Several factors explain the low effectiveness. One is that Agricultural Stabilization and Conservation Service employees at the local level are caught in the fallacy of composition. That is, producers in their county will receive greatest incomes if payments are generous and diversions lax, whereas for the nation E will be greatest under the opposite circumstances, given a fixed national budget for programs. A second reason is that some programs entailed a large direct payment component. This is illustrated in data from the Department of Agriculture, separating the functions which commodity programs payments served in 1968 into "supply management" and "income supplement" functions.[23]

---

[20] R. P. Christensen and R. O. Aines, "Economic Effects of Acreage Control Programs in the 1950s," Agricultural Economic Report no. 18 (Washington, D.C.: Economic Research Service, USDA, 1962).

[21] A. Barry Carr and Luther Tweeten, "Comparative Efficiency of Selected Voluntary Acreage Control Programs in the Use of Government Funds," Oklahoma Agricultural Experiment Station Research Report P-696 (Stillwater, Oklahoma: Oklahoma State University, 1974).

[22] Tweeten, *Foundations of Farm Policy*, p. 345.

[23] John Schnittker, "Direction of Federal Farm Program Alternatives," summary of remarks to management training and development conference of the Bank for Cooperatives, Edwardsville, Illinois (Washington, D.C.: Schnittker Associates, 1970).

Program	Supply Management		Income Supplement	
	Dollars (in millions)	Percent	Dollars (in millions)	Percent
Cotton	276	35	508	65
Feed Grains	1,221	89	148	11
Wheat	384	51	362	49
Three Programs	1,881	65	1,018	35

Note that feed grain payments in 1968 were almost entirely devoted to limiting output (supply management), while only one-third of total cotton payments served that function. One-half of all wheat payments in 1968 were income supplements.

Even if for acreage diversion programs $E = 1$, it can be shown that they are more cost-effective than direct payment programs. Cost-effectiveness CE in raising net income per Treasury dollar is given by the formula:[24]

$$CE = 1 - E(1 + F) + S$$

where E is effectiveness as defined above, F is the price flexibility of demand, and S is production cost savings per dollar of program cost. Each dollar increment in government diversion payments raises net income $1 from the payment itself, $3 through the macroeconomic impact $E(1 + F)$ where $E = 1$ and $F = -4$ plus $S = \$.50$ saved in production expenses. Thus each dollar spent on the diversion or set-aside program raises net farm income an estimated $1 + \$3 + \$.50 = \$4.50$. This compares with $CE = \$1.00$ for a direct payment program requiring no diversion. While in theory this is a conservative estimate, it is notable that on the average, $100 spent on feed grain programs in the early 1960s actually increased farm income only $168.[25] In spite of the theoretically high cost-effectiveness of diversion programs, the record is not impressive.

Acreage diversion has advantages other than cost-effectiveness, including making program payments more acceptable to farmers who feel they are doing something to receive them, by holding reserve capacity for future use and by conserving soil. But in view of the low cost-effectiveness of diversion programs, the high slippage factor, high

---

[24] Tweeten, "Objectives of U.S. Food and Agricultural Policy and Implications for Commodity Legislation," Appendix A.

[25] Legislative Reference Service, Library of Congress, "Farm Program Benefits and Costs in Recent Years," Senate Committee on Agriculture and Forestry, 88th Congress, 2d session (Washington, D.C., 1964).

social cost, and inequities in program payments among producers or concentration of diverted acres on selected geographic areas, perhaps it is time to consider direct payments seriously as an alternative to production controls.

Summary and Conclusions

The review of farm programs and their economic implications warrants several conclusions:

(1) Government commodity programs for agriculture have contributed significantly to stability in farm commodity and food prices in the short and long run. This has benefitted both farmers and consumers.

(2) Programs avoided a substantial drop in short-run farm income during periods of rapid advances in productivity and low foreign demand. Programs probably reduced long-term farm income and the number of farms and farm residents.

(3) Excess or reserve capacity has been highly beneficial for utilization in several emergencies such as wars, droughts at home and abroad, and pestilence, such as the corn blight of 1970.

(4) Accumulation of buffer stocks and their release at propitious times has been largely a matter of blind luck rather than sagacious foresight. A buffer stock acquisition and release policy is clearly overdue— the options, of course, include sole reliance on the private trade.

(5) Benefits of farm programs have been obtained at considerable Treasury cost and short-run social cost of reduced goods and services produced. To these can be added "costs" of transfer payments from lower income taxpayers to higher income farmers.

(6) A crisis in farm policy calling for substantial new directions could come from a collision between farm interests on the one hand and consumer–taxpayer interests on the other. The latter may feel that the costs in (5) are too high a price to pay for the benefits of commodity programs. A confrontation seems unlikely to end in a free market—the role of government in providing stability in the farm and food economy is widely accepted. But a confrontation could lead to establishment of a national farm and food policy featuring a buffer stock policy, income security for low-income farmers through direct payments (perhaps as part of a national income maintenance program), elimination of provision for production controls in legislation, and provision for export controls or other devices to limit the rise in food prices in times of national emergency.

(7) Inefficiency engendered by commodity programs was reduced in the past because economic security and capital provided by the pro-

grams speeded consolidation of farms and exodus of excess farm labor. (Benefits did not rise proportionately with output, hence programs did not increase economies of size.) Because excess labor has been eliminated for the most part from farming, future commodity programs of the relative magnitudes used in the past will entail larger real economic costs.

(8) Success in raising farm income with production controls has been mixed. Farm production capacity is like a balloon filled with water. Prior to the 1960s, production controls focused on specific crops with little attention to cross compliance that would have idled cropland withheld from production of controlled crops. The result was compressing one part of the balloon but allowing the balloon to expand elsewhere, depressing prices of noncontrolled commodities. Programs that required idling of cropland by conversion to soil-conserving uses let water out of the balloon and raised prices received and receipts of farmers. Programs prior to the 1960s removed little production capacity and contributed to farm income mainly as direct payments. Despite programs to drain water from the balloon by idling land since 1960, the record in raising farm receipts by reducing overall output has fallen short of expectations based on cost-effectiveness measures in this paper. Even in the case of feed grains, where payments were more heavily focused on supply control, cost-effectiveness of program dollars has been extremely low in relation to reasonable standards based on theory.

(9) In the absence of shocks to shift the direction of farm policy, it appears that target prices and loan rates will be contained in forthcoming commodity programs. History and analysis suggest guidelines for setting such prices and rates. Tweeten has shown that, given time for land prices to adjust, average full cost per unit of production will exceed the average price per unit of the commodity.[26] Setting the target price at the full cost (current land value) of production raises land values and the full cost of production, leading to a spiral of escalating target prices and production costs. To avoid stimulation of land values, overproduction, excessive Treasury costs and/or requirements for stringent production controls, target prices should be set no higher than the long-term expected average price under a free market. (For 1977, it appears such a price for corn is $2 per bushel or slightly higher, for wheat is $3 per bushel or lower, and for cotton is $.55 per pound or slightly higher.) Target prices can be adjusted after 1977 for year-to-year changes in the cost of production.

While the principal purpose of target prices and deficiency payments is to maintain viability of efficiently managed farms of adequate

---

[26] Tweeten, *Foundations of Farm Policy*, pp. 178ff.

size, the principal purpose of loan rates is to hold whatever reserves are deemed appropriate in the form of buffer stocks and, if desired, set aside acreage. Loan rates are best set to allow competition in markets, particularly the export market without export subsidies, and to allow substitution of wheat for coarse grains as feed. To avoid undue accumulation of reserves, loan rates need to be highly flexible and tied to reserve levels or set by the secretary of agriculture rather than tied to a fixed percentage of target prices. Inasmuch as the purpose of the loan rate is to adjust reserves, it is possible for loan rates intermittently to exceed target prices.

COMMENTARIES

Howard W. Hjort

Dr. Johnson commented on the changes in farm income and the sources of change in farm operators' income. I would encourage some additional discussion of the gain in income since 1972, due to the escalation in crop prices, and the relationship between that phenomenon and the second topic that he takes up, changes in the labor market.

I think this may have major significance in terms of farm policy directions. And, of course, it touches on the question that is referred to throughout both of the papers—the productivity of American agriculture.

Is it possible that the slowing of the rate of decrease of farm operators is due to the relatively high commodity prices recently? And, is this only a temporary pause? If prices stay near the current levels, or supplies again become excessive, will we then see an acceleration in the rate of decrease in farm numbers? Or have we, in fact, reached a point of enduring stability in that segment of the sector?

With respect to the comparative advantage question that was raised, the conclusion that U.S. grain and soybean producers are dependent upon international trade is certainly true. And that has important implications for reserve or inventory policies—whatever term one wants to use—as well as for price policies. Prices need to be viewed both from the standpoint of international trade and from the balance-of-payments implications of the situation. The big increase in exports and the favorable balance of trade on agricultural products has been a great plus to the U.S. economy.

Now, for a few comments on marketing. The brief discussion about marketing seems to pose the same question we are wrestling with in the other segments of the sector—Have we run out of sources of productivity change?

As has been stated, there is a lot of rhetoric about that. Isn't this an area that should have some serious research and study?

I think the same thing has to be said about productivity growth. Dr. Johnson makes the case for a serious research effort on the whole question of productivity growth in agriculture. I would agree—as he states in a footnote—that the weather factor must be fully taken into account in making that assessment.

In the last part, on farmland prices and the sharp escalation in nominal prices in recent years, there are significant implications for agricultural policy, and not just price and income policy. I was a little surprised to discover that over two-fifths of our crop acres are now farmed by those who are renting land. What happens when we go through a period of high prices like this one? We bid up the price of land very sharply. Are we in a situation where the ownership of land is profitable, but farming is not necessarily so? There is part of our dilemma.

In terms of policy, we probably should be thinking seriously of dividing the question and focusing on the transfer of land apart from the income and price support levels in commodity programs. The transfer process cannot be carried out merely by boosting the support levels, price or income, to a level that permits the transfer to continue taking place. As Luther Tweeten and others have pointed out, that simply escalates the price of land. While the price of land rises, so does the cost of production to the renter. This opens the whole question of the structure of American agriculture. What structure do we want? Do we want a system where ownership and operation are separated? It seems to me that is the direction in which we are headed.

I would underscore one point Luther Tweeten makes—that the loan levels should be geared to the market, and that there should be an income transfer to make up the difference between the loan levels and the income criteria, whatever that is. As I read the hearings and several of the bills that have been introduced, I found that was not being recognized.

Several bills say the loan rates shall be 90 percent of the last three-year or four-year average of prices, or some proportion of the cost of production, or some percentage of parity. If we get into those rigid relationships, then we will have a gap between the price support (loan) level for wheat and corn.

I would like to hear Luther Tweeten examine the implications of that. This has great significance in terms of the operation of programs. If we have that gap, there may be conditions when we have to revert back to rigid allotments and set-asides for individual crops. We have to give up the idea that a farmer can use his resources as he sees fit, after meeting an initial set-aside requirement.

Bruce L. Gardner

These papers surveyed a very broad array of events. To fit in with the rest of the conference, it would be helpful to highlight what the interpretations of history by Gale Johnson and Luther Tweeten tell us about the pitfalls and promises of the alternatives facing us now. Although the authors did not spell this out explicitly for the most part, a couple of points were clear.

First, Johnson and Tweeten both emphasize the late 1940s and early 1950s as a negative example. The message is, Don't get locked into high price supports.

Second, both of these authors apparently believe that the cost of policy error is greater today than it has been in the past. Johnson's analysis gives a reason for this, on the supply side. It can be reduced to the idea that the supply function for agricultural products is more elastic than it used to be. And, considering what has happened to exports, the demand function is also more elastic than it used to be.

These changes mean that pricing errors lead to bigger quantity distortions and higher welfare costs than had been the case. They also mean, of course, that incorrect quantity restrictions would produce smaller price distortions and smaller welfare costs. However, since the proximate targets for farm policy typically seem to be prices, I think the assessment is correct, that the cost of error is bigger now than it used to be.

I found Gale Johnson's categories of underlying forces behind change in U.S. agriculture generally helpful. He might have given more weight to the rising value of human time as a factor both in the labor market changes and in the shifts in the technology of food consumption and marketing, as well as, perhaps, the increased specialization of farm enterprises.

The relevance for policy of this set of changes is apparent, and it came out in some of the data that Tweeten presented. The main fact is that the mainstream commercial producers of farm products are no longer poor people; and while there are poor people in agriculture, these poor people will not have their lot significantly improved by high commodity prices.

Incidentally, I think Tweeten may be overstating the significance of the 1961 legislation in his text, though he did not discuss this today, and understating the degree of change in the 1973 act. The Agriculture and Consumer Protection Act of 1973 was significant in taking a final step in dichotomizing income support from market management by basing deficiency payments on a fixed allotment base, so there could be high payments without causing economic mischief.

I also doubt Tweeten's suggestion that policies under the compromise act of 1970 were widely accepted. In the early 1970s, the set-aside acreage and the annual payments of around $4 billion to farmers were crystalizing discontent with farm policy as much as ever, among general economists anyway. Evidence of that can be seen in the policy monographs of the time by Hendrik Houthakker and Gale Johnson, and in one by Charlie Schultze that I am referring to more and more lately. Perhaps the best reading of the times is an article in *The Wall Street Journal* in early July 1972, about a week prior to the Russian grain sales. It was a major article in which eminent agricultural economists were surveyed. The view of the state of things and of the prospects for ever changing anything in farm policy was quite pessimistic. The headline was: "Will we ever end farm subsidies?"

Whatever we think about particular programs, the fundamental shift in the 1960s and 1970s as seen from today's perspective is a continuous flow towards market orientation from, say, 1963 on by means of cuts in support prices. Inflation masks the extent to which support prices were actually cut during this time. But if those prices are deflated, the extent of change is readily apparent. In 1972 dollars, the support price for wheat fell by more than a half between 1962 and 1972, from about $2.80 to $1.25; and the real support price for corn in the same period fell by roughly a third. Indeed, as Tweeten mentioned, if we go back to the mid-1950s, we can see that the trend towards declining real support prices started then.

Both authors give surprisingly little attention to the events of the last five years. I take this as a judgment that the price fluctuations since 1972, say, were large but transitory aberrations, perhaps like those of World War II, and do not represent any fundamental change in the world or the U.S. agricultural economy. I infer that the authors believe that the upheavals of these past few years do not have important implications for the conduct of farm policy. If that is true, then the support price trend is important to maintain. Unfortunately, the increase in the loan rate on wheat last fall brings the real support price on wheat back up to the level of the mid-1960s. And that support level was causing problems at the time. So, if there has been no fundamental change, we may get back into those problems.

Let me now turn to a few of the particular interpretations of past events contained in the papers.

First, we have to recognize the great difficulty of the questions that the authors are asking. One that they both consider is the effects of attempts to control acreage on agricultural output in the period from the mid-1950s to 1972.

For some earlier periods and programs, this question would have been less difficult, of course. In those old days there was sometimes a more direct approach; for example, if policy makers decided there were too many baby pigs, then some were bought up and killed. But under the more sophisticated recent crop supply and management schemes, the question is much more difficult. Johnson estimates at 2 percent or less the reduction in farm output; Tweeten has a 5 percent reduction. What the discussion brings out is how difficult these counter-factual questions are. We want to know what would happen if we did not have the programs, but we have no way of observing that.

There are so many different counter-factual questions one can ask that it may not be worth spending a whole lot of time on any particular one. For example, what if we considered the situation not only without the grain programs, but also without the tobacco, peanut, and rice programs, which had restrictive acreage effects, or the dairy supports and import restriction programs, or the beef import restrictions, or the sugar program? Maybe we would want to ask how the whole situation would have been different without various subsets of these programs.

Moreover, Johnson brings in the very interesting suggestion—which we owe principally to Ed Schuh—that a more appropriate counter-factual question might be, How would things have been different without farm programs *and* without an overvalued dollar which constituted a de facto tax on agricultural and other exports? It is tempting to suppose with reference to this question that farm programs might have approached some kind of second-best situation; that the overvalued dollar depressed exports and lowered U.S. farm prices, and the farm programs offset this by increasing farm prices. But a moment's reflection will reveal that farm programs under this sort of interpretation actually made a bad situation worse, as far as resource allocation is concerned. This is because the overvalued dollar resulted in reduced demand for U.S. products, and, hence, less farm output at lower prices, while the addition of programs which reduce supply results in *still less* output at higher prices. Thus, we have price effects which are offsetting and farm income effects which may be offsetting, as Johnson says, but the output reductions are cumulative. We are trying to cure a situation of too little farm output by reducing it further.

One other issue reveals an interesting contrast between the two papers. Johnson argues that we have not yet measured factor productivity with enough precision even to discuss trends in it. Tweeten goes ahead and presents estimates of how farm programs affected it. I am not prepared to say who is more nearly correct, but I think it is a useful division of labor.

I found a few items in Tweeten's summary unsatisfying. His first item says that farm programs benefited both farmers and consumers by stabilizing prices. But we really did not have an adequate discussion of the basis for this conclusion in the text. We need more on how big these benefits are; how they are measured; did they exceed the cost of carrying the stocks which created the stability; and so on.

Also, Tweeten mentions *short-run* social costs in terms of goods and services lost. It is not clear to me what this *short-run* means in a historical context; at least, it is not clear that it means what it does when we draw theoretical supply or demand curves, because in the context of past events, the losses either existed or they did not. I interpret *short-run* as meaning that the costs existed for a few years and then they disappeared. If that is true, in which years did they occur, and how did this all fit into the historical record?

There should have been more discussion of the effects of farm programs on consumer prices of food. Some of the elasticities Tweeten uses can allow us to make our own estimates. But I would have liked more detail on his judgment of how much income or wealth was transferred to farmers indirectly by means of higher prices.

In regard to the issue of who gets what, Tweeten discusses the purpose of farm programs. He says the principal purpose of deficiency payments and target prices is to maintain the viability of efficiently managed farms of adequate size. While our job as economists may sometimes be to spell out this sort of reason or more plausible ones for government programs, at some point we have to recognize that the purpose of legislation is better described in political terms. The purpose is to take from those who have less political clout and give to those who have more. I do not want to overstate this point, but we sometimes have to think about the political aspect too.

Finally, I think, Tweeten gives a possibly misleading picture of the state of agricultural policy today by emphasizing a few of the large continuing interventions which can be patterned as part of a general policy design. What is missing is the flavor of ad hockery, or even chaos, in the menu of intervention that we have had and still have. Just a listing of current programs makes the point—import restraints on beef, sugar, and dairy products; production controls on peanuts and tobacco; encouragement of exports of rice and other products under P.L. 480 and CCC Credit; domestic commodity distribution programs; marketing orders and agreements for milk and all those fruits, vegetables, and specialty crops; the state marketing boards for milk and different fruits and vegetables; these new research and promotion boards for cotton and beef.

That list can be topped with a set of policy moves that is surely a significant new trend in the last five years, namely the increase in regulation of agriculture under EPA, OSHA, fair labor practice laws, and such activities as the Grains Standards Act of 1976, as well as the increased regulation of food processing and distribution. Then, I think, we have a truer picture of the state of agricultural policy.

Hendrik S. Houthakker

The problem of having to discuss two such excellent papers is that it is hard to criticize them, except perhaps to point out some of the disagreements between them, and these are not major. So let me make a few remarks which are not intended to be critical of the papers, but which deal more with the general policy problem.

The very low cost-effectiveness of diversion programs found by Luther Tweeten fits in with the thesis that the farm problem has always been a problem of excess labor. The question is whether that is still the case right now. There never was excess land, because it is so easy to change the inputs into agricultural production. The whole idea of controlling production through restrictions on land use never made much sense.

The second point in this regard is that increasing productivity is, by itself, an adverse development, as far as the farm problem is concerned. By increasing productivity, some farmers, and perhaps most farmers, are generally made worse off. Gale Johnson has some tentative remarks on this question of productivity. On the problem of whether there still is excess labor in agriculture I am inclined to think (in agreement with Gale Johnson, I believe) that there cannot be very much. Nevertheless, we cannot be sure.

Farm incomes, of course, rose very high in 1974, and, to some extent, in 1975. In 1976 they had quite a severe fall. According to most recent figures, real farm income per farm (the simplest indicator short of an elaborate analysis) is now back to the level of about 1969, which was by no means a disaster year. On this basis one could say real farm income per farm is still just about what it should be, especially since income in the nonfarm sector has not gone up much.

Nevertheless, I would like to see a more detailed analysis of whether there is still excess labor in agriculture. Even if there were, this would not justify the farm programs that are now being talked about. My impression is that the new administration plans to revert to the rather extensive government intervention of the 1950s and 1960s with some new, different twists. If true this is a very unfortunate development. For one thing, it would be contrary to the case President Carter made in his election campaign, namely that government is too big, and should become smaller. The only thing that will make government smaller is greater reliance on the market.

This simple truth is too often overlooked, not only in the farm area but also in various other areas, such as energy. If the market is not used, somebody else has to make the allocations, that is, government officials by the hundreds of thousands. We cannot get a smaller government unless market forces are allowed to do the job that would be done otherwise by the bureaucracy.

I would hope that we will not return to a highly regimented agriculture, as we had until 1966. The 1966 bill was the first major departure from such regimentation. The justification for regimentation is, if anything, less now than it was before.

Luther Tweeten's paper has some interesting figures on the distribution of benefits. These figures are not the whole story as I am sure he would admit. They are quite old, and they also do not cover the full income scale.

For one thing, the highest income in any of the groups he considers is about $40,000. In the recent period of high prices, there were many farmers whose incomes were $100,000 or over. Somehow we never hear much about those. I once made myself very unpopular in farm circles by pointing this out. As a result I got some irate letters from congressmen. Evidently, this is not the kind of thing they want mentioned, because if other members of Congress got wind of it, they might not be quite so willing to vote for farm programs. Nevertheless, this kind of information should be more widely circulated.

Luther Tweeten has done a good job in showing that the programs are, in fact, transferring money to high-income farmers from consumers, most of whom have much lower incomes; and that low-income farmers do not benefit from them. I had also pointed this out many years ago in one of my occasional excursions into the subject.

I believe there is some scope for government intervention in agriculture. In other words, I am not saying that the government should stay out of it completely. Following the lead of Gale Johnson, I would say the government has a role in stabilizing farm prices and farm income. This is a rather limited role, but an important one, and one can talk at great length about how it is to be done.

In *Economic Policy for the Farm Sector*, a study written for the American Enterprise Institute about ten years ago, I advocated the use of future markets for this purpose, primarily because I felt that government intervention in the cash market is bound to be burdensome, expensive, and inefficient in various technical ways. This idea has not made a great deal of headway. Those who had any knowledge of farm policy at all said it would be a return to the Federal Farm Board of the early 1930s. The Federal Farm Board, as Luther Tweeten's paper points out, was an aspect of Hoover's approach to the farm policy.

The Federal Farm Board was not very successful, for various reasons. It tried to corner the markets when they were plunging rapidly. It succeeded in cornering May wheat in 1931, but that did not help farm prices generally.

In our history we have had quite a number of episodes like this, which somehow rule out everything remotely similar. I was very encouraged, just the other day, by a related story on the subject of Teapot Dome. For many years, whenever the Naval Petroleum Reserves there were mentioned, somebody would bring up the Teapot Dome scandal, and that finished all further consideration of the reserves. Now, more than fifty years after the scandal, Teapot Dome will at last be developed. If that can be done after a lapse of fifty-three years, maybe the Federal Farm Board is now also sufficiently far back in history for us to consider a program like this.

The main point is that this kind of intervention, if done judiciously and under appropriate rules, is important. Most other kinds are harmful or, at best, not very helpful to the people who really need help.

I would like to have seen a little more discussion of international aspects in the two papers before us. However, both authors have dealt with them in other places.

One particularly important point is the question of export subsidies. When I was in the government several years ago, I carried on a great campaign against export subsidies. Indeed, when I left the government in 1971, I thought that the Department of Agriculture had agreed not to use them anymore.

However, no sooner had I lifted my heels than the export subsidies were back again to play a major role in the Russian wheat sales of 1972. If it had not been for export subsidies, the Russians could not have bought the huge amounts they did without raising prices. The government should have been out of the market at that time, but it was not; and as a result, it bears a considerable share of the blame for that unfortunate episode. That is the kind of farm program we definitely should not have.

My own opposition was especially influenced by Gale Johnson's demonstration that export subsidies did not lower export prices, but rather increased our domestic prices. And, since I was then at the Council of Economic Advisers, that was a matter of great concern to me.

I hope we have learned something from the past. I am an incurable optimist, and sometimes no amount of evidence can convince me to the contrary. If we have not learned anything, it certainly is not the fault of the two papers before us.

PART TWO

FOOD PRODUCTION, PROCESSING, DISTRIBUTION, AND CONSUMPTION

AGRICULTURAL PRODUCTION, PRICES AND COSTS: HOW HAVE THE FARMERS FARED?

George E. Brandow

Statistics on farm income and assets readily show that agricultural producers collectively have fared very well indeed in the past five years, though farm income in early 1977 was well below the peak reached in 1973. The years since 1972 contrast with the preceding two decades, when farm income might loosely be said to be low to moderate. The reason for the sharp change in farmers' fortunes in 1972 was change in the economic environment in which agriculture operated. The most dramatic development was a surge in export demand, but inflation in the economy at large and some poor weather for crops contributed to improved farm income after 1972.

The year 1972 also marked a change in the role of farm policy. Prior to that year, government programs to support farm prices and incomes had been almost constantly in effect for much of agriculture. When new economic circumstances lifted farm prices above supports in the 1970s, most of the leading farm programs became inoperative though still legally in place. The principal exceptions were in dairying, peanuts, tobacco, and rice, for which programs continued to be at least sporadically important.

As we try to gain perspective on farmers' economic position in 1977, we will compare farm income and net worth with corresponding data for the period before 1972 when farmers were not faring very well. And we will gain some idea of how much government programs were contributing to farm income in that era. Then we will take a closer look at income, prices, costs, production, and net worth in the years since 1972, which may or may not foreshadow the future.

Two Decades Prior to 1972

The "farm problem" as it existed during the 1950s and 1960s became clear in 1953. Excess stocks of farm products accumulated rapidly, and farm prices and incomes fell back from earlier peaks. For nearly twenty years, beginning in 1953, prices and incomes were generally weak, and various government programs struggled with farm surpluses.

The root of the farm problem during the two decades was a rapid advance in technology that increased crop and livestock yields faster than markets expanded, and faster than could be accommodated by orderly withdrawal of labor and land from agriculture. Much of the new technology substituted capital for labor and increased the size of farm needed for efficient operation by one family. Under the economic pressures stemming from the technological revolution, the farm labor force—including both family and hired labor—was much reduced during the period. The acreage of harvested crops declined mainly because of land retirement programs operated by government to control surpluses. The number of farms fell steadily while the average size of farms increased.

Prices, Costs, and Income. Prices received by farmers from 1953 to 1971 were more stable than they were before or after that period. The U.S. Department of Agriculture's index of farm prices of crops (1967 = 100) fluctuated within the narrow range from 97 to 107 (annual averages). Price support programs of the government were directed mainly to the major crops. The range of the index of prices of livestock products, some subject to strong cycles, was three times as wide as the range for crops. Except for dairy products, prices of livestock products were not supported.

Prices paid by farmers for production inputs (goods, wages, interest, taxes) rose moderately during the two decades because of increasing real farm wages and slow inflation in the economy at large. But inputs required per unit of output in farming declined. Cost per unit of output apparently fell gradually from 1953 to the early 1960s and then began to rise.[1] The increase was attributable to more rapid inflation of prices related to production inputs in the latter 1960s and to a slowing of the rate of increase in productivity. The ratio of prices received by farmers to unit cost of production reached its low in the mid-1950s and was somewhat improved, though it remained variable, from the early 1960s to 1971.

The ratio of prices received by farmers to prices paid for all items (both for production and for family living) declined irregularly throughout the period. This price ratio when calculated from a 1910–1914 base is the famous parity ratio. A ratio of 100 is often advanced as the

---

[1] The calculation of unit costs is at best a crude approximation because of dissimilarities in items included in the prices-paid and physical input indexes and because of the tenuous character of a total productivity index when technology is changing rapidly.

appropriate target for farm policy, even though the ratio does not take into account changes in agricultural productivity, in revenue other than that from sales, and in levels of living in the nonfarm economy. The parity ratio was 92 in 1953 and 70 in 1971.

Total net farm income as the two-decade period began was well below the peak reached in 1948. Net income declined a little further before inching upward from the early 1960s to 1971. Real net farm income, computed by adjusting dollar net income for changes in prices paid by farmers for family living items, declined at the outset of the period but fluctuated without any clear trend from the late 1950s to 1971.

Enormous disparity among census-defined farms makes it difficult to interpret aggregate income for producers in terms of the welfare of farm people. "Commercial farms" is a common term for farms that, with good management, are capable of producing sufficient income from farming alone to be viable economic units. In this paper, commercial farms are defined as farms that in 1971 had sufficient resource bases of labor and capital to generate (and that did generate) sales of at least $10,000 per farm at that year's prices. Noncommercial farms sold less than $10,000 of farm products in 1971. This classification is crude but is the best available way of making an essential distinction between two segments of agriculture.

In 1971, commercial farms constituted 34 percent of all farms and accounted for 88 percent of all cash receipts from farming. Net income from farming in the commercial segment was $11,778 per farm.[2] Income from off-farm sources averaged $4,445, bringing total income from all sources to $16,223 per farm.

The great majority of commercial farms are family enterprises. Included in commercial farm income, however, is income received by large-scale (not family-held) corporations. On a number of commercial farms, more than one family (for example, father-son or brother-brother partnerships) share the farm income. Thus, income per family on family operated commercial farms was less than $16,223, but exactly how much less is not known. On the smallest 39 percent of commercial farms,[3] however, where one family probably was associated with one farm in almost all cases, income per farm was $5,924 from farming, $4,585 from off-farm sources, making $10,509 in total. The conclusion seems

---

[2] U.S. Department of Agriculture data for realized net income have been adjusted to approximate total net farm income wherever necessary throughout this paper. The adjustment for any group of farms was made by applying the ratio of total net income to realized net income for all farms to the group in question.

[3] Farms with sales between $10,000 and $19,999 accounted for 39 percent of commercial farms.

warranted that average income per family on family operated commercial farms approximated the median family income in the nation, which was estimated to be $13,668 for 1971 by a method since revised.[4]

On smaller farms—noncommercial farms—net income from farming averaged only $1,586 in 1971, but off-farm sources brought the total income per family to $9,068. Many operators of small farms were primarily industrial or professional workers with medium or high incomes. Others were dependent almost entirely on farm income and were in poverty. Comparisons with earlier data, however, show that the extent of small-farm poverty substantially diminished during the 1960s as the number of noncommercial farms declined and as income from off-farm sources rose.

Assets, Debt, and Net Worth. Investment in production assets per worker and per dollar of sales is higher in farming than in most nonagricultural industries. Total farm assets include, also, farm residences and other assets used for living. In 1971, production assets were 82 percent of total assets, and farm real estate, chiefly land, accounted for 75 percent of the total value of production assets.

An important aspect of farmers' economic position during the two decades preceding 1972 was the strong advance in farmland values. The average value of farm real estate per acre rose 142 percent between 1953 and 1971. Some of the early increase could be attributed to a lagged adjustment to previous increases in farm income but, clearly, reasons other than farm income were raising farmland prices during the period. Principally because of the advance in land values, capital gains on farm physical assets during the years 1960–1971 amounted to 72 percent of farm proprietors' equity as 1960 began and to 85 percent of all net farm income earned during the interval.[5]

Farm debt more than tripled during the two decades. But debt amounted to only 10 percent of the value of farm assets in 1953 and was still at the favorable level of 17 percent at the end of 1971. The absolute value of proprietors' equity in the farming sector nearly doubled during the period.

---

[4] The median family income in the nation has at least two defects as a standard of comparison. Median income is less than average income because of the skewness of income distributions; comparing average farm family income with the national median somewhat overstates the relative position of farm families. Peculiarities in the national median series during the 1970s, together with revisions introducing noncomparability over time, impair the usefulness of farm-national median comparisons made later in the paper for 1976.

[5] Data on assets, debt, equity, and capital gains are taken from *Balance Sheet of the Farming Sector*, suppl. no. 1, U.S. Department of Agriculture, Agriculture Information Bulletin no. 389, April 1976. About one-third of capital gains went to nonoperator landlords (see later text).

Imputation of Farm Income to Factors of Production. On the great majority of farms, net farm income is the return to the farm family for its labor, management, and capital. This is in sharp contrast with most of industry, where all wages of labor and salaries of management ordinarily are expenses and do not enter net income (large corporate farms follow industrial practice). Estimates of how net farm income might be apportioned to labor, management, and capital are extremely unreliable but give some insight into rates of return earned in farming and into the welfare aspects of income distribution.

In 1971, at the close of the two-decade period under review, average rates of return realized on unpaid resources in farming were distinctly modest. A calculation by the U.S. Department of Agriculture valued family labor at the wage rate paid to hired farm workers and made a charge of 5 percent of cash receipts for management; residual income was expressed as a percentage of proprietors' equity in production assets. The value thus placed on family labor was $1.73 per hour; in contrast, hourly earnings in manufacturing were $3.57 in 1971. The value of management on the average commercial farm was implied to be $2,543. Residual income after allocations to labor and management represented a 3.4 percent rate of return on proprietors' equity in production assets valued at 1971 prices. The yield on medium grade corporate bonds in the same year was 8.56 percent.

Rates of return probably were higher on commercial farms than in all farming, but the difference apparently was not great because most income and resources were on commercial farms and because the method of calculation tended to exclude unproductive resources in noncommercial agriculture. Valuation of proprietors' equity at current asset prices raises a question, however: in standard business accounting, assets are valued at cost prices. If farm assets had been valued on a cost basis, residual income treated as return on investment would have amounted to 6.8 percent of proprietors' equity.[6]

Roughly 60–66 percent of the substantial capital gains on commercial farms in the 1960s and early 1970s went to farm operators. The remainder went to nonoperator landlords, many of whom presumably were retired farmers or farmers' widows. Another large portion of the remainder went to nonfarm investors who had no other immediate tie with farming. Capital gains were being made outside of agriculture during the same period, for example, in the stock market and urban real

---

[6] The USDA calculation is given in the source cited in footnote 5. The rate of return on proprietors' equity at asset cost is based on an estimate that in 1970 proprietors' equity at market value of assets was twice proprietors' equity at cost value (*The Balance Sheet of the Farming Sector, 1970*, U.S. Department of Agriculture, Agriculture Information Bulletin no. 350, 1971).

estate. A study applying nonfarm rates of earnings to farm-furnished factors of production in 1966 found that inclusion or exclusion of capital gains did not greatly change conclusions about how rates of earnings on commercial farms compared with earnings outside of agriculture.[7]

Income of Hired Farm Labor and of All Farm Residents. Hired farm labor is near the bottom of the American labor force in skills, earnings, and social status. Hourly pay is usually low, fringe benefits are scarce, and obtaining sufficient hours of work is a major obstacle to making an acceptable annual income. Yearly earnings from all sources typically are well below the average annual income of noncommercial farmers. Farm wage rates were rising somewhat more rapidly than wages in private non-agricultural industry near the close of the two-decade period, but the gap between incomes of hired farm workers and incomes of most farmers or most industrial workers remained wide.

The ratio of personal disposable income per person in the farm population to personal disposable income per person in the nonfarm population fell to its postwar low of 48 percent in the mid-1950s. Thereafter, the ratio rose strongly and reached 75 percent by 1971, just before a sharp turn in farmers' favor occurred in 1972.

Farm Production. Total farm production rose about 1.7 percent per year during the two decades ending in 1971. Methods of production and the input mix changed substantially while output persistently increased. The use of farm labor was more than cut in half between 1953 and 1971. New kinds of machinery went into use, but total input of mechanical power and machinery rose only a little. Use of agricultural chemicals increased sharply. Greater specialization in farming and output expansion increased interfarm transfers of feed, seed, and livestock. The U.S. Department of Agriculture's index of total inputs used in farming declined slightly betwen 1953 and 1971.

The changing input mix in agriculture during the two decades meant a sharp increase in the use of purchased inputs and a decline in farm-furnished inputs. Between 1953 and 1971, purchased inputs rose 42 percent while farm-furnished inputs declined 36 percent. Other things being equal, the change made net farm income more sensitive to fluctuations in the ratio of prices received by farmers to prices paid for production inputs. By the close of the period, farming had developed specialized animal, dairy, and poultry enterprises dependent upon stable livestock-feed price ratios, and crop producers had high cash costs that made them vulnerable to sharp drops in crop prices.

---

[7] *Parity Returns Position of Farmers*, report by U.S. Department of Agriculture, 90th Congress, 1st session, August 1967.

Crop production per acre rose 55 percent between 1953 and 1971, and production per livestock breeding unit also increased strongly. Total productivity, the ratio of total output to total input, advanced persistently until the mid-1960s and then appeared to slow down. How much of the apparent change might be due to technical imperfections of the indexes is not clear, but some genuine retardation of the advance of agricultural productivity took place near the close of these two decades.

Effects of Farm Policy. If farm programs in effect during the period had only minor effects on prices, income, and production, then actual markets reflected fairly well the underlying economic pressures bearing on agriculture. But if programs had important effects, the price, income, and production experience during the period is not an accurate indication of the free market impact of the circumstances then existing or of expected consequences should they recur in the future.

Studies during the period showed that excess capacity dealt with in one way or another by farm programs reduced the volume of farm output flowing to commercial markets by roughly 5 to 10 percent.[8] Since demand for farm output is highly inelastic, that amount of output reduction served at any one point in time to keep farm prices substantially higher than they would have been.

Five independent estimates made in the early 1960s indicated that the short-term effect of abandoning farm programs would be to reduce farm prices materially (17 percent was the median estimate) and to cut net farm income on the order of one-third. The greatest impact would be on crop producers; producers of hogs, poultry products, and feedlot beef, after comparatively short periods of adjustment, would find both their feed costs and product prices reduced. The devices that collectively had these effects included price supports, government accumulation of stocks, export subsidies, concessional sales to poor countries, domestic consumption subsidies, marketing orders, acreage restraints, and direct payments to farmers.

The long-term effects of programs were much less clear. Lower prices and incomes resulting from abandoning programs would be expected to discourage production eventually, and reduced output would bring about some recovery of prices and incomes. The empirical base for estimating lagged relationships required to appraise the effects of farm programs over, say, five- to ten-year periods is very weak. Three simula-

---

[8] Sources of data used in this section are given in G. E. Brandow, "Policy for Commercial Agriculture: A Review of Literature, 1945–71," in *A Survey of Agricultural Economics Literature: Traditional Fields of Agricultural Economics, 1940s to 1970s* (Minneapolis: University of Minnesota Press, 1977).

tion studies comparing hypothetical free-market agriculture with agriculture as it was during the 1950s and 1960s tell more about the lack of consensus among economists concerning the relevant economic relationships than about the effects of farm price and income programs.

The study by Rosine and Helmberger (empirically the weakest) indicated that most of the effects of farm programs were small during the two decades under review. Programs were estimated to have increased output by 4.7 percent, price of output by 4.4 percent, labor input by 6.5 percent, and wages earned by hired and family labor by 2.6 percent.[9] Ray and Heady presented results for principal crops and for total livestock in the form of 1959–1967 averages. The estimated effect of a free market as contrasted with programs was to reduce prices of leading crops by 21 to 59 percent and of livestock products collectively by 11 percent. Estimated free-market production was virtually the same as program production except for tobacco, which declined 26 percent, and for cotton, which rose 24 percent. Gross farm income expected in a free market was down 15 percent, and net farm income was down 47 percent.[10]

Nelson and Cochrane portrayed what would have been a long, strong cycle if farm programs had been eliminated in 1953. The effect in the 1950s and early 1960s would have been to increase market supplies of all crops and of all livestock by 5.5 percent and 4.3 percent, respectively, to reduce the index of all farm prices nearly one-fourth, and to lower net farm income by about 40 percent. As a lagged response to such adverse circumstances, however, supply available to the market during the five years 1968–1972 would have been cut below the program level by 9.5 percent for crops and 3.9 percent for livestock. Farm prices then would have been 27.7 percent higher than with program prices, and net farm income would have been 40.3 percent above that with program income.[11]

This writer's judgment is that the pattern shown by the Nelson and Cochrane study is the most realistic but that the expected decline of prices and income in the 1950s and early 1960s is somewhat overstated,

---

[9] John Rosine and Peter Helmberger, "A Neoclassical Analysis of the U.S. Farm Sector, 1948–1970," *American Journal of Agricultural Economics*, vol. 56, no. 4 (November 1974), pp. 717–29. The percentages given here are averages of percentages obtained by the authors for the years 1953–1970 from two alternative versions of how best to represent the effects of certain farm programs.

[10] D. E. Ray and E. O. Heady, "Government Farm Programs and Commodity Interaction: A Simulation Analysis," *American Journal of Agricultural Economics*, vol. 54, no. 4, pt. 1 (November 1972), pp. 578–90.

[11] F. J. Nelson and W. W. Cochrane, "Economic Consequences of Federal Farm Commodity Programs, 1953–72," *Agricultural Economics Research*, vol. 28, no. 2 (April 1976), pp. 52–64.

while the expected recovery of farm prosperity in 1968–1972 is much overstated. If no farm programs had existed during the 1950s and 1960s, market prices of farm products in 1971 might have averaged about the same or a little higher than they actually were, while net farm income might have been 10–20 percent lower.

Economists are virtually unanimous in agreeing that much of the income benefit of farm programs becomes capitalized in land values. This has clearly been shown for crops such as tobacco, for which acreage quotas were in use in the 1950s and 1960s. Such capitalization is shown in each of the two studies, cited above, that considered the question. Reinsel and Krenz found that the implied interest rate at which benefits were capitalized was perhaps 1.5 to 3 times the farm mortgage rate of interest. An alternative way of stating their finding is that an important portion of benefits is imputed to labor and management if commercial interest rates are taken to be the rates used for capitalization into land values. Reinsel and Krenz estimated that about 8 percent of farm real estate values in 1970 was attributable to capitalized benefits of farm programs.[12]

Capitalization has important long-run implications for the effectiveness of farm programs and for welfare of farm people. To the extent that benefits are imputed to land or other fixed asset, most future entrants into agriculture while underlying circumstances stay the same will have higher costs and will need higher prices to remain solvent. Imputation of benefits to land owners can be expected to be less favorable to lower-income people in farming than would imputation of benefits to labor.

Summary of Farmers' Economic Position Just Prior to 1972. In the years immediately preceding the dramatic turn of agriculture's fortunes in 1972, farm production was being restrained by acreage controls, prices of several leading farm products were being modestly supported by government loans and output restrictions, large stocks of grains were being held off the market by government financing, and net farm income was being materially aided by government programs then in effect. The commercial sector of agriculture accounted for one-third of all farms and for nearly 90 percent of the market supply of farm products. Average family income on commercial farms approximated the median family income for all families in the nation. In the noncommercial part of agriculture, income from off-farm sources far exceeded farm income. Many small farmers were truly poor; average family income in noncommercial

---

[12] R. D. Reinsel and R. D. Krenz, *Capitalization of Farm Program Benefits into Land Values*, U.S. Department of Agriculture ERS-506, October 1972.

agriculture was about two-thirds percent of the national median. Hired farm labor was the clearly disadvantaged group in agriculture.

Capital gains, principally because of rising land values, were an important source of economic strength to commercial farmers. Rates of return on family labor, management, and investment were modest— below nonfarm standards—in the commercial farm sector. The comparatively large labor and capital resources of the average commercial farm family enabled it to equal the median family income in the nation despite below average rates of return on resources.

The once strong rise in total resource productivity in farming had shown signs of slowing down since the mid-1960s. An inherently unstable industry, agriculture was benefiting from the steadying influence of price supports, large stocks of grains, and reserve acreage withheld to control surpluses. Though a variety of ills affected farming and the public was unhappy about the high cost of government farm programs, agriculture as a whole was solvent, was able to produce a little more than the market would take at modest prices, and was shedding its image as a disadvantaged sector of the American economy.

1972–1976: The Agricultural Transformation

Within a year beginning in mid-1972, grain surpluses that had seemed so burdensome disappeared, excess production capacity was replaced by shortage, farm prices and incomes turned sharply upward, and important farm programs became inoperative. A strong surge of farm exports was the leading cause of the about-face in agriculture. Inflation in the nonfarm sector of the economy swelled consumers' incomes and demand for farm products, especially meat. The year 1973 was a fantastic year for agriculture in general if not for every producer group. By 1976, a more normal state of affairs was asserting itself, but farm prices, costs, incomes, and net worth were at much higher levels than in 1971.

Prices, Costs, and Incomes. Grains and soybeans were most immediately affected by the strong surge of export demand. In 1973, prices of all crops averaged 73 percent higher than their pre-1972 level (Table 1). Exceptionally poor weather for crops in 1974 drove crop prices considerably higher. The crop price index fell back in 1975, and in 1976 it was just short of double the pre-1972 position.

Prices of livestock and livestock products rose much less sharply and in 1976 were only 50 percent higher than before the upsurge began. An important influence on livestock prices was the turning point in the decade-long cattle cycle in 1974. Beef production increased substan-

Table 1

AGRICULTURAL PRICE INDEXES, 1969–1976

Year	Prices Received by Farmers			Prices Paid by Farmers			Ratio, Prices Received to Paid
	Crops	Live-stock products	All prod-ucts	Produc-tion[a]	Living items	Total index	
1969–71 = 100							
1969–71	100	100	100	100	100	100	100
1972	113	115	114	112	108	110	104
1973	173	155	163	132	117	127	128
1974	221	140	175	150	133	145	121
1975	199	146	169	165	146	160	106
1976	195	150	169	178	155	171	99

[a] Products purchased, wages, interest, taxes.
Source: U.S. Department of Agriculture.

tially, and cattle prices plummeted and put downward pressure on prices of other meat animals and poultry.

Prices paid by farmers for production inputs rose strongly because of inflation in the general economy and soaring energy costs. In addition, prices paid by farmers for feed, seed, and purchased livestock reflected changes in other farmers' selling prices of crops and livestock. Prices paid for production inputs had risen a little more than prices received by farmers for all farm products by 1976, but rough adjustment for higher productivity of inputs indicates that unit costs of production rose slightly less than prices of farm products between 1969–1971 and 1976.

Net farm income more than doubled between 1969–1971 and 1973 (Table 2). It had fallen back nearly one-fourth by 1975 and slipped further in 1976. The much greater increase in cash receipts from crops than from livestock, including dairy and poultry, indicates that the higher net income after 1971 went mainly to crop producers. Adjustment of dollar net income for prices of farm family living items shows that real net farm income, which had doubled by 1973, was back at the pre-1972 level in 1976.

Data carrying forward the commercial-noncommercial distinction made for 1971 in an earlier section are not available. Classification of farms by dollar sales, which continues to be done, is useless for comparisons over time when prices rise as much as they have risen in the past five years. Change in total net farm income and data for farms that

Table 2

CASH RECEIPTS FROM MARKETINGS AND NET
FARM INCOME, 1969–1976

Year and Units	Cash Receipts from Marketings and CCC Loans			Total Net Farm Income	
	Crops	Live-stock products	Total	In current dollars	In 1969–71 dollars
Billion dollars					
1969–71	20.95	29.57	50.53	14.36	14.36
1976	47.8	47.0	94.8	22.0	14.2
Indexes, 1969–71 = 100					
1969–71	100	100	100	100	100
1972	122	121	121	130	120
1973	196	155	172	232	198
1974	245	140	183	185	139
1975	223	145	177	178	122
1976	228	159	188	153	99

Source: U.S. Department of Agriculture.

in 1975 sold more than $20,000 worth of farm products do give some indication of incomes on commercial and noncommercial farms as defined for 1971. To repeat, commercial farms are farms that have sufficient labor and capital resources to be viable economic units; at 1971 prices, they have sales of $10,000 or more.

As roughly estimated by the writer, net income from farming amounted to $17,000 per commercial farm in 1976, and income from off-farm sources was $7,000. Total income per commercial farm was perhaps $24,000. Income per commercial farm *family* was less, as previously explained, but apparently was well above the median family income in the nation. On noncommercial farms, net farm income probably was about $2,000 per farm, but income from off-farm sources brought average family income to the neighborhood of $15,000, at least equal to the national median family income (but see footnote 4). Noncommercial farmers continued to range from poverty stricken people dependent on farming, at one extreme, to wealthy farm residents at the other extreme.

Three of the many possible methods of imputing net farm income in 1975 to factors of production not paid for in a market give the results shown below:

Factor and return rate	Method 1	Method 2	Method 3
Unpaid labor, dol. per hr.	$2.39	$2.39	$4.81
Unpaid management, dol. per commercial farm	$3,940	$3,940	—
Proprietors' capital, interest rate earned	4.9%	12-13%	7%

Method 1 is based on the calculation by the U.S. Department of Agriculture described earlier: unpaid (family) labor is valued at the wage rate paid to hired farm labor; management is valued at 5 percent of cash receipts; and return on proprietors' investment is residual income expressed as a percentage of proprietors' equity in production assets when assets are valued at 1975 prices. Method 2 is the same except the estimated cost value of production assets is used in computing proprietors' return on capital. For method 3, hourly earnings of manufacturing workers are used to value family labor; no additional charge is made for family management; and residual earnings are expressed as a percentage of proprietors' equity in production assets when farm real estate is valued at 1971 prices and other assets are valued at 1975 prices.[13]

The hourly rate used for valuing family labor by method 1 is low, especially in view of the absence of common fringe benefits; hourly earnings in manufacturing averaged $4.81. Valuation of unpaid management is highly arbitrary, but the estimate for the average commercial farm seems modest. Return on proprietors' investment is well below the 10.39 percent yield on medium grade corporate bonds in 1975. In method 2, return on proprietors' capital is somewhat higher than the corporate bond standard. In method 3, manufacturing workers' wages are used as the standard for family labor and management combined, while a compromise is used for valuation of assets. Net farm income was lower in 1976 than in 1975. It may be concluded that net farm income received on commercial farms in 1976 did not represent rates of returns on unpaid factors of production that were in excess of rates that might reasonably be accepted as standards.

Assets, Debt, and Net Worth. The total value of farm assets more than doubled between 1969–1971 and January 1, 1977 (Table 3). By far

---

[13] The calculations are extremely rough, and for method 2, depend upon estimates of cost values of assets derived from figures for 1970 that probably were not themselves very firm. Uncertain as they are, the numbers seem adequate for the general conclusion derived from them. For USDA data used directly or indirectly, see footnotes 5 and 6.

Table 3

ASSETS, DEBT, EQUITY, AND CAPITAL GAINS IN THE FARMING SECTOR, 1969–1977

Year[a] and Units	Total Farm Assets	Total Debt	Propri- etors' Equity	Capital Gains of Proprietors	
				Total on all physi- cal assets (in billions of dollars)	Percent to farm operators
Billion dollars					
1969–71	306.3	52.7	253.6	14.6	—
1977	634	101.5	532.5	—	—
Indexes, 1969–71 = 100					
1969–71	100	100	100	14.6	70
1972	112	112	112	41.1	71
1973	126	124	127	82.2	71
1974	155	141	158	42.0	71
1975	170	155	173	62[b]	c
1976	191	172	195	47[b]	c
1977	207	193	210	—	—

[a] Asset, debt, and equity values are for January 1.
[b] Rough estimates by the writer.
[c] Not estimated.
Source: U.S. Department of Agriculture except as noted.

the principal contributor to this strong increase was farm real estate, whose value per acre rose 131 percent between 1969–1971 and late 1976. Apparently, prices of farm land were increased during the period by higher net farm income, by the increasing influence of urban values on much farm real estate, and by the attractiveness of farmland as an investment during a time of rapid inflation in the economy at large.

Both short-term and real estate debt rose rapidly during the period as working capital requirements in farming increased with higher prices and as farms changed ownership at higher values. The ratio of debts to assets, which averaged 17.2 percent in 1969–1971, was about 16 percent on January 1, 1977. Both ratios show a high degree of solvency in the farming sector as a whole though not, of course, for every farmer. As the debt figures imply, the equity of farm proprietors, which was 84 percent of assets as 1977 began, rose at a slightly faster rate than the value of farm assets during the period.

Capital gains in the farming sector were large (Table 3). For the period 1972–1976 as a whole, capital gains were twice as large as net farm income and almost equalled proprietors' equity as 1972 began. Capital gains were divided between farm operators and nonoperator landlords approximately in the proportion 71 to 29. Capital gains were also made outside of agriculture during the inflationary period but not, overall, in the stock and bond markets.

Hired Farm Labor and All Farm Residents. Farm wage rates rose somewhat faster than hourly earnings in manufacturing between 1969–1971 and 1976. For the first time in more than half a century of decline in the farm labor force, the trend in employment of hired farm labor appeared to turn upward while employment of family labor continued to fall. Some further improvement in the generally substandard working and living conditions for hired employees apparently was made. Nevertheless, hired farm labor remained near the bottom of the American labor force in economic and social standing.

Per capita disposable income of all farm residents collectively, which was 75 percent of per capita disposable income of the nonfarm population in 1971, exceeded the nonfarm level in 1973. In 1975, the ratio of farm to nonfarm per capita disposable income was 90 percent. Probably the ratio declined little in 1976. There was no longer any reason to single out farms as a location characterized by generally substandard incomes.

Production. Several developments affected agricultural production during the period 1972 to 1976, as indicated in the following summary:

(1) Harvested acreage was increased over the 1972 area by return to cultivation of 40 to 45 million acres withheld under acreage retirement programs in effect in 1972. This amount was less than the 60 million acres for which payments were made in 1972.

(2) Weather was exceptionally poor for grain and soybean production in 1974 and seemed somewhat below normal for crops collectively in 1975 and 1976.

(3) Productivity, the ratio of total output to total input, continued to advance but more slowly than in the 1950s and early 1960s.

(4) High prices of fertilizer, due mainly to the energy situation, had a mildly adverse effect on crop production, particularly in 1975.

(5) Export demand for grain and oilseeds raised prices of those crops and of livestock feed, tending to divert grain and oilseed meal from production of livestock products for domestic consumption to the export market.

(6) More or less independently of the foregoing developments,

the cattle cycle reached a characteristic turning point in 1974 at which cattle marketings rose substantially and cattle prices declined. The large market supply of grass-fed beef in 1974 to 1976 was a negative influence on production of other meats and of dairy and poultry products. It also helped to make grain utilization low in relation to the volume of livestock products reaching consumers.

Table 4 shows that crop production rose substantially while output of livestock and livestock products fluctuated without any clear trend. The gain in productivity was irregular and slow. By 1976, total crop acreage was as large as it was likely to be at the then existing price relationships, virtually all of output was moving to markets, and excess capacity in the sense of withheld but readily available output did not exist in agriculture.

National inventories of grains were lower in 1976 than in 1972. Feed grain stocks, which were 50 million tons at the beginning of the 1972–1973 crop year, were 19 million tons at the outset of the 1976–1977 crop year. Wheat stocks were down from 985 million bushels as the 1972–1973 crop year began to 664 million bushels at the start of the 1976–1977 crop year. Experience during the period demonstrated both the large stocks that would be necessary to achieve year to year stability of prices and domestic utilization and the limited capacity of private traders to carry stocks without marked depression of prices.

Stability and Feed—Livestock Relationships. The period 1972–1976 was one of great instability in agriculture because of strong but uneven ex-

---

Table 4

FARM OUTPUT AND PRODUCTIVITY, 1969–1976

	Farm Production			
Year	Crops	Livestock products	Total	**Total Productivity**
	Indexes, 1969–71 = 100			
1969–71	100	100	100	100
1972	107	103	105	104
1973	114	100	107	105
1974	104	101	103	103
1975	115	96	106	108
1976	115	98	108	108[a]

[a] Estimated by the writer.
Source: U.S. Department of Agriculture except as noted.

port demand, exceptionally poor weather in 1974, inflation in the economy at large, energy shortages, the disappearance of once large grain stocks, and the rise of most farm product prices above levels at which government supports could exert a stabilizing influence. As indicated earlier, export demand for grains and oilseeds raised prices of the crops, increased costs of feed concentrates to producers of meat animals, dairy products, and poultry products, and increased crop production relative to livestock production. In general, net incomes of crop producers were raised more than incomes of livestock producers (though many farmers are both).

Short-term movements of farm prices of five crops are illustrated by the fourth-quarter averages given in Table 5. The price-raising effect of poor grain and soybean crops in 1974 is obvious. Prices in the closing quarter of 1976 were below corresponding prices in 1974 by one-third for corn, one-half for wheat, and one-fifth for soybeans. Farm prices of cotton, however, reached their fourth-quarter peak in 1976. For most crops, the increase in prices between 1971 and 1976 was highly erratic rather than a steady advance.

Of the livestock prices, only egg prices in the fourth quarter of 1976 were double prices in the fourth quarter of 1971; egg prices were cyclically low in 1971. The collapse of cattle prices in 1974 is very evident and was a reason for a slight decline in several other livestock prices in 1974. Milk prices exhibited the steadiest advance in the livestock group between 1971 and 1976.

Ratios of livestock prices to feed prices, which are crude indicators of short-term changes in profitability of livestock production, are shown in Table 6. The price ratio varied widely for each class of livestock, especially for beef and hogs. The poor crops of 1974, combined with low carryover of feed grains from the preceding year, squeezed all livestock producers; and producers' reactions were an important reason for higher livestock prices in the following year.

The highly uneven impact of price and production changes upon different producer groups during the period is demonstrated by these data and by the income statistics of Table 2. In addition, weather did not affect all producers within a group alike. A cash grain producer in the Corn Belt who had near-average crops in 1974 had a bonanza; a producer who had especially poor crops was not fully compensated by higher prices. As 1977 began, drought and cold in important producing areas caused difficulties and threatened production later in the year.

Effects of Farm Policy. The large grain stocks on hand in early 1972, then widely regarded from force of habit only as burdensome surpluses, were a reason for the incautiously large sale of grain to Russia in 1972

Table 5

FOURTH QUARTER FARM PRICES, 1971–1976

Year	Corn (bu.)	Wheat (bu.)	Soybeans (bu.)	Cotton (lb.)	Tobacco[a] (lb.)	Hogs (cwt.)	Cattle Beef (cwt.)	Milk (cwt.)	Eggs (doz.)	Broilers (lb.)
1971	$1.02	$1.32	$2.91	$ .278	$ .79	$19.33	$29.83	$6.15	$ .310	$ .125
1972	1.27	2.08	3.49	.264	.80	27.93	34.07	6.48	.374	.143
1973	2.25	4.40	5.47	.417	.90	39.87	40.00	8.59	.609	.210
1974	3.35	4.79	7.55	.485	1.13	37.43	28.83	8.37	.566	.232
1975	2.44	3.67	4.55	.496	1.03	51.63	33.07	9.99	.584	.265
1976	2.20	2.48	6.19	.646	1.13	33.43	31.67	9.92	.652	.198

a Averages, types 11–37.
Source: U.S. Department of Agriculture.

Table 6

RATIOS OF FARM PRICES OF LIVESTOCK AND LIVESTOCK PRODUCTS TO PRICES OF FEEDS CONSUMED BY THE LIVESTOCK, FOURTH QUARTER, 1971–1976

| | Livestock or Livestock Product[a] | | | | | |
Year	Hogs	Beef	Milk	Eggs	Broilers	Turkeys
1971	19.0	28.3	1.86	7.4	2.63	4.9
1972	22.0	25.7	1.72	7.9	2.73	4.4
1973	17.8	16.8	1.59	8.5	2.57	5.0
1974	11.2	11.0	1.21	6.8	2.50	3.3
1975	21.2	17.6	1.64	8.1	3.30	4.4
1976	15.2	17.2	1.61	8.5	2.33	3.6

[a] Price ratios: 100 pounds of hog to bushel of corn; 100 pounds of steer (Omaha) to bushel of corn; one pound of milk to one pound of concentrate ration; one dozen eggs to one pound of laying feed; one pound of broiler to one pound of broiler grower feed; one pound of turkey to one pound of turkey grower feed.
Source: U.S. Department of Agriculture.

and for the pricing policies associated with it. But the basic fact was that Russia and some other populous countries were short of grain and were turning to imports to alleviate their problems. Export demand for American grain and soybeans would have expanded sharply even if direct sales to Russia had been much smaller than they were. The external demand for American farm products was largely if not wholly independent of American policy. The United States did, of course, have options about how to respond to that demand.

Large grain stocks, accumulated under price support operations, and 40–45 million acres of cropland held back to prevent surplus production were important means by which the strong surge of export demand and rising domestic demand could be met. Stocks were drawn down quickly in 1972 and 1973, and by 1974 all land retirement programs had been eliminated. Even this unusual capacity to respond to strong demand did not prevent sharp price increases. Prices for feed grains, wheat, soybeans, and cotton rose sufficiently so that loan programs had no appreciable influence in supporting their prices, and no payments to farmers under the feed grain, wheat, and cotton programs were made except for disaster relief. After 1973, government programs were significant mainly for peanuts, tobacco, and rice among the crops and for milk and wool among livestock products. Prices, costs, production, stocks, and incomes in agriculture after 1973 were largely though not completely the result of underlying economic conditions operating through free markets.

Summary for 1972–1976. After nearly two decades of economic adversity, agriculture experienced a sharp turn in its favor in 1972. Strong export demand for grains and soybeans was the principal element in the new situation, and producers of those crops most strongly felt the impact in higher prices and incomes. Producers of meat animals and of dairy and poultry products saw feed prices climb as crop prices rose; despite short periods of favorable price relationships, livestock producers were less favored by the turn of events than were crop producers. Cattlemen were especially hard hit by a cyclical depression of prices beginning in 1974. Crop production rose 15 percent between 1969–1971 and 1976, but livestock production declined slightly. The new pattern of demand, operating through the price system, shifted aggregate farm output toward the export market.

Farm costs rose with general inflation, the energy shortage, and higher purchase prices of feed, seed, and livestock. The slower pace of advancing productivity in agriculture, noted in the latter 1960s, continued in the 1970s and only modestly tempered the effect of rising input prices on production costs.

Net farm income soared in 1973 but had fallen back in 1976 to 53 percent above the pre-1972 level. The average income of families operating commercial farms exceeded the national median family income. Families on noncommercial farms collectively received far more income from off-farm than farm sources; despite the persistence of a poverty subgroup, average family incomes in noncommercial agriculture at least equaled the national median. Hired farm labor continued to earn low incomes. In 1976, the once wide gap between per capita disposable incomes of the farm and nonfarm populations was nearly closed.

Capital gains in agriculture, about 70 percent going to farm operators, were double net farm income over the five years 1972–1976. Rapidly rising farmland values were the principal scource of capital gains. Farmers' debts rose almost as rapidly as asset values. As 1977 began, proprietors' equity in farm assets amounted to 84 percent of the value of assets.

Buffeted by strong external shocks and for a time lacking the steadying influence of large stocks and of operational price supports, agriculture was highly unstable from 1972 to 1976. Instability was most evident in wide fluctuations of crop prices and in the ratios of livestock product prices to feed costs. Changes in livestock product output induced by variable crop prices were important reasons for instability of prices and incomes in the livestock portion of the farm economy.

As 1977 began, virtually all aggregate measures of the welfare of agriculture showed it to be in a strong economic position. Net income, however, had receded much below the 1973 peak. Some groups within agriculture were experiencing temporary gains or losses, and others were in historically favored or disadvantaged situations. Prices, production, and incomes were largely though not entirely determined in markets unaffected by the farm programs that had been so important in the 1950s and 1960s. Excess capacity had disappeared, and output seemed approximately in balance with market outlets in the aggregate if not for each commodity. Continuation of that balance depended greatly upon strong and growing export demand. In light of all the variables—economic, political, acts of God—likely to affect exports, there was no assurance that the economic position of agriculture as it was at the outset of 1977 would persist far into the future.

FOOD PROCESSING AND DISTRIBUTION: THE ROLE OF THE MIDDLEMEN

Joel Popkin

Introduction

Brandow has described the dramatic improvement in farm income that began in 1972 when farm prices started their sharp rise. The improvement reflects a larger rise in prices received than in prices paid by farmers, from mid-1972 through 1974. While prices paid caught up with the slightly declining prices received after 1974, the rise in farm output in those years served to maintain farm income at about two-thirds of the level it had reached in 1974. This paper is concerned with how the large rise in farm prices from mid-1971 through 1974 and the subsequent small decline were reflected in the prices food manufacturers and retailers obtained for their products.

Prices and Costs—Manufacturers and Retailers

Figures 1 and 2 present data on the behavior of food price indexes at the manufacturers' and retailers' level from 1960 through 1975. Two other variables are also plotted in the charts. One is an index of prices manufacturers and retailers pay for the food products they process or distribute. The other index is a weighted sum of the prices each pays for all the commodities it purchases—food, other commodities (such as fuel), and labor.[1] The data are plotted as percentage changes over four calendar quarters, in order to depict longer term changes in prices and their relationship to unit input costs.[2]

---

[1] These data were prepared for a project funded by the National Science Foundation. They have not been updated beyond 1975. The inputs are weighted by their relative importance in the 1967 input-output table for the U.S. economy.

[2] The issue of the short-run speed of response to costs at various levels of food processing and distribution is discussed in U.S. Council on Wage and Price

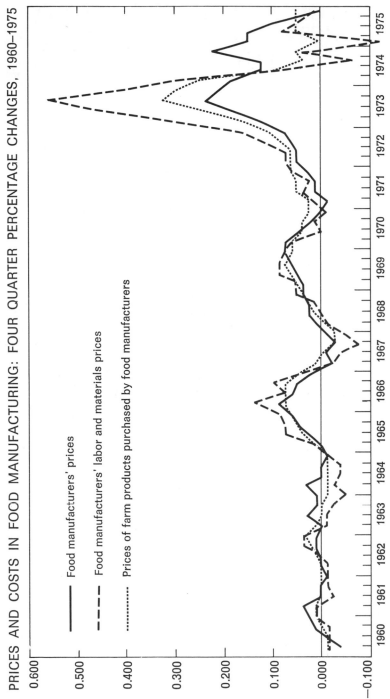

Figure 1

PRICES AND COSTS IN FOOD MANUFACTURING: FOUR QUARTER PERCENTAGE CHANGES, 1960–1975

——— Food manufacturers' prices

– – – Food manufacturers' labor and materials prices

·········· Prices of farm products purchased by food manufacturers

Figure 2

PRICES AND COSTS IN FOOD RETAILING: FOUR QUARTER PERCENTAGE CHANGES, 1960–1975

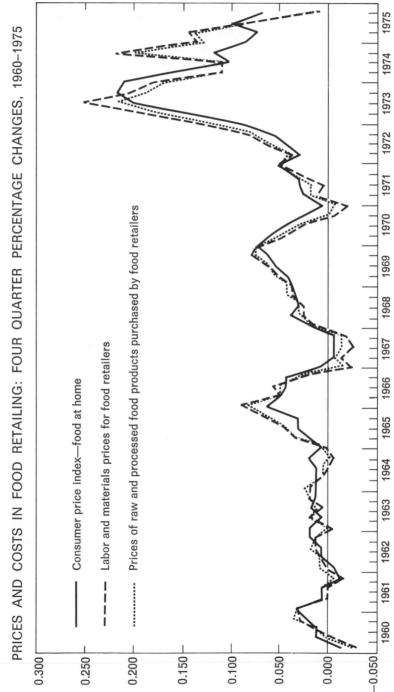

—————— Consumer price index—food at home

– – – – – Labor and materials prices for food retailers

·············· Prices of raw and processed food products purchased by food retailers

Weighting variable input (labor and materials) price indexes by their relative shares in the total value of output, or sales, and comparing the changes in the resulting index with those of the output price index, provides some indication whether the combined share of profits and fixed costs as a percentage of sales is changing or remaining the same. It is only an indication, however, since such weighting assumes that the relative quantities of labor and materials remain constant over time. If the elasticity of substitution between materials and labor is not zero, or if technological change affects the two inputs in different ways, true quantities will, of course, change. Changes in the combined share of profits and fixed costs do not imply that the profit share is changing in the same direction. In fact the profits and fixed cost shares usually are moving in opposite directions, depending on what is happening to output. So the comparative movements of the indexes in Figures 1 and 2 indicate at best only what is happening to the combined share of profits and fixed costs, and say nothing about profit margins.

Manufacturers. For manufacturers, the data show a very close correspondence in the movements of input and output prices between 1960 and 1971. In 1972 and 1973, when farm prices, and those of other inputs, were rising steeply, output prices rose less rapidly than input prices—by 4 percentage points in 1972 and by 6 percentage points in 1973. In 1974, when farm prices first decelerated and then turned down, output prices rose more rapidly than input prices—by 15 percentage points.

Data available from the Bureau of Economic Analyses on profits and profits plus capital consumption allowances confirm this picture. Between 1960 and 1971 profits with inventory valuation adjustment but without capital consumption adjustment rose gradually from $2.1 billion to $3.3 billion, presumably reflecting increasing volume but fairly constant sales margins. In the next two years they declined, reaching $2.2 billion in 1973, about the level of 1960; this reflected the sharper rise of input as compared with output prices. In 1974 profits began to rise again as output price increases outstripped input price increases.

Retailers. In food retailing the picture was different in two respects. First, there was a greater tendency for retail price changes to lag behind input price changes somewhat, particularly when the latter were rising.

Stability, *The Responsiveness of Wholesale and Retail Food Prices to Changes in the Costs of Food Production and Distribution*, Staff Report, November 1976. This report was based in part on Dale Heien, "A Study of the Relation Between Farm-Level Prices and Retail Prices," report written for the Council on Wage and Price Stability, 1976.

Second, like behavior at the manufacturing level, input price increases outstripped retail price increases during 1972 and most of 1973, but there was no catch-up in 1974, viewed as a whole. Some catch-up was manifested in late 1973 and early 1974, but the subsequent spurt in food input prices more than offset these gains. It was not until 1975 that some catch-up was obvious at the retail level.

Analysis of the behavior of food processing and distribution margins in the period since the new farm policy took effect is clouded by the fact that wage and price controls and their aftermath also affected most of the period. Kosters has undertaken some analysis of margins in the food industry during controls.[3] The analysis is confined to the farm-retail spread; data on spreads are not calculated by the Department of Agriculture for processing and distribution separately, except for a few items. He finds a sharp rise in margins during Phase IV— July 1973–April 1974. In that period the percentage increase in margins outstripped that in farm prices, while in Phases I, II, and III, the reverse was true. Kosters attributes this change in pattern to the fact that during Phase IV, prenotification requirements on intended price increases were dropped for food processors, resulting in an almost immediate pass-through of cost increases, built up during the earlier phases of the controls program, but not yet reflected in prices. He concludes that the increase in the farm-retail spread in 1974 appears to be due to a widening of processors' margins. His findings are consistent generally with those based on the data for manufacturers in Figure 1 and for those of retailers in Figure 2.

The data in Figures 1 and 2 covering the entire 1960–1975 period show that at both the retail and the wholesale levels the ratio of input to output prices rose at an annual rate of 0.3 percent. A study by the Bureau of Labor Statistics (BLS) suggests that output per labor hour in food retailing grew at an annual rate of 2.0 percent between 1960 and 1975.[4] Presumably there has been improvement as well in labor productivity among food manufacturers. A study by Kendrick, based on data from 1960 to 1966, shows that labor productivity rose at an annual rate of 3.2 percent during that period.[5] Such improvement, together with relatively constant gross margins for processors and distributors may mirror one or more of several possible developments.

---

[3] Marvin H. Kosters, *Controls and Inflation: The Economic Stabilization Program in Retrospect* (Washington, D.C.: American Enterprise Institute, 1976).

[4] U.S. Department of Labor, Bureau of Labor Statistics, "Output Per Unit of Labor Input in the Retail Food Store Industry," *Monthly Labor Review*, January 1977.

[5] John W. Kendrick, *Postwar Productivity Trends in the United States, 1948–69* (New York: National Bureau of Economic Research, 1973).

(1) The improvement in output per labor hour attributable to the infusion of new capital in food processing and distribution may reflect a rise in the ratio of capital to labor coupled with the fact that the elasticity of substitution between capital and labor may not be unity.

(2) The structure of the markets through which farm products pass on their way to the consumer may have changed.

(3) The mix of products and services may have changed—presumably toward more highly processed products at the manufacturers' level and less service at retail.

Regression Analysis

The structure of price determination in food processing and retailing can be studied through regression analysis. To do so requires making some assumptions about the underlying behavior, deriving the mathematical form implied, and testing it with the relevant data. It is assumed that manufacturers process and retailers distribute food products subject to the widely used Cobb–Douglas production function, with constant returns to scale. Further, it is assumed that in the long run they seek to maximize profits subject to this production function with input prices given. These assumptions would imply that over the long run the combined share of profits and fixed costs is constant. In the short run, however, it can vary when demand shifts induce changes in the degree to which the fixed (in the short run) capital stock is utilized and when price departs from that which would clear markets. Price disequilibrium implies that unfilled orders and/or finished goods inventories are changing to take up the slack between purchases (or orders) and production. Such a model, in log (ln) and log change ($\Delta\ ln$) form, is given by:

$$\Delta\ ln\ p_t = ln\ \beta_0 + \beta_1\ \Delta\ ln\ \sum_t^{t-i} \omega_i \left[\left(\frac{\alpha_2}{1-\alpha_1}\right) w + \left(\frac{\alpha_3}{1-\alpha_1}\right) m\right] \quad (1)$$

$$+ \beta_2\ \Delta\ ln\ \sum_t^{t-i} \omega_i \left[\frac{X}{K}\right] + \beta_3\ ln\left(\frac{X}{K}\right)_{t-1} \left(\frac{NO}{X}\right)_{t-1} + u_t,$$

where:

p = is price
w = the wage rate
m = the price of materials
X = output
K = capital stock

NO = new orders
u = a random disturbance term[6]

The ω_i reflects distributed lag weights estimated using the Almon technique assuming a four-period adjustment process and constant or unidirectionally changing weights. The constant term, β_0, includes the technical progress term which has an expected negative algebraic sign. Other factors might obscure this, however, including changes in market structure. If the data fit the Cobb–Douglas constant returns to scale assumptions, β_1 should equal unity and β_2 should equal the capital share divided by the noncapital share $\left(\dfrac{\alpha_1}{1-\alpha_1}\right)$. The algebraic sign of β_3 is the implied positive constant in the exponent of NO/X, X/K. In other words, when price is in disequilibrium, new orders will not equal output. The amount of price change required to eliminate the disequilibrium will be greater the higher production is relative to capacity (capital) if the slope of the demand and/or supply curve increases at an increasing rate.

If both β_2 and β_3 turn out to be positive, competitive behavior is implicit.[7] If they are negative, noncompetitive behavior is implied. However, since the results depend importantly on the appropriateness of the underlying assumptions, it would be more prudent to interpret the algebraic sign of the estimates of β_2 and β_3 merely as indicators of whether margins behave procyclically or anticyclically or are cyclically neutral.

Equations of the form given by (1) above are estimated for a number of time periods in order to study the period since the passage of the new agricultural program and take account of the effect of the controls period. The sample period starts in 1959:2 for manufacturers and 1960:2 for retailers, reflecting the availability of data. The equa-

---

[6] Equation 1 relies on the long-run pricing rule derived by Nordhaus in *The Econometrics of Price Determination*, Otto Eikstern, ed. (Washington, D.C.: Federal Reserve Board, 1973), pp. 18-49, for the Cobb-Douglas case. It is modified to incorporate short-run equilibrium by substituting for r the cost of capital in Nordhaus's formulation, $\dfrac{\alpha_1\, pX}{K}$, which is the marginal productivity condition. The variable (NO/X) is introduced after the equation is stated in log change form to reflect short-run disequilibrium. (NO/X) is a proxy for the change in unfilled orders minus the change in finished goods inventories, so the first difference of it need not be taken.

[7] Laden has shown that, in industries using average cost pricing, β_2 would be positive above the point of minimum average cost, but negative in the large range below it. Ben E. Laden, "Perfect Competition, Average Cost Pricing and the Price Equation," *Review of Economics and Statistics*, February 1972.

tions for both sectors are fit initially through 1971:2, the precontrols period. Then the sample period is extended, a year at a time, beginning in 1972, until 1975 is encompassed.

The input and output price data are those in Figures 1 and 2 (total food instead of CPI food-at-home is substituted as the dependent variable in the retail equations). Manufacturers output is measured by the Federal Reserve Board's (FRB) production index and retail output by deflated retail sales. A capital stock proxy is used in the retail equation and the disequilibrium variable used is a proxy for changes in retail food store inventories. The observations are based on quarterly data. The parameters are estimated by ordinary least squares. Simultaneous equation bias has been found to be quite small by those who have estimated similar equations with price change on the left-hand side and current values of changes in wage rates and materials prices on the right.

The initial results indicated that the coefficients of neither the output-capital ratio or the disequilibrium variable were significant. This mirrors the earlier finding that in the aggregate, and over quarterly periods, changes in costs rather than changes in demand are the major influence on food price changes at the processing and distribution levels.

Equation (1) was reestimated deleting the variables $\Delta \ln \dfrac{X}{K}$ and $\left(\dfrac{X}{K}\right)_{t-1} \left(\dfrac{NO}{X}\right)_{t-1}$. The input prices—$w$ and m—were split into two separate variables. Lags were estimated as described above. The results are shown in Table 1. For both manufacturers and retailers, materials price coefficients are always significant. The values of these coefficients are somewhat lower for retailers than for manufacturers. Wage rate coefficients are not always significant, particularly for manufacturers. Toward the end of the sample period—1974 and 1975—wage rate coefficients for manufacturers begin to take on significance. But the fact that both materials prices and wages were rising sharply in part of both years suggests that the observed changes in the coefficients of the two variables may be affected by multicollinearity.

For manufacturers, the sum of the labor and materials coefficients is less than unity for the sample period through 1973 and greater than unity thereafter. For retailers, the sum is greater than unity until data for 1975 are added to the regression. It is interesting to note that the constant terms change to offset changes in the sum of the coefficients, in order to produce the result stated earlier based on the analysis of data in Figures 1 and 2—that input prices rose slightly more than output prices during 1960–1975. But the difference is small, a fact that contributes to the result that the constant terms in the equations are rarely significant.

Table 1

REGRESSION RESULTS FOR PRICE BEHAVIOR OF FOOD PROCESSORS AND RETAILERS, SELECTED PERIODS

Sample Period Ending[c]	Constant Term	Materials Input Price Coefficient	Labor Input Price Coefficient	$\bar{R}^2$
Manufacturers				
1971:2	.002	.679[a]	.004	.501
1972:4	.003	.661[a]	−.126	.572
1973:4	.003	.535[a]	−.057	.789
1974:4	−.011[a]	.475[a]	1.263[a]	.628[b]
1975:4	−.006	.545[a]	.754[a]	.585
Retailers				
1971:2	−.004	.493[a]	.720[a]	.657
1972:4	−.004	.465[a]	.698[a]	.614
1973:4	−.005	.557[a]	.732[a]	.793
1974:4	−.003	.585[a]	.623[a]	.826
1975:4	.000	.567[a]	.332	.763

[a] Coefficient significant at 5 percent level.

[b] Significant autocorrelation for this period.

[c] Sample period begins in 1959:2 for manufacturers, 1960:2 for retailers.

A more meaningful test of structural change than analyzing coefficients individually is to consider each equation in Table 1 as a whole. Tests developed by Chow show that for manufacturers there was a significant change in the structure of price behavior between 1973 and 1974, a change apparent in the preceding, less formal analysis.[8] The reasons for this have already been discussed.

For retailers, the structure of price behavior appears to have changed in 1973, and again in 1975. The first year was one of controls and marked the beginning of a period of sharp increases in farm and processed food prices. In 1975 the rate of increase in such prices slowed markedly. That the structure of retail price behavior changes significantly during 1973–1975 probably reflects the fact that retailers tended to absorb more food input price increases and to pass through less than the full decreases. When these input prices move sharply up and down, as they did in 1973–1975, the swings in the spread become more pronounced and show up as structural change.

[8] G. C. Chow, "Tests of Inequality between Sets of Coefficients in Two Linear Regressions," *Econometrica*, vol. 28 (1960), pp. 591-605.

Major Group and Detailed Commodity Analysis

Another way to look at the behavior of margins is through spread data developed by the Department of Agriculture. Such data for the consumer market basket and its major components are shown in Table 2, for

Table 2
RETAIL COST, FARM VALUE, FARM-RETAIL SPREAD AND FARMERS' SHARE: TOTAL MARKET BASKET AND SELECTED COMPONENTS

Years	Retail Cost	Farm Value	Farm-Retail Spread	Farmers' Share
Market Basket of Farm Food Products				
1960	996	393	603	39
1965	1,037	416	621	40
1970	1,228	478	750	39
1971	1,250	479	771	38
1972	1,311	524	787	40
1973	1,537	701	836	46
1974	1,750	747	1,003	43
1975	1,876	784	1,092	42
1976	1,895	749	1,146	40
Meat				
1960	287	163	124	57
1965	307	181	126	59
1970	381	210	171	55
1971	377	207	170	55
1972	422	246	176	58
1973	523	331	192	63
1974	533	299	234	56
1975	583	348	235	60
1976	584	315	269	54
Dairy				
1960	177	79	98	45
1965	178	79	99	44
1970	219	104	115	47
1971	225	106	119	47
1972	229	109	120	48
1973	249	124	125	50
1974	296	146	150	49
1975	303	150	153	50
1976	331	170	161	51
Bakery, Cereal				
1960	153	19	134	12
1965	161	22	139	14
1970	186	30	156	16
1971	193	30	163	16
1972	192	32	160	17

Table 2 (continued)

Years	Retail Cost	Farm Value	Farm-Retail Spread	Farmers' Share
1973	214	48	166	22
1974	277	69	208	25
1975	304	57	247	19
1976	299	46	253	15
Fruits, Fresh				
1960	42	15	27	36
1965	43	13	30	30
1970	51	15	36	29
1971	56	17	39	30
1972	59	17	42	29
1973	67	22	45	33
1974	73	22	51	30
1975	75	23	52	31
1976	76	21	55	28
Vegetables, Fresh				
1960	57	19	38	33
1965	70	25	45	36
1970	81	26	55	32
1971	83	27	56	33
1972	88	28	60	32
1973	109	38	71	35
1974	119	40	79	34
1975	114	40	74	35
1976	121	40	81	33
Fruits & Vegetables (Processed)				
1960	107	19	88	18
1965	106	22	84	21
1970	119	22	97	18
1971	125	23	102	18
1972	128	24	104	19
1973	135	26	109	19
1974	166	36	130	22
1975	187	40	147	21
1976	190	39	151	21
Fats & Oils				
1960	34	10	24	29
1965	37	12	25	32
1970	41	12	29	29
1971	45	14	31	31
1972	45	12	33	27
1973	50	19	31	38
1974	76	35	41	46
1975	81	28	53	35
1976	70	22	48	31

Source: U.S. Department of Agriculture.

selected years from 1960 to 1970, and annually thereafter through 1976. Focus is on the columns containing the farmers' share, the complement of which is the processing and distribution margin. While the spread data are extremely useful, they provide no breakdown of margins between those of manufacturers and those of retailers, except in the case of beef and pork. They are available through 1976, however, providing an additional observation, beyond that of the input and output price series analyzed above, of behavior after the new farm policy was implemented and after the controls period ended.

There is a noticeable stability in the farmers' share and, of course, its complement, during the period covered in the table except for 1973, when the effect of controls, particularly on processing margins, seems to be evident. Farmers' shares for meat, bakery and cereal products, and fats and oils, all processed goods, follow the same pattern. For raw foods, fruits, and vegetables, the pattern of margins is relatively constant, even during controls and their aftermath. This is to be expected because of the exclusion of raw products from controls and the liberalization throughout the controls program of the requirements for passing through price increases for the volatile commodities. Margins for processed fruits and vegetables also remained relatively constant, while those for dairy products trended upward during the entire period.

Over the period 1960–1976, the market basket of farm food products rose in price at an annual rate of 4.1 percent. The farm value and the spread rose at the same rate. This similarity of trend is implied by the constancy of the farmers' share over the period.

Yet another glimpse at the behavior of margins can be obtained by analyzing the spread data on a detailed commodity basis. These data are shown in Table 3 for twenty major commodities for selected time periods from 1960 to 1970 and annually thereafter.

There are no systematic characteristics in these data, with respect either to the period of controls, to the period since the advent of the new agricultural policy, or to anything else, for that matter. The only conclusion that one can reach based on the analysis of these data is that farm prices and margins for these selected commodities appear to react in a highly individualized manner, undoubtedly reflecting supply at the farm level and demand at the retail level. And demand at the retail level for each commodity is undoubtedly affected by the opportunities for substitution in the market basket in response to relative price changes. It is interesting but probably not surprising, however, that despite the margin changes for individual commodities, sales margins for the market basket as a whole are fairly constant over time. This suggests that price substitution effects are indeed strong so that, when the farm level price for one commodity rises because its supply di-

Table 3
RETAIL COST, FARM VALUE, FARM-RETAIL SPREAD AND FARMERS' SHARE: SELECTED COMMODITIES

Period	Retail Price	Wholesale Value (carcass)	Net Farm Value	Farm-Retail Spread			Farmers' Share (percent)
				Total	Wholesale-retail	Farm-wholesale	
CHOICE BEEF (cents per pound)							
1960	80.2	59.5	52.1	28.1	20.7	7.4	65
1965	80.1	58.0	51.8	28.3	22.1	6.2	65
1970	98.6	68.3	61.5	37.1	30.3	6.8	62
1971	104.3	75.7	67.8	36.5	28.6	7.9	65
1972	113.8	80.1	72.4	41.4	33.7	7.7	64
1973	135.5	98.1	89.9	45.6	37.4	8.2	66
1974	138.8	97.4	86.1	52.7	41.4	11.3	62
1975	146.0	105.5	92.9	53.1	40.5	12.6	64
1976	138.9	88.6	77.9	61.0	50.3	10.7	56
PORK (cents per pound)							
1960	55.9	44.2	28.7	27.2	11.7	15.5	51
1965	65.8	52.6	38.1	27.7	13.2	14.5	58
1970	78.0	58.8	39.4	38.6	19.2	19.4	51
1971	70.3	52.1	32.3	38.0	18.2	19.8	46
1972	83.2	65.3	47.7	35.5	17.9	17.6	57
1973	109.8	87.3	71.5	38.3	22.5	15.8	65
1974	108.2	77.4	60.8	47.4	30.8	16.6	56
1975	135.0	103.8	86.9	48.1	31.2	16.9	64
1976	134.3	93.6	78.4	55.9	40.7	15.2	58

Table 3 (continued)

Period	Retail Price	Farm Value	Farm-Retail Spread	Farmers' Share (percent)
		CHICKENS		
		(cents per pound)		
1960	41.6	23.8	17.8	57
1965	39.0	21.0	18.0	54
1970	40.6	18.5	22.1	46
1971	41.0	19.3	21.7	47
1972	41.4	20.0	21.4	48
1973	59.6	35.0	24.6	59
1974	56.0	31.6	24.4	56
1975	63.2	37.0	26.2	59
1976	59.7	32.8	26.9	55
		GRADE A EGGS		
		(cents per dozen)		
1960	56.9	37.1	19.8	65
1965	52.3	32.2	20.1	62
1970	61.2	38.3	22.9	63
1971	52.8	30.2	22.6	57
1972	52.4	30.0	22.4	57
1973	78.0	54.4	23.6	70
1974	78.3	53.2	25.1	68
1975	77.0	50.8	26.2	66
1976	84.1	58.0	26.1	69
		BUTTER		
		(cents per pound)		
1960	73.9	53.4	20.5	72
1965	74.8	53.9	20.9	72
1970	86.6	61.9	24.7	71
1971	87.6	59.5	28.1	68
1972	87.1	59.1	28.0	68
1973	91.6	60.8	30.8	66
1974	94.3	57.0	37.3	60
1975	102.5	67.3	35.2	66
1976	126.1	81.3	44.8	64
		MILK, SOLD IN STORES		
		(cents per half gallon)		
1960	47.4	22.2	25.2	47
1965	46.9	21.8	25.1	46
1970	57.4	28.8	28.6	50
1971	58.9	29.6	29.3	50
1972	59.8	30.2	29.6	51
1973	65.4	33.9	31.5	52
1974	78.4	40.8	37.6	52
1975	78.5	41.2	37.3	52
1976	82.7	46.2	36.5	56

Table 3 (continued)

Period	Retail Price	Farm Value	Farm-Retail Spread	Farmers' Share (percent)
		APPLES (cents per pound)		
1960	16.7	6.1	10.6	37
1965	17.6	5.9	11.7	34
1970	21.8	6.0	15.8	28
1971	23.3	7.0	16.3	30
1972	25.0	7.9	17.1	32
1973	30.4	11.1	19.3	37
1974	34.1	11.3	22.8	33
1975	34.2	12.0	22.2	35
1976	33.2	10.6	22.6	32
		ORANGES (cents per dozen)		
1960	74.6	26.2	48.4	35
1965	77.8	20.6	57.2	26
1970	85.9	18.3	67.6	21
1971	94.2	23.5	70.7	25
1972	94.0	21.8	72.2	23
1973	105.3	24.8	80.5	24
1974	110.9	25.9	85.0	23
1975	115.2	25.8	89.4	22
1976	114.2	23.5	90.7	21
		FRESH TOMATOES (cents per pound)		
1960	31.6	11.4	20.2	36
1965	34.1	12.0	22.1	35
1970	41.9	15.0	26.9	36
1971	46.5	18.8	27.7	40
1972	46.8	16.7	30.1	36
1973	48.2	19.8	28.4	41
1974	54.8	21.0	33.8	38
1975	57.9	23.8	34.1	41
1976	57.7	23.8	33.9	41
		CANNED TOMATOES (cents per #303 can)		
1960	15.9	1.9	14.0	12
1965	16.3	2.4	13.9	15
1970	21.3	2.6	18.7	12
1971	22.6	2.6	20.0	12
1972	22.8	2.7	20.1	12
1973	24.7	2.8	21.9	11
1974	30.0	3.7	26.3	12
1975	35.1	4.9	30.2	14
1976	35.1	4.8	30.3	14

Table 3 (continued)

Period	Retail Price	Farm Value	Farm-Retail Spread	Farmers' Share (percent)
FROZEN ORANGE JUICE CONCENTRATE				
(cents per 6 oz. can)				
1960	22.2	8.2	14.0	37
1965	23.4	10.6	12.8	45
1970	22.5	7.8	14.7	35
1971	23.4	7.3	16.1	31
1972	25.0	10.3	14.7	41
1973	25.0	8.6	16.4	34
1974	25.9	9.2	16.7	36
1975	28.2	8.6	19.6	30
1976	28.7	10.7	18.0	37
FROZEN FRENCH-FRIED POTATOES				
(cents per 9 oz.)				
1960	N.A.	N.A.	N.A.	N.A.
1965	16.8	4.8	12.0	29
1970	16.5	2.9	13.6	18
1971	16.3	2.6	13.7	16
1972	16.6	2.3	14.3	14
1973	17.2	3.9	13.3	23
1974	22.5	6.6	15.9	29
1975	25.6	4.7	20.9	18
1976	27.5	5.5	22.0	20
LETTUCE				
(cents per head)				
1960	21.6	8.4	13.2	39
1965	25.5	8.8	16.7	35
1970	29.8	9.4	20.4	32
1971	34.0	11.6	22.4	34
1972	34.1	11.5	22.6	34
1973	41.8	14.2	27.6	34
1974	42.3	13.2	29.1	31
1975	41.7	13.8	27.9	33
1976	47.7	17.1	30.6	36
POTATOES				
(cents per 10 pound bag)				
1960	69.4	24.3	45.1	35
1965	93.6	36.9	56.7	39
1970	89.0	25.7	63.3	29
1971	85.9	21.2	64.7	25
1972	92.4	24.3	68.1	26
1973	136.6	44.4	92.2	32
1974	166.4	59.4	107.0	36
1975	134.4	42.2	92.2	31
1976	145.9	44.9	102.0	31

Table 3 (continued)

Period	Retail Price	Farm Value	Farm-Retail Spread	Farmers' Share (percent)
	WHITE BREAD			
	(cents per pound loaf)			
1960	19.8	2.8	17.0	14
1965	20.8	3.2	17.6	15
1970	24.2	3.4	20.8	14
1971	24.8	3.5	21.3	14
1972	24.7	3.8	20.9	15
1973	27.6	5.5	22.1	20
1974	34.5	7.9	26.6	23
1975	36.0	6.8	29.2	19
1976	35.3	5.6	29.7	16
	LONG GRAIN RICE			
	(cents per pound)			
1960	20.5	6.9	13.6	34
1965	21.6	7.3	14.3	34
1970	23.1	7.3	15.8	31
1971	23.8	7.7	16.1	32
1972	24.0	8.7	15.3	36
1973	30.8	15.8	15.0	51
1974	51.6	19.7	31.9	38
1975	47.1	14.8	32.3	31
1976	43.2	10.0	33.2	23
	MARGARINE			
	(cents per pound)			
1960	25.9	7.0	18.9	27
1965	27.6	8.5	19.1	31
1970	29.8	8.6	21.2	29
1971	32.7	10.0	22.7	31
1972	33.1	8.5	24.6	26
1973	37.4	14.0	23.4	37
1974	57.4	27.8	29.6	48
1975	62.9	21.1	41.8	34
1976	52.6	16.5	36.1	31
	VEGETABLE SHORTENING			
	(cents per 3 pound can)			
1960	80.5	24.6	55.9	31
1965	87.3	29.9	57.4	34
1970	88.8	30.9	57.9	35
1971	96.9	35.9	61.0	37
1972	97.4	30.2	67.2	31
1973	110.1	48.8	61.3	44
1974	179.0	98.1	80.9	55
1975	190.7	74.0	116.7	39
1976	153.6	56.9	96.7	37

Table 3 (continued)

Period	Retail Price	Farm Value	Farm-Retail Spread	Farmers' Share (percent)
		SALAD OIL		
		(cents per 24 oz.)		
1960	N.A.	N.A.	N.A.	N.A.
1965	47.4	13.6	33.8	29
1970	56.8	14.2	42.6	25
1971	63.5	16.5	47.0	26
1972	64.3	13.7	50.6	21
1973	70.5	21.9	48.6	31
1974	107.4	44.6	62.8	42
1975	115.6	35.0	80.6	30
1976	95.4	26.8	68.6	28
		SUGAR		
		(cents per 5 pounds)		
			(unadjusted for government payment and taxes)	
1960	57.1	20.3	36.8	36
1965	58.6	21.2	37.4	36
1970	65.0	26.7	38.3	41
1971	68.1	29.7	38.4	44
1972	69.5	29.4	40.1	42
1973	75.5	33.4	42.1	44
1974	161.2	97.3	63.9	60
1975	185.4	80.8	104.6	44
1976	119.8	46.6	73.2	39

Note: Some farm equivalents vary over the years covered. Soft drinks and chocolate bars are not included because of a lack of farm value data on each. Fresh orange juice, a seasonal product whose price spread is not readily available, is also not included here.
Source: U.S. Department of Agriculture.

minishes, processors (particularly horizontally integrated ones) and retailers obtain less unit profit on the item, but more on the commodities that substitute for it.

Summary

This study attempts to show that while the margins for specific food commodities tend to fluctuate markedly in response to supply and demand factors unique to each, the result is that the distribution of consumer expenditures on food between farmers and middlemen has remained fairly constant over any substantial period of time during 1960–1976. This suggests that there are strong cross-price elasticity effects among individual food products on the demand side. The advent of the new agricultural policy does not appear to have disturbed the relationships among these stage-of-process sectors. The only major disturbance in shares appears to have occurred during and just after the controls period of 1972–1974, and it seems to have impacted most on food processors. The study also shows that prices charged by food retailers and manufacturers have risen slightly less than price indexes of the variable inputs they purchase. This suggests that some issues left for further study are the role of capital in productivity improvements in food processing and distribution, the possibility that there have been changes in market structure, particularly international influences, and the likelihood that the relationship of prices to costs has been affected by the apparent shift to more highly processed manufactured foods and to more self-service in its distribution.

TRENDS IN FOOD CONSUMPTION, PRICES, AND EXPENDITURES

J. Dawson Ahalt

In early 1977, a number of people asked the question: Is the United States in for another inflationary surge like that of 1972–1975, which will have major effects on consumer food costs and food consumption patterns? Although retail food price pressures moderated significantly in the past year, adverse weather, economic factors, and several policy issues raise questions about the prospective food situation facing consumers.

Studying the behavior of food consumption, price, and spending provides a useful perspective for understanding why consumers reacted the way they did during the "economic storm."[1]

In the post–World War II period, steady income gains, together with large supplies and moderate increases in food prices, allowed consumers to enjoy an unprecedented upgrading in diets of both crop and livestock foods (Tables 1 and 2). This upgrading reflected a shift toward more preferred and more expensive foods, mainly meats, poultry, and processed items. Total per capita food consumption made only modest gains from the mid-1950s through the mid-1960s, and retail food prices increased annually at about 1.5 percent (Table 3).

As income gains accelerated during the mid-1960s, the index of per capita food consumption (weighted by retail prices) rose more rapidly (about 1 percent per year from 1965 to 1970). Food prices, which in the previous decade had lagged behind retail prices for non-food items, began catching up and in some years led price advances in the nonfood sector. For the 1965–1970 period, the advance in retail food prices averaged 3.6 percent per year. This faster pace was due to

The views expressed in this paper are those of the author and may or may not be consistent with those of the U.S. Department of Agriculture. The author appreciates the helpful comments of Rex Daly, Larry Summers, and others in the Economic Research Service of the Department of Agriculture. Larry Summers and Terry Barr also assisted with the computational tasks.

[1] A term often used by Don Paarlberg to describe the inflationary period of 1972–1975.

Table 1
PER CAPITA FOOD CONSUMPTION INDEXES, 1955–1976
(1967 = 100)

Selected Years	Meat	Poultry	Fish	Eggs	Dairy Products[a]	Fats and Oils			Fruits[b]		
						Animal[a]	Vegetable	Total	Fresh	Processed	Total
1955c	95	61	98	115	110	140	75	98	120	90	104
1960c	92	78	99	105	106	126	80	96	112	94	102
1965c	96	90	99	98	103	109	95	100	100	88	94
1970	104	108	109	99	99	90	116	107	101	103	102
1971	107	109	105	97	99	90	113	105	98	106	102
1972	105	113	113	95	100	84	122	109	94	105	100
1973	98	107	119	91	99	78	127	110	93	110	102
1974	105	109	112	89	99	76	124	107	98	106	102
1975	101	106	111	86	100	73	127	108	104	113	109
1976f	107	115	115	85	100	68	136	112	103	111	107

Selected Years	Vegetables[d]			Potatoes and Sweet Potatoes		Cereal Products	Sugar and Sweeteners	Coffee, Tea, and Cocoa	All Food		
	Fresh	Processed	Total	Fresh	Processed				Animal products	Crops[e]	Total
1955c	111	78	100	N.A.	N.A.	107	96	97	98	96	97
1960c	106	84	98	N.A.	N.A.	103	98	101	96	97	96
1965c	99	94	97	N.A.	N.A.	100	100	100	98	98	98
1970	100	104	101	91	121	98	106	94	102.5	103.1	102.8

1971	99	105	101	87	124	99	106	92	103.8	102.8	103.3
1972	99	108	102	89	123	98	108	98	103.6	104.1	103.8
1973	100	113	104	82	126	98	110	96	99.1	105.3	101.9
1974	100	110	103	79	131	96	107	93	101.9	103.8	102.8
1975	101	109	104	92	131	97	103	88	99.9	104.9	102.2
1976f	102	113	106	85	130	99	109	88	103.7	106.8	105.1

Note: Civilian consumption only. Quantities of individual foods are combined in terms of 1957–1959 retail prices.
a Includes butter.
b Excludes melons and baby food.
c Three-year average.
d Excludes soup, baby food, dry beans and peas, potatoes, and sweet potatoes.
e Includes melons, dry beans and peas, nuts, soup, and baby food, in addition to groups shown separately.
f Preliminary.
Source: U.S. Department of Agriculture, Economic Research Service.

Table 2

ALL FOOD: PER CAPITA CONSUMPTION, RETAIL WEIGHT EQUIVALENT, 1960–1975

(in pounds)

| Year | Meat, Poultry, Fish | | | | Eggs | Dairy Products | | Fats and Oils | | | |
| | Meat[a] | Poultry | Fish[b] | Total | | Excluding butter | Including butter | Excluding butter | Including butter | | |
									Animal	Vegetable	Total
1960	146.9	34.4	13.2	194.5	42.4	376	384	41.1	19.9	28.6	48.5
1961	145.4	37.7	13.7	196.8	41.7	370	377	41.0	20.7	27.7	48.4
1962	147.1	37.3	13.6	198.0	41.4	368	376	41.7	20.1	28.9	49.0
1963	152.0	38.0	13.7	203.7	40.3	368	374	42.6	19.6	29.9	49.5
1964	155.7	39.0	13.5	208.2	40.4	367	374	43.9	18.7	32.1	50.8
1965	148.3	41.3	13.8	203.4	39.8	366	373	44.5	18.3	32.6	50.9
1966	151.4	43.8	13.9	209.1	39.7	365	371	47.2	16.8	36.1	52.9
1967	158.3	45.5	13.6	217.4	40.7	357	362	47.0	17.1	35.4	52.5
1968	162.4	45.0	14.0	221.4	40.1	358	364	48.7	17.8	36.6	54.4
1969	161.4	47.1	14.2	222.7	39.3	355	360	49.8	15.9	39.2	55.1
1970	164.6	48.9	14.8	228.3	39.5	349	354	50.9	15.1	41.1	56.2
1971	170.0	49.2	14.5	233.7	39.9	350	355	50.2	15.3	40.1	55.4
1972	166.5	51.4	15.5	233.4	39.1	352	356	52.6	13.9	43.6	57.5
1973	154.7	49.6	15.9	220.2	37.3	347	352	52.8	12.4	45.1	57.5
1974	165.2	50.4	15.1	230.7	36.6	335	346	51.8	12.6	43.8	56.4
1975[d]	158.1	49.3	15.1	222.5	35.3	343	348	51.6	11.0	45.6	56.6

	Fruits			Melons[e]	Fruits, Melons, Baby Food	Vegetables				Total[e]
	Fresh	Processed	Total			Fresh[e]	Processed			
							Canned	Frozen	Total	
1960	89.6	50.3	139.9	28.2	170.2	150.0	43.4	7.0	50.4	200.4
1961	85.8	49.0	134.8	27.4	164.4	146.8	43.5	6.9	50.4	197.2
1962	81.0	49.8	130.8	24.9	157.9	143.6	45.2	7.4	52.6	196.2
1963	72.2	48.3	120.5	26.3	149.1	143.5	46.1	7.2	53.3	196.8
1964	76.9	46.5	123.4	24.8	150.5	141.0	45.8	7.6	53.4	194.4
1965	79.3	48.1	127.4	25.4	155.1	140.8	46.9	8.0	54.9	195.7
1966	79.6	49.4	129.0	24.0	155.3	138.4	47.3	8.8	56.1	194.5
1967	79.1	52.0	131.1	24.3	157.7	140.8	49.0	9.0	58.0	198.8
1968	76.4	50.9	127.3	24.9	154.5	143.6	50.5	9.6	60.1	203.7
1969	76.8	55.9	132.7	24.6	159.6	140.5	51.6	9.1	60.7	201.2
1970	79.5	55.6	135.1	25.2	162.6	141.0	51.1	9.6	60.7	201.7
1971	77.7	55.7	133.4	24.5	160.2	141.8	51.2	9.7	60.9	202.7
1972	75.1	54.1	129.7	23.9	155.9	140.7	52.8	9.9	62.1	202.8
1973	73.8	56.6	130.4	23.7	156.4	142.8	54.3	10.6	64.9	207.7
1974	76.1	54.4	130.5	21.2	154.0	143.4	53.5	10.1	63.6	207.0
1975[d]	80.3	55.7	136.0	21.5	159.8	142.9	53.4	9.7	63.1	206.0

117

Table 2 (continued)

	Vege-tables, Soup, Baby Food^f	Potatoes and Sweet Potatoes^e,k	Beans, Peas, Nuts, Soya Products^e,g	Flour and Cereal Products^h	Sugars and Other Sweet-eners^i	Coffee, Tea, Cocoa	All Foods^j		
							Animal products	Crop products	Total
1960	210.6	97.7	16.5	147	108.8	15.1	633	794	1,427
1961	207.6	97.5	16.8	147	109.2	15.4	629	786	1,415
1962	206.7	93.8	16.9	146	110.0	15.4	628	776	1,404
1963	207.4	96.2	17.0	144	110.5	15.6	632	770	1,402
1964	205.0	91.6	17.0	144	111.6	15.4	634	767	1,401
1965	206.3	86.5	16.4	144	111.7	15.1	628	768	1,396
1966	205.1	92.2	15.8	143	113.0	15.1	631	776	1,407
1967	209.4	82.4	16.5	144	112.6	15.2	632	773	1,405
1968	214.3	87.5	16.4	144	116.2	15.3	637	785	1,422
1969	211.8	84.9	16.6	145	116.9	14.5	633	788	1,421
1970	212.3	83.4	15.8	141	119.7	14.3	632	790	1,422
1971	213.3	82.4	15.9	142	120.0	14.0	639	788	1,447
1972	213.4	82.8	16.7	140	122.8	14.8	638	790	1,448
1973	218.3	78.7	18.1	140	125.3	14.3	617	796	1,413
1974	217.6	75.9	17.7	138	121.5	13.2	615	781	1,396
1975^d	216.6	84.4	18.4	139	114.5	12.4	612	790	1,402

Note: Final consumer products from a combination of primary food groups, such as bakery products, are measured and reported in the form of their primary ingredients, such as flour, shortening, and eggs. Civilian consumption only.
a Includes game and edible offal.
b Includes 2.9 pounds per capita of game fish in 1960; 3.0 pounds thereafter.
c Includes product weight of butter and margarine; other items in terms of fat content.
d Preliminary.

e Includes consumption of home garden produce.
f Excludes estimated quantities of meat, poultry, and fish-base soups duplicated elsewhere.
g Soya products approximated at 1.3 pounds until 1973.
h Corn sugar and sirups are with sugars and other sweeteners.
i Excludes sugar used in production of canned and frozen fruit, canned fruit juices, canned vegetables, and unskimmed sweetened condensed milk.
j Includes spices and herbs.
k Data have been revised to reflect conversion from fresh weight equivalent to processed weight for dehydrated potatoes, potato chips, and shoe strings.
Source: Economic Research Service, U.S. Department of Agriculture.

an expansion in demand for food, particularly livestock products, as well as general price inflation fueled partly by large increases in deficit spending associated with the Vietnam War.

So much for prices, but what about expenditures? From the mid-1950s through 1965, abundant food supplies and relatively modest price increases had let consumers upgrade diets with an average increase in expenditures per person on food of about 2.3 percent per year. In the last half of the 1960s, however, the per capita food spending rate picked up to about 5 percent per year, reflecting stepped-up consumer demand and higher prices, particularly for livestock food products. Even so, increases in outlays for food grew at a slower rate than disposable incomes. So the share of income spent for food declined steadily.

Despite the slowdown in economic activity at the close of the 1960s, inflation continued to be a major concern for the public and policy makers in the new decade. Part of this concern stemmed from the tightening of supplies and the acceleration in retail food prices in 1969 and 1970, which jumped to annual rates of increase of over 5 percent. These sharp advances, reflecting a strong demand for meat and poultry products in the face of a cyclical drop in pork production, probably dramatized the impact of inflation on the minds of consumers.

Even with fluctuations in supplies and prices, per capita food use rose annually from 1965 to 1972, for the longest span of year to year increases on record. The driving forces behind this expansion were large output gains for food commodities, coupled with steady increases in consumer demand that lifted consumption of meat, and poultry products in particular, to new highs. The share of income spent on food, however, continued to decline and by 1971 accounted for only 16.4 percent of after-tax income.

On the eve of the 1972–1975 economic storm, consumers were enjoying substantially upgraded diets from a smaller portion of their budget. Thus, when meat and other food prices escalated sharply in 1972 and, especially, in 1973, these pressures were viewed as a threat to continuing or even maintaining improvements in diets, as well as a signal that spending patterns in general might have to be altered.

Food Consumption

Major Trends. Consumption of red meats by 1971 had risen to an all-time high of 192 pounds per person, some 30 pounds more than a decade earlier. Consumption of chicken had climbed to over 40 pounds per person, up more than a third in a decade. Consumption of beef and poultry was also stimulated by growth in fast-food merchandising. Consumption gains for these products more than offset declines for eggs and

J. DAWSON AHALT

Table 3

PERCENTAGE CHANGE IN RETAIL, WHOLESALE, FARM, AND MARKET BASKET PRICES, 1955–1976

Item	1955–1960[a]	1960–1965[a]	1965–1970[a]	1970	1971	1972	1973	1974	1975	1976
Retail prices[b]										
All goods & services	1.8	1.4	4.1	5.9	4.3	3.3	6.2	11.0	9.1	5.8
All items less food	2.2	1.4	3.4	6.0	4.6	3.0	3.9	9.9	9.3	6.6
All foods	1.4	1.6	3.6	5.5	3.0	4.3	14.5	14.4	8.5	3.1
Food at home	1.1	1.4	3.4	5.1	2.4	4.5	16.3	14.9	8.3	2.1
Food away from home	2.8	2.4	5.5	7.6	5.2	4.0	7.9	12.7	9.3	6.8
Wholesale prices[b]										
All commodities	1.3	0.5	2.6	3.7	3.2	4.6	13.8	18.9	9.2	4.6
Industrial	1.7	0.3	2.6	3.8	3.6	3.4	7.7	22.2	11.5	6.3
Farm products	−0.6	0.6	2.2	2.0	1.6	10.7	41.0	6.9	−0.5	2.4
Processed foods	1.0	1.4	3.0	4.1	2.1	5.4	18.5	19.9	8.0	−4.1
All foods[c]	0.7	1.1	3.3	3.6	1.8	5.5	20.6	18.7	6.6	−3.8
Prices received by farmers[d]	0.4	0.8	2.0	2.8	2.7	10.6	43.2	7.3	−3.1	0.0
Crops	−1.1	1.0	−0.7	3.1	8.0	5.6	53.5	28.0	−10.3	−1.5
Livestock	1.5	0.6	4.1	0.9	0.0	15.2	34.6	−9.8	4.2	+2.9
Market basket of U.S. Farm foods[e]										
Retail costs	1.4	1.0	3.2	4.2	1.8	4.9	17.2	13.9	7.2	1.0
Farm-retail spread	2.3	0.9	3.2	7.4	2.8	2.1	6.2	20.0	8.9	5.0
Farm value	0.2	1.2	3.1	−0.6	0.2	9.4	33.8	6.6	5.0	−4.4

[a] Average annual compound rate of change centered on three-year average.
[b] Department of Labor, Bureau of Labor Statistics.
[c] Includes all processed foods plus eggs and fresh dried fruits and vegetables from the farm products group.
[d] Statistical Reporting Service, U.S. Department of Agriculture.
[e] Economic Research Service, U.S. Department of Agriculture.
Source: Compiled by the Economic Research Service, U.S. Department of Agriculture.

dairy products (particularly items high in milk fat)—foods that had been adversely affected by changes in eating habits and concern for animal fats in the diet.

On the crop side, consumption had also risen significantly during the 1960s. Expanding demand for more built-in services provided much of the boost for processed fruits and vegetables (including potato products), sugars, and other sweeteners. The use of vegetable oils during this period also rose substantially because of the growth in fast-food restaurants, as well as health considerations. Gains in these products more than made up for declines in fresh produce, flour and cereal products, and coffee.

Although the index of food consumption per person on a price-weighted basis has risen over a long period of time, the amount of food energy consumed per person (measured in terms of calories) has declined. This decline is mainly in response to shifts to urban life styles and less strenuous physical activity. However, caloric intake bottomed out somewhere in the late 1950s and early 1960s at around 3,100 calories per person per day. From then on it rose steadily, and by the early 1970s, it was back up to over 3,300 calories, roughly in line with intake levels of World War II. Consumption of carbohydrates and proteins behaved in a similar, though less pronounced, manner, while consumption of fats in the diet continued to rise.

These overall trends were altered abruptly beginning with developments in late 1972. Up to that time, combined domestic uses (food, feed, and industrial) of agricultural commodities accounted for around 85 percent of the total U.S. farm output, leaving around 15 percent for export markets. But with widespread shortfalls in world grain output in 1972, coupled with a sharp expansion in worldwide economic activity and devaluations of the dollar in 1971 and 1973, U.S. agricultural exports expanded sharply, led by timely and huge grain purchases by the Soviet Union. Since 1973 agricultural exports have accounted for roughly one-fifth of the total annual disappearance of U.S. agricultural commodities (about one-fourth of total U.S. crops are utilized abroad, but only 3 percent of animal products). With export markets bidding strongly against domestic uses for available supplies, prices rose sharply, and consumer buying patterns shifted.

Although worldwide commodity inflation began in grain and oil-seed markets in 1972, initial effects on domestic food markets were relatively modest. Market supplies of animal products contracted slightly that year, mainly because of a sharp cyclical cutback in pork and a drop in egg production. Hurricane Agnes in the East and spring frosts in the West also hurt fruit and vegetable output in 1972, but ample stocks enabled food use to hit a new high.

1973—The Year of Sharp Adjustments. Inflation began taking its toll early in 1973. Farm and food commodity prices surged to record levels at most points in the production-distribution chain because of unprecedented increases in foreign demand, coupled with an acceleration in domestic demand.

The effects of excess demand on domestic food use in 1973 were in line with what economic theory would suggest. The index of food consumption declined 2 percent from the 1972 level, for the first year to year drop since 1965 and the sharpest decline since the inflationary period of 1951. But the sharp drop in per capita food consumption was the result of more than simply a downgrading in the diet due to tight markets and high prices.

The Nixon administration had imposed wage and price controls in mid-1971. During that season and throughout most of 1972, inflation moderated mainly as a result of ample food supplies and gains in productivity, which offset cost-push price pressures in manufacturing. As raw commodity prices surged upward in late 1972 and in 1973, however, the Nixon administration took a number of actions to expand supplies and also to tighten price controls on the food sector. With respect to controls, mandatory regulations were, at first, continued on the food sectors, while most of the rest of the economy was shifted to "voluntary" restraints. Later, however, price ceilings were imposed on meats, followed by a second price freeze in June 1973. These actions had some counterproductive effects. With ceilings on prices, farmers reduced marketings, particularly of livestock products and produce. These actions helped push prices up sharply and forced consumers to downgrade purchases in order to stretch their budgets.[2]

The substitution effects were enormous. Consumption of animal products—which tend to be the most expensive and the most income responsive items in the diet—fell 4.3 percent on a per capita basis, with all items except fish participating in the drop. The consumer boycott against meat may also have contributed. This cutback, however, was partially offset with more crop foods—items lower in cost—especially processed fruits and vegetables (goods already in processor and marketer inventories were not permitted to reflect higher raw material costs). Consumption adjustments in 1973 were so dramatic that the pounds of food consumed per person experienced their greatest drop in over a decade.

---

[2] Marvin H. Kosters, with J. Dawson Ahalt, *Controls and Inflation: The Economic Stabilization Problem in Retrospect* (Washington, D.C.: American Enterprise Institute, December 1975) and Glen L. Nelson, "Food and Agricultural Policy in 1971–74, Reflection on Controls and Their Impact," prepared for the Office of Economic Stabilization, Department of the Treasury, December 1974.

In regard to supply actions, the Nixon administration took a number of steps in early 1973 to expand output and supply of agricultural and food commodities.[3] The effects of these actions were mostly longer-run in nature. However, the temporary increase in import quotas on cheese and nonfat dry milk had fairly immediate effects. While the controls temporarily restrained consumption in 1973, once they were relaxed late in the year, farmers boosted marketings, and supplies rose dramatically. This caused prices to drop and consumption to pick up in the closing months of 1973. This pattern continued in 1974 as meat supplies recovered sharply from the curtailed levels in 1973.

1974—The Effects of Passing Through Higher Costs. While raw commodity prices peaked in 1973, substantial cost pressures still existed in the marketing system in 1974. Thus, processed foods which were a relatively good buy in 1973 became less attractive to consumers as raw material costs worked through the system. With larger marketings of meat and poultry products and only slight increases in prices in 1974, consumers shifted back to more animal products while cutting down on processed fruits and vegetables. This move was further stimulated in 1974 as sugar prices soared because of a worldwide tightening of supply and demand conditions. Consumption of cereal products and vegetable oils also fell considerably during the year. The drop was sharp enough to pull the per capita index of crop foods back to the 1970 level (see Table 1).

The year 1974 is also remembered because the poor U.S. crop yields had long lasting effects on meat, poultry, and milk supplies. Feed grain and soybean production fell by about one-fifth because of extremely high temperatures, reduced moisture during the growing season, and an early fall frost. Feed costs, which had been rising since 1972 because of increased foreign demand, thus escalated further. The squeeze already underway on livestock feeding, as a result of disrupted marketings from the previous season, tightened and forced many livestock producers into loss positions. Hog and poultry producers began liquidating breeding stock, and cattle feeders sharply reduced placements in feedlots. Nonfed beef, for example, which in 1971 and 1972 accounted for 7 percent of steer and heifer slaughter, in the second half of 1974 comprised more than 20 percent of the kill. Later in the year, cow slaughter also rose sharply, and the liquidation process of the cattle cycle was underway. This meant that consumers were to have temporarily abundant supplies of beef, particularly hamburger and lower priced cuts, at relatively low prices for several years.

---

[3] Council of Economic Advisers, *Economic Report of the President, 1974*, table 24 (February 1974), p. 93.

1975 and 1976. By the fourth quarter of 1974, the ratio of aggregate livestock product prices relative to feed costs was more than 40 percent below the corresponding period in 1971, before the emergence of world-wide inflation. Cattle feeding dropped sharply in 1975. But market supplies and beef consumption rose for the year because of stepped-up slaughter of animals with relatively little grain feeding, as well as slaughter of the breeding stock. At the same time, production of hogs was curtailed quickly because of profit losses (consumption of pork in 1975 dropped nearly one-fifth from the previous year). Reduced output of poultry and eggs also caused consumption declines in 1975. With the recession holding down real income gains, and retail prices for animal products staying high, consumers again switched to crop foods (see Table 1).

The continued liquidation of cattle and relatively stable meat prices allowed consumers to expand consumption of animal foods in 1976. The recovery in hog production and record poultry output, coupled with the largest gains in milk production in more than two decades, also helped. These increases together with ample gains for crop food supplies enabled the overall per capita food consumption index to recover by 3 percent and to an overall level even above the preinflationary record.

What Lessons Have Been Learned? In view of the behavior of food consumption during the 1972–1975 period of widespread inflation, and the subsequent return to less sudden adjustments, what conclusions can be reached? Have there been basic alterations in the way consumers respond to changes in prices and incomes? What about alterations in demand for particular foods or food products? How did economic factors interact with other longer-term considerations in determining food consumption patterns? These are difficult questions; the answers to some of them are tenuous at best, while the answers to others will be learned only through additional analysis and experience.

During 1972–1975, the shocks to the agricultural and food system transcended anything most consumers had been accustomed to. The wide swings in prices and incomes forced substantial adjustments in food consumption patterns. Analysis of the aggregate relationship between consumption, prices, and incomes, however, suggests that there has been relatively little alteration in basic demand. Apparently, export demand shifted sharply, pulling stocks down and pushing prices up. Consumers reacted by purchasing less expensive foods, as well as by cutting back on some nonfood spending. Only time will enable us to learn whether or not basic demand relationships were altered.

With regard to alterations in the long-term consumption trends, some fundamental changes may be underway.[4] For example, over time consumers have switched from high-priced fresh fruits and vegetables to the more convenient processed items. In the case of vegetables, however, the decline in consumption of fresh items may have bottomed out and may possibly be turning upward because of the expanded demand for salad vegetables. It should be noted that most of the gain in consumption of processed vegetables has been due to the increased use of canned tomato products. Future growth in this area may have less potential.[5] The consumption of alcoholic beverages, which on a price-weighted basis exceeds nonalcoholic drinks, appears to have gained more ground in recent years.

There has been some controversy whether or not there has been any major shift in the demand for beef. Increasing evidence suggests that the changes reflect variations in prices, prices of substitutes, and incomes rather than fundamental changes in underlying demand relationships. Consumers, however, appear to be eating a larger portion of their beef in the form of hamburger, perhaps as much as 40 percent.[6] Moreover, declines in retail beef prices in the past few years appear to have been much larger for the higher priced cuts than for hamburger and some of the lower priced cuts. It will be interesting to see how consumer demand responds to reduced output of beef in the future as herds are rebuilt.

Although economic factors are important in determining food consumption changes in the short run, demographic considerations continue to play an important role especially in the longer run. The significant increase in young adults in the postwar period was a major factor affecting per capita consumption of meats, fluid milk, vegetable oils, and processed potatoes. With a smaller portion of young adults in the future, consumption trends for these foods could be altered.[7] Also, the population growth rate is expected to continue to diminish in the future.

Concern about nutrition escalated during the inflationary period as higher prices limited the flexibility of consumers in adjusting their diets,

---

[4] Rex F. Daly, "Economic Activity, Consumer Income and Demand for Meat," prepared for *Western Livestock Roundup*, Economic Research Service, U.S. Department of Agriculture, January 1977.

[5] C. W. Porter, "The Dominant Trends in the U.S. Vegetable Industry," Economic Research Service, U.S. Department of Agriculture (Speech delivered in Vineland, New Jersey, January 1977).

[6] William C. Helming, "The Livestock Outlook and Demand for Meat" (Paper presented to the National Independent Meat Packers Association, Marco Island, Florida, January 27, 1977).

[7] Corrine LeBovit, "Trends in Food Consumption" (Paper presented to the Institute of Food Technologists, Chicago, Illinois, November 8, 1976).

especially for poor people and young marrieds. Data on nutrient consumption, however, indicate that consumption patterns, together with new standards for white bread, have been maintained.[8]

Food Prices

Both the supply and the use of farm and food commodities are relatively slow in responding to changes in prices and other economic variables. Conversely, small changes in supply or demand can cause proportionately larger swings in prices. Moreover, the fact that food supplies are highly dependent on weather, are subject to perishability, and are vulnerable to pests and diseases, implies an element of inherent instability in the system.

Over long periods of time, prices for food tend to move roughly in line with prices for nonfood commodities. In the short run, however, the relatively inelastic supply and demand for food and farm products compared with nonfarm commodities implies much larger adjustments in prices in response to changes in market conditions and other variables.

With this concept in mind, it is interesting to compare the performance of food prices with prices in the nonfood sector before, during, and after the inflationary period.

Prices before Inflation. While food prices were a basis for concern because of inflation in 1969 and 1970, the year 1971 was an expansive one for agriculture. Retail food prices rose only 3 percent for the year, compared with 4.6 percent for nonfood items, and accounted for 16 percent of the overall rise in the consumer price index (CPI).

Prices during Inflation. During the entire 1972–1975 period, retail food prices accounted for slightly over one-third of the overall rise in CPI. To understand what happened, it helps to look at year to year developments in the food sector. In 1972 the picture began to change. The overall increase in retail food prices was only 4.3 percent, but more than 60 percent of the rise was due to spiraling meat prices (Tables 4 and 5).[9] The composition of the advance in food prices in 1972 was also in sharp contrast to developments in the previous two years. Raw farm commodity prices, which normally explain about 40 percent of the

---

[8] Ruth Marston and Berta Friend, "Nutritional Review," *National Food Situation*, Economic Research Service, U.S. Department of Agriculture, NFS-158 (November 1976).

[9] Meat prices account for a little over one-fourth of the weight in the food-at-home component of the CPI.

value of a market basket of food, in 1972 accounted for 80 percent of the rise.[10]

Because raw commodity prices have a larger effect on grocery store prices than do restaurant prices, the index for home food rose more rapidly than for prices of away-from-home eating for the first time since 1965. The cost of away-from-home eating is more dependent on service costs—such as labor costs—than are prices of food commodities. Hence, when farm commodity prices rise sharply, grocery store food prices tend to increase more than the cost of restaurant meals. This is what happened in 1972–1974.

Although farm commodity prices started rising in late 1972, real inflation began in 1973. Not only did the upsweep in farm, food, and other commodity prices create widespread distortions in 1973, it caught most analysts and policy makers by surprise. The basis for the unprecedented inflation in farm and food prices and the reasons why forecasters were caught off guard have been documented.[11] What has not been adequately explored is what would have happened if analysts had predicted that farm and food price increases in 1973 would be as large as they actually were. For example, would policy makers have believed the estimates? If they had, what action would they have taken?

As it turned out, the supply actions that the administration took in 1973 were in the right direction. Some of the other moves the administration made, however, particularly regarding price controls in the food area, turned out to be counterproductive. These actions have been documented by several economists.[12] The point is that there were few additional options left open to the administration at that late stage in 1973.

Retail food prices during that tumultuous year jumped 20 percent, from December 1972 to December 1973. The average year to year increase was 14.5 percent, with food prices accounting for over half the increase in the overall CPI (see Tables 3 and 4).

Most of the food price increases in 1973 were from items involving relatively small amounts of processing. For example, price increases for meats, eggs, poultry, and fresh vegetables accounted for nearly two-thirds of the overall rise in prices for home food. Moreover, almost 80 percent of the increase in prices of food in the market basket was due

---

[10] The market basket of farm produced foods excludes fish and imported foods included in the BLS food component of the CPI.

[11] Karl A. Fox, "An Appraisal of the Deficiencies in Food Price Forecasting for 1973, and Recommendations for Improvement," paper prepared for the Council of Economic Advisers (Ames: Iowa State University, November 1973).

[12] Kosters and Ahalt, *Controls and Inflation*; Nelson, "Food and Agricultural Policy in 1971–74."

Table 4

PERCENTAGE CHANGES IN RETAIL FOOD PRICES, 1955–1976

Item	1955–1960[a]	1960–1965[a]	1965–1970[a]	1970	1971	1972	1973	1974	1975	1976
All food	1.4	1.6	3.6	5.5	3.0	4.3	14.5	14.4	8.5	3.1
Food at home	1.1	1.4	3.4	5.1	2.4	4.5	16.3	14.9	8.3	2.1
Meats	2.3	1.4	4.1	5.5	-0.8	10.7	24.7	1.9	8.4	0.2
Fish	2.0	1.4	5.3	10.0	10.3	9.0	14.7	15.3	8.3	11.8
Poultry	-4.5	0.0	1.3	-0.5	0.6	1.3	40.2	-5.1	10.6	-4.7
Eggs	-1.4	0.0	1.7	-1.0	-13.7	-0.6	48.7	0.4	-1.9	9.5
Dairy	1.8	0.8	4.0	4.8	3.1	1.6	9.2	18.8	3.1	8.1
Fresh fruits	2.3	2.8	3.0	1.2	6.0	5.5	12.0	8.8	6.8	-.2
Fresh vegetables	1.8	4.1	4.0	7.3	2.7	6.1	22.2	7.2	-1.1	4.5
Processed fruits & vegetables	2.0	1.0	2.0	2.6	6.4	3.7	8.0	31.0	4.5	2.6
Cereal & bakery products	2.0	1.7	2.8	5.5	4.6	0.7	11.3	30.1	11.3	-2.3
Sugar & sweets	1.6	2.1	3.0	5.5	3.6	1.3	6.1	52.1	26.1	-11.4
Nonalcoholic beverages	-3.9	2.1	2.5	12.2	3.6	-0.2	7.3	19.5	15.0	19.6
Food away from home	2.8	2.4	5.5	7.6	5.2	4.0	7.9	12.7	9.3	6.8

[a] Average annual compound rate of change centered on three-year average.
Source: Department of Labor, Bureau of Labor Statistics.

129

to higher prices of raw farm food products. Following the pattern set in 1972, prices for grocery store foods rose more rapidly than the cost of away-from-home eating.

With excess domestic and foreign demand driving prices for farm food products up more than a third in 1973, prices for processed foods at wholesale and retail were destined to rise sharply in 1974. In fact the year to year advance in retail food prices turned out 14.4 percent in 1974, only fractionally under the previous year's near record rise (see Table 4). In 1974, however, the increase in retail food prices accounted for only 30 percent of the overall increase in the consumer price index, as energy and other nonfood costs also soared.

The basis for the rise in food prices in 1974 was considerably different from that of the previous year. Meat and poultry supplies had been withheld from the market in 1973, but then came on stream in 1974. Retail prices for meats rose less than 1 percent for the year, and prices for poultry products actually declined. On the other hand, prices for processed foods, such as processed fruits and vegetables, cereal and bakery products, sugar and sweets, and dairy products, climbed sharply as firms passed along the raw commodity and other cost increases incurred from the previous year. In addition, some of the increases reflected pent-up cost increases that industry allegedly was unable to pass on until after the Economic Stabilization Act expired in April 1974.

Unlike the previous year, price increases for processed foods in 1974 (most of which were of crop origin) accounted for nearly three-fourths of the rise in the cost of home food.[13] For the year, over 80 percent of the increase in retail food prices was associated with processing and marketings spreads, compared with 20 percent in 1973. Although food price increases in grocery stores were larger than increases for away-from-home eating, the latter were catching up in 1974, with a year to year average advance of nearly 13 percent.

Prices after Inflation. Retail food prices steadied materially in the first half of 1975. Except for a spurt at mid-season, associated with concern over another shortfall in Soviet grain production, food prices continued relatively stable through 1976. This slowing of inflation in food prices resulted from several forces. On the supply side, output of food commodities responded to the high product prices generated in 1973 and 1974. In addition, the liquidation of cattle added to beef supplies. These supply adjustments, coupled with the recession in business activity, pushed farm products prices down in 1975 and, coupled with the expansion in world grain production, led to further declines in 1976.

---

[13] These items have a basic weight in the food-at-home component of about 40 percent.

Table 5

PROPORTION OF PRICE CHANGE IN FOOD AT HOME, ALL FOOD, AND ALL ITEMS OF THE CPI, 1955–1976

Item	1955–1960	1960–1965	1965–1970	1970	1971	1972	1973	1974	1975	1976
Food at home										
Meat	54.5	26.4	31.5	28.2	−8.7	62.2	39.7	3.3	26.5	2.4
Fish	4.5	2.9	4.1	5.1	11.2	5.1	2.3	2.7	2.5	14.3
Poultry	−15.5	0	1.5	0	.8	1.1	9.3	−1.3	4.8	−7.2
Eggs	−3.6	0	1.5	−.1	−16.6	−.4	8.8	.1	−.7	13.3
Dairy	26.4	9.3	18.8	15.1	20.8	5.8	9.1	20.3	6.0	61.9
Fresh fruits	9.0	8.6	3.8	.1	11.0	5.3	3.3	2.6	3.6	0
Fresh vegetables	9.0	16.4	6.5	8.0	6.3	7.6	7.7	2.6	−.7	11.9
Fresh fruits & vegetables	11.8	5.0	3.8	3.3	12.9	5.6	3.3	13.9	3.6	8.1
Cereal & bakery	24.5	16.4	11.2	14.9	26.3	2.2	9.5	27.8	18.6	−15.1
Sugar & sweets	4.5	5.0	2.9	3.5	5.0	1.0	1.2	11.3	10.2	−17.6
Beverages	−20.0	8.6	4.1	13.5	8.0	.2	2.5	7.4	10.2	52.4
Other	−5.5	1.4	10.3	7.8	17.9	4.4	3.3	9.2	15.3	−23.8
All food										
Food away from home	41	32	30	28	37	20	11.5	18.6	23.1	53
Food at home	59	68	70	72	63	80	88.5	81.4	76.9	47
CPI all items										
All food	17	26	20	21	16	30	52	30	26	14
All less food	83	74	80	79	84	70	48	70	74	86

Source: Compiled by the Economic Research Service, U.S. Department of Agriculture.

Although retail food prices averaged 8.5 percent higher in 1975, the rise was less than the 9.3 percent boost in nonfood items. Higher prices for pork, poultry, cereal and bakery products, sugar, and beverages provided most of the upward pressure. The increased cost of processing and marketing food in 1975 accounted for nearly 73 percent of the overall increase in the market basket. And, for the first time since 1971, food prices in grocery stores rose less rapidly than prices for food consumed away from home.

Food prices in 1976 averaged only 3 percent higher for the year. This moderation was due to very small increases for meats, fruits, and vegetables, coupled with declines for poultry, cereal and bakery products, sugar and sweets, and other items. As in the two preceding years, the farm-retail spread made up for an unusually large share of the increase in retail food prices. Moreover, retail food prices in 1976 rose only half as much as nonfood prices, and accounted for only 14 percent of the increase in the overall CPI (see Table 5). Hence, food price stability was a major factor behind the moderation in inflation in the past year. Farm food commodity prices in 1976 were actually lower for the year, but the cost of away-from-home eating rose more than three times as much as the cost of grocery store foods.

A Question about Performance. Did the CPI accurately measure the magnitude of the price changes? Since the CPI uses 1960–1961 quantity weights in measuring price changes, it would be interesting to know if the large price advances in 1973 and 1974 were accurately reflected. Alden Manchester compared the food-at-home component published by the Bureau of Labor Statistics (BLS) with a recomputed index using the 1972–1973 weights from the BLS consumer expenditure survey (CES).[14] He also built another index using foods not currently included in the CPI. The results showed that in 1973–1974 the index using the updated weights was only 1 percent lower, while the "more comprehensive" index was slightly higher than the current BLS series. Several other of his comparisons show that price increases in 1973 and 1974 were greater for "low" cost foods than for other food.

Food Expenditures

The highly inelastic relationship between income and total food consumption is a universal phenomenon. This linkage allows consumers to

---

[14] Alden C. Manchester, "Relationships of Food Costs, Expenditures, and Prices, 1960–74," Economic Research Service, U.S. Department of Agriculture, Agricultural Economic Report no. 329 (March 1976).

Table 6

PERCENTAGE CHANGES IN DISPOSABLE INCOME PER CAPITA, 1955–1976

Year	Percentage Change of Per Capita Disposable Income (seasonally adjusted annual rate)				
	I	II	III	IV	Year
Current Dollars					
1955–60	N.A.	N.A.	N.A.	N.A.	3.2
1960–65	N.A.	N.A.	N.A.	N.A.	4.6
1965–70	N.A.	N.A.	N.A.	N.A.	6.6
1970	6.1	11.7	6.6	1.8	7.6
1971	12.3	8.3	3.3	5.0	7.2
1972	7.8	5.5	9.2	15.2	6.9
1973	14.2	10.9	8.7	11.2	11.7
1974	4.0	8.5	11.5	7.0	8.3
1975	2.5	26.7	.2	9.9	9.1
1976	9.2	8.3	5.3	8.4	8.5
1972 Dollars					
1955–60	N.A.	N.A.	N.A.	N.A.	0.9
1960–65	N.A.	N.A.	N.A.	N.A.	3.2
1965–70	N.A.	N.A.	N.A.	N.A.	2.8
1970	1.5	7.5	3.0	−3.6	3.0
1971	7.6	3.6	−1.1	2.1	2.6
1972	3.4	2.9	5.8	11.3	3.3
1973	8.2	2.9	1.8	1.1	5.9
1974	−7.5	−3.6	−.2	−4.5	−2.3
1975	−3.4	20.9	−6.6	4.1	1.0
1976	5.4	4.0	−.1	2.8	3.3

Source: Computed from the *Economic Report of the President, 1977.*

upgrade diets with a steadily declining share of their income as families move up the income scale, and as economies achieve higher standards of living in time (see Tables 6 and 7).

In the United States, food spending has risen steadily since the post–World War II period. In 1976, outlays for food, including alcoholic beverages, totaled $224.5 billion. Viewed in perspective with other aggregates in the national income accounts, food expenditures about match the amount spent annually on fixed investment.

When inflation and food prices accelerated in 1973 and 1974, expenditures on food increased at rates double those experienced in the late 1960s (see Table 7). Even though consumers attempted to shift

Table 7

EXPENDITURES FOR FOOD IN RELATION TO DISPOSABLE INCOME, 1955–1976

| Year | Disposable Personal Income | Personal Consumption Expenditures for Food[a] | | | | | |
| | | For Use at Home[b] | | Away from Home[c] | | Total | |
		Amount (in billions of dollars)	Percentage of income	Amount (in billions of dollars)	Percentage of income	Amount (in billions of dollars)	Percentage of income
1955	275.3	N.A.	N.A.	N.A.	N.A.	58.3	21.2
1960	349.3	56.3	16.1	14.2	4.1	70.5	20.2
1965	472.2	66.8	14.2	19.0	4.0	85.8	18.2
1970	685.9	91.8	13.4	26.8	3.9	118.6	17.3
1971	742.8	94.2	12.7	27.8	3.7	122.0	16.4
1972	801.3	100.5	12.5	30.1	3.8	130.6	16.3
1973	901.7	112.9	12.5	33.9	3.8	146.8	16.3
1974	982.9	128.5	13.1	38.4	3.9	166.9	17.0
1975	1,080.9	141.0	13.0	43.8	4.1	184.8	17.1
1976[d]	1,181.8	150.6	12.7	48.1	4.1	198.7	16.0

a Data include beverages and food donated by government agencies to schools and needy persons, and nonpersonal spending for food, such as business purchases of meals, food furnished to inmates of hospitals and institutions, and food included with transportation tickets and camp fees.
b Includes food consumed on farms where produced.
c Includes food served to military and employees of hospitals, prisons, and food service establishments.
d Preliminary.

Source: Compiled by the Economic Research Service, U.S. Department of Agriculture, using U.S. Department of Commerce, Bureau of Economic Analysis data.

Table 8

CONSUMER EXPENDITURES FOR U.S. FARM FOODS AS A
PERCENTAGE OF PERSONAL DISPOSABLE INCOME, 1960–1976

Consumer Expenditure	1960	1965	1970	1971	1972	1973	1974	1975	1976[a]
All farm food	19.1	17.2	15.4	14.9	14.7	14.8	15.2	14.7	13.8
Meat	5.3	4.7	4.7	4.5	4.7	4.7	4.4	4.0	3.9
Beef	2.9	2.8	2.8	2.7	3.0	3.0	2.7	2.4	
Pork	2.1	1.7	1.7	1.6	1.5	1.6	1.6	1.4	
Other red meats	.4	.3	.2	.2	.2	.2	.2	.2	
Dairy	3.5	2.8	2.4	2.2	2.2	2.1	2.2	2.1	2.0
Fluid milk & cream	2.0	1.6	1.3	1.2	1.2	1.0	1.1	1.0	
Other dairy	1.4	1.2	1.1	1.1	1.0	1.1	1.1	1.1	
Poultry	1.5	1.3	1.3	1.1	1.1	1.3	1.1	1.1	1.1
Poultry	.8	.8	.8	.7	.7	.9	.7	.7	
Eggs	.7	.6	.5	.4	.4	.5	.4	.4	
Fruits & vegetables	4.2	3.8	3.2	3.1	2.8	3.1	3.2	3.1	2.9
Fresh fruits	.8	.6	.6	.6	.5	.5	.6	.6	
Fresh vegetables	1.4	1.2	1.0	.9	.9	1.0	1.0	.9	
Processed fruits	.8	.6	.5	.5	.4	.5	.4	.5	
Processed vegetables	1.3	1.3	1.1	1.1	1.0	1.1	1.2	1.1	
Grain mill products	.7	.6	.5	.4	.4	.5	.5	.5	.5
Bakery products	2.0	1.7	1.4	1.5	1.5	1.4	1.6	1.7	1.5
Miscellaneous	2.0	2.2	2.1	2.0	2.0	1.8	2.2	2.2	1.9
Fats & oils	.5	.6	.6	.6	.6	.6	.8	.7	.6
Other foods	1.5	1.7	1.5	1.4	1.4	1.2	1.5	1.5	1.3

[a] Preliminary.
Source: Economic Research Service, U.S. Department of Agriculture.

to lower cost items, the upsurge in food costs halted the declining share of income spent for food in 1973; the portion actually increased in 1974 and 1975 for the first time since 1958.

During the 1972–1975 period, the annual increment in consumer food spending averaged $15.7 billion per year, more than double the level in preceding years. Some critics of U.S. food and farm policy at that time argued that even though over $3 billion annually in direct payments to farmers was being eliminated by the expansion in world demand, the regressive effects of higher food, particularly on low-income families, was too great a cost. This argument seems to have ignored the benefits to the U.S. economy from expanded exports, which produced a net trade balance on U.S. agricultural commodities of over $11 billion annually beginning with 1973, compared with a $1–2 billion level prior to that time.

How Budgets Were Adjusted. With consumers no longer able to enjoy the luxury of devoting a smaller portion of their income for food, it is interesting to examine how food budgets were adjusted. Through time, expenditures for virtually all farm produced foods as a percentage of disposable incomes have declined, explaining the aggregate behavior (see Table 8). In 1972, however, consumer demand pushed the portion of income spent on beef up 11 percent from the previous year's level. This ratio held in 1973 while the share of income spent on pork, poultry, fruits, vegetables, and grain mill products increased. The portion of income spent on all other items continued to decline or remain the same as in previous years. In 1974 dairy products, fruits and vegetables, bakery products, and miscellaneous items captured a larger portion of income, while the shares devoted to other items decreased or remained steady. As real income gains recovered and price changes moderated in 1975 and 1976 the percentage of income spent on most foods again dropped, except for fresh fruits and grain mill products, which held about even with the 1973–1974 period. The portion of income spent on red meats, particularly beef, showed an unusually large decline in 1975 and 1976.

In addition to the substantial adjustments in long-term food consumption and spending patterns, inflation and the subsequent recession forced a decline in savings rates in 1973 and a substantial alteration in the allocation of the total consumer budget. Over time, the portion of consumer spending on nondurables (including food) has declined, while services have accounted for a rising share of total outlays. Durables, on the other hand, have fluctuated significantly in response to changes in incomes, previous purchases, and prices.

Food began taking a bigger bite of personal consumer outlays on a

Table 9

PERSONAL CONSUMPTION EXPENDITURES BY MAJOR CATEGORY, 1960–1976

(percentages)

Expenditures	1960	1965	1970	1971	1972	1973	1974	1975	Est. 1976
Durable goods	13.3	14.6	13.7	14.5	15.2	15.3	13.7	13.5	14.6
Motor vehicle & parts	6.1	6.9	5.6	6.5	6.9	6.8	5.4	5.4	6.6
Furniture & household equip.	5.4	5.7	5.9	5.9	6.1	6.3	6.2	5.9	5.9
Other durables	1.8	1.9	2.1	2.1	2.3	2.2	2.2	2.2	2.1
Nondurable goods	46.5	43.6	42.8	41.6	40.8	41.2	42.4	42.0	40.8
Total food	21.7	19.9	19.2	18.3	17.8	18.1	18.8	19.0	18.5
Nondurables less food	24.8	23.9	23.6	23.3	23.0	23.1	23.6	23.0	22.3
Clothing & shoes	8.2	7.8	7.5	7.6	7.5	7.6	7.4	7.2	6.9
Gasoline & oil	3.7	3.4	3.6	3.5	3.5	3.4	4.1	4.0	3.8
Fuel oil & coal	1.2	1.0	.9	.8	.9	1.0	1.1	1.0	1.0
Other nondurables	8.5	8.6	8.8	8.6	8.5	8.5	8.5	8.3	10.6
Alcoholic beverages	3.3	3.1	2.9	2.8	2.7	2.6	2.6	2.5	
Services	40.2	41.6	43.5	43.9	44.0	43.6	43.9	44.4	44.6
Housing	14.8	15.2	15.2	15.4	15.3	15.2	15.4	15.4	15.4
Household operation	6.2	6.1	6.2	6.2	6.3	6.2	6.3	6.6	6.5
Transportation	3.3	3.2	3.4	3.6	3.5	3.4	3.5	3.5	3.5
Personal care	1.8	1.7	1.4	1.3	1.2	1.1	1.1	1.0	
Recreation	2.0	2.0	2.1	2.0	2.0	2.0	2.0	1.9	
Personal business	4.4	4.6	5.1	5.1	5.1	5.0	5.0	5.2	
Medical care	4.7	5.6	6.7	6.9	7.1	7.2	7.4	7.7	19.2
Private education	1.2	1.3	1.6	1.6	1.6	1.6	1.5	1.5	
Religious & welfare	1.5	1.4	1.4	1.4	1.4	1.3	1.3	1.2	
Foreign travel	.4	.4	.5	.5	.5	.5	.4	.4	

Source: Computed from U.S. Department of Commerce, Bureau of Economic Analysis data.

current dollar basis in 1973 (see Table 9). Gasoline and oil purchases captured a larger share beginning in 1974. So did housing and home operating costs, transportation, and medical care expenses. With these important items taking a larger portion of total income, consumers curtailed shares spent on durable goods, clothing and shoes, private education, personal care items, and miscellaneous services. The total level of durable purchases, particularly for autos, even declined in 1973. However, as inflation subsided in 1976, the share of consumer spending for food declined again while durable goods, particularly autos, recouped a part of the overall budget lost during the inflationary years. Nondurables (excluding food), on the other hand, continued to take a smaller portion of outlays in 1976, while services continued to consume a larger piece of the budget.

It is interesting to note that as price pressures moderated and inflation in general slowed, expenditure patterns adjusted toward the basic relationships that existed in the preinflationary period.

Food and Nutrition Programs. In addition to the effects of changes in prices and incomes on food spending, federal food programs in recent years have played an expanding role in consumer food markets. Few federal programs have grown as rapidly as the Food Stamp Program. Its acceleration actually began in 1970 when the concept of the program was liberalized to insure low income people a "minimally nutritious diet." The child nutrition programs have also expanded rapidly, and together they have more than offset the phasing down of the food distribution program. In FY 1965 the federal outlays on food programs totaled $789 million. By FY 1971 expenditures had jumped to $3.1 billion, and by FY 1975 increased participation, liberalized benefits, and higher food prices had pushed the cost to $6.8 billion annually.

The economic effects of these programs have been significant. The federal contribution in recent years has been equal to about 3 to 4 percent of total consumer food expenditures. However, the programs have raised food spending by a smaller amount. Research shows that a $1 increase in bonus food stamps will raise food spending by around 50 cents. The remaining 50 cents goes for nonfood items.[15] In 1975, the $6.8 billion food programs are estimated to have increased food expenditures by around 2 percent. Using input-output analysis, Nelson and Perrin showed that in 1972 an income transfer of slightly less than $2 billion in food stamps increased GNP by a net amount of slightly

---

[15] Robert B. Reese et al., "Bonus Stamps and Cash Income Supplements," Economic Research Service, U.S. Department of Agriculture, MRR no. 1034 (October 1974).

over $300 million.[16] Similar results were obtained from an analysis of the school lunch program.

Studies show that the food programs have increased the demand for products such as meats, fruits and vegetables, milk, and bakery products. One estimate shows that the demand for beef in the 1970s has been increased as much as 3 to 4 pounds per person by the food stamp program.[17] Hence while in normal times, it has enabled low-income consumers to upgrade diets, in inflationary periods it has enabled them to maintain consumption levels above what would have existed in the absence of the program. The extent to which the food programs have raised prices, of course, depends on the market conditions at a given time.

What Lies Ahead

The abundant market supplies, particularly of meats, poultry, and dairy products, are expected to continue through the first half of 1977. Weather problems virtually wiped out the tender winter vegetable crop in Florida, damaged the citrus crop, and currently are raising serious concerns with regard to crops produced in California and parts of the Midwest. Even so, current expectations are that food supplies will continue to be ample, and prices for the year are likely to average somewhere in the 4 to 6 percent range above 1976, compared with a 3.1 percent increase in the past year, despite the sharp milk support price hike and indications of a less optimistic first-half meat output than had been seen earlier.

Prospects for the second half of 1977 are uncertain. The potential impact of weather on the 1977 U.S. and world crops, plus the difficulty in predicting when the liquidation phase of the cattle cycle will end in late 1977 or early 1978, make forecasts at this time highly tentative.

Certain developments can be expected to leave their mark in the future. One thing that can be foretold with reasonable certainty is that beef supplies will become smaller, and prices will become higher as cattlemen begin rebuilding herds. However, pork and broiler supplies will help maintain consumption of livestock foods and will act as a damper on upward price pressures. Another possible moderating force

---

[16] Paul E. Nelson and John Perrin, "Economic Effects of the U.S. Food Stamp Program, Calendar Year 1972 and Fiscal Year 1974," Economic Research Service, U.S. Department of Agriculture, Agricultural Economic Report no. 331 (July 1976).

[17] Leo V. Blakley, "Domestic Food Costs," *American Journal of Agricultural Economics*, vol. 56, no. 5 (December 1974), pp. 1103–12.

is that, if consumers prefer a larger share of their beef in the form of hamburger, grain feeding may be less intensive. Therefore, the adjustment of animal products to changes in grain prices could be less than history might suggest.

Other factors affecting food prices will be the pattern and behavior of input costs, particularly energy; the flexibility within the food production, processing, and marketing system to adjust to changes in costs; and the extent to which improvements in technology can continue to be reaped in the future. Weather may be more variable in the years ahead. This factor could play an important role in determining consumer food costs in the future.

An analysis of these forces suggests that the increased focus on policies aimed at reducing variability in farm prices and food costs is a worthwhile goal. Recall, for example, that most of the fluctuations in food costs in 1972–1975 came from swings in export demand, which affected grain prices and in turn livestock supplies and prices. However, the resiliency and the flexibility of both producers and consumers in food markets should be kept in mind in pursuing stabilization and its attendant costs.

COMMENTARIES

Kenneth J. Fedor

The papers by Dawson Ahalt and the others range over a wide spectrum of interesting and useful topics for discussion. I will limit my remarks to what happened during the period of the economic storm, to use Don Paarlberg's phrase, which lasted from 1972 through 1974, or 1975. I would like to focus on the lessons that might be applicable to future economic storms.

My first comment has to do with the paper presented by Professor Brandow. Its principal implication is that the decline of real income in the farm sector relative to the nonfarm sector in much of the period from 1950 through the late 1960s is, in some ways, a problem of the past. This problem, according to Professor Brandow, has given way to problem of instability of income in the farm sector, which rose approximately 80 percent in 1973 and has fallen back, if estimates of 1976 are right, to the pre–1972 level of farm income measured in real terms.

That is an abrupt change in income distribution, which seems to have major implications for farm legislation.

There is a question whether or not that implication from the Brandow paper is right. There will be a good deal of discussion about the extent to which farm income in the future will be as unstable as it has been over the last three or four years.

As a result of the lack of a consensus among agricultural economists, there is a great temptation to draft a piece of farm legislation that leaves a good deal of discretion to the Department of Agriculture. I think everyone who made a speech this morning succumbed to that temptation.

Although I am not going to come out against discretion, I think that there ought to be some limitations. The extraordinary discretion that the administration had in 1973 was not able to prevent the dramatic increase in food and farm prices during that year. There was little that could be done when the problem had already developed in the economy, no matter how much flexibility the government had. As a consequence, I am drawn to the point of view that a reasonably clear specification of the goals of agricultural legislation is needed. In particular, we should admit that the kind of dramatic increase in farm prices and income experienced in 1973 will not be acceptable in the future to this or, I would submit, any other administration. The government should recognize that it will have to "do something about it," to use the jargon of Washington, and it would be more prudent if it admitted that beforehand. Then it will not have to resort to unacceptable ad hoc policies, such as the export restraints, which have been used even after wage and price controls were ended.

If there is some agreement on the need to increase stability in the food and agricultural market, as Dawson Ahalt said at the end of his remarks, we ought to think clearly and carefully about how we will achieve that stability. Simply to say we will leave a lot of discretion to the secretary of agriculture does not get us very far in solving that problem.

We have to take the next step and identify the causes of the problem. Dawson Ahalt's paper pointed out that the rise in agricultural exports, related to the change in weather-related crop production throughout the world, made the U.S. food industry a good deal more susceptible to shocks from outside the country. This problem has not been dealt with so far, in terms of agricultural legislation, and it may not be dealt with unless we recognize that future administrations will not be able to "do nothing" in the face of increases in food prices as substantial as the increases of 1973 and 1974.

Perhaps an obvious point is that some sort of reserve system should be put in place to help cushion the effect of changes in food production and exports from the United States. It would be very helpful to implement a reserve policy in anticipation of the problem, rather than just reacting after the administration has been forced to do something about a rise of 10 or 15 percent in food prices.

The other problem with discretion was implied in Joel Popkin's paper, where he analyzed how the system actually adjusted to changes in prices at the farm level. I was particularly interested in his comment about what he identified as the traditional way of looking at margins, that is, to look at spread data. The reason people look at spread data is that they are available on a current basis. But, everybody who has used spread data agrees that they are probably the worst set of data to use in trying to discern exactly how the system is adjusting.

This underscores the need to make better information and data available on a timely basis to the people in government who must make decisions, especially when exercising the discretion they have been granted. To the extent that new data systems can be put in place to anticipate future instability, to the extent that the industry can agree on the kind of data to be used and collected on a continuing basis, we would make a good deal of progress.

Popkin brought out another point which I am repeating for emphasis because principally I agree with it. During the 1972–1975 period, economists did not learn what causes lags, but they did learn about the significance of lags, in terms of the ability of the marketing system to wait patiently, and to display flexibility. By the marketing system, I mean the food processors, the food retailers, and, most importantly, the consumers, in terms of their ability to adjust to changes in prices.

Joel Popkin pointed out in his paper and in his remarks that he was really investigating the long-term relationships in the industry. I would submit that the short-term relationships are also important. And I do think a good deal of substitution did take place, especially in the use of alternative inputs by food processors. One illustration is the extent to which the Quaker Oats Company found it could use a good deal less sugar in its products when sugar prices went up by a factor of five. We were surprised how much we could adjust to those kinds of changes, as well as how rapidly the consumers adjusted, substituting one product for another, when prices of individual items were going up rapidly.

In 1973–1974, within certain product groups, such as cereals, there were discernible changes in twenty- or thirty-year trends as consumers switched to buying items that had a good deal less value added. Since then, consumption patterns have returned to what they had been prior to 1973.

I differ with Dawson Ahalt's analysis of consumer reaction on only one point. Consumers have become a good deal more price sensitive now than they were before. That does not mean that consumers are unwilling to pay for convenience, nutrition, or any other value added at the processing level. But when prices change, consumption patterns seem to react a good deal faster than they did before the 1972–1973 experience.

As a final observation about consumer reaction to rapidly changing prices, I would point to the restaurant industry. It offers a classic illustration of the extent to which consumers were willing to trade down but not give up the conveniences they had come to expect in food consumption. Fast-food restaurant chains continued to achieve record sales levels in 1973–1974, when meat prices were going up rapidly, and also in 1974–1975, when incomes were declining.

A medium-priced, high-quality restaurant chain experienced the same thing. Its sales increased rapidly in 1974–1975, as consumers traded down from the higher-priced French restaurants.

In summary, I think the 1972–1975 period provided many lessons for the future. The lessons I emphasized reflected two aspects of the market system. Both producers and consumers exhibited a good deal more flexibility and responsiveness to changes in prices and costs than had been anticipated.

W. E. Hamilton

I have been impressed by the conclusions reached by the authors. It would not be a good use of my time or your time to try to discuss the technical aspects of these papers, but I would like to stress some points that appealed to me and seemed to have policy implications.

I was particularly impressed with Dawson Ahalt's concluding statement, in which he said that the resiliency and the flexibility of both producers and consumers in food markets need to be kept in mind in pursuing stabilization objectives and their attendant costs. I like that statement because it stresses both that consumers and producers have considerable capacity to adjust and that stability does cost something.

We have a very large and diverse agricultural economy, and consumers always have considerable flexibility and an opportunity to make choices. Adjustments in agricultural production require varying amounts of time. Some producers have more capacity to adjust than others, but as a whole, agriculture has a tremendous capacity to adjust production to fit the product mix consumers want.

People who disagree with this cite cases where it is difficult for producers to adjust, maybe impossible. My rejoinder is that adjustments do not have to take place where producers are the most severely restricted by climate, soil, topography, or other factors. Adjustments do take place where producers do have alternatives, and there are many such areas.

One reason we have a great deal of flexibility in our agricultural economy is that a large portion of it consists of livestock products. I often say that livestock is the balance wheel of agriculture. Under relatively free market conditions, producers tend to adjust agricultural production to market demand by varying the quantities of grain, forage, and other feedstuffs that are fed to livestock. We have heard something here about shifts in demand, including shifts between hamburger and steak, which are a part of this picture.

Dr. Popkin's analysis seems to support Dr. Ahalt's emphasis on the resiliency and flexibility of producers and consumers. In his summary he concluded that, while margins for specific food commodities tend to fluctuate markedly in response to supply and demand factors unique to each, the distribution of consumer expenditures for food between farmers and middlemen remained fairly constant over any substantial period of time during 1960–1976. He said this suggests that there are strong cross-price elasticity effects among individual food products on the demand side. In less academic language, it suggests that consumers have numerous choices with respect to food, and that they do change the mix of their purchases when it appears advantageous to do so.

While Dr. Popkin's conclusions appear to be somewhat cautious and tentative, his research generally supports the conclusion that, in the aggregate, food processing and distribution are fairly competitive. Changes in costs are the major influence on changes in food prices. The idea that food middlemen are profiteering at the consumer's expense is largely a myth.

Our food marketing system is not perfect. It is always easy to find prices that differ from what producers, consumers, or economists think they should be. At any given moment, some prices may be out of line with what they logically should be, but, on the whole, the system seems to work fairly well. The reason it works as well as it does, I think, is that consumers usually have a choice.

Of course, there are lags, and this is one of the problems that make it difficult for producers and consumers to see what is happening at any given moment. From the standpoint of producers, middlemen have contributed to some of this confusion. The meat packers like to put some of the blame on the chain stores for prices that are unpopular with producers. The chain stores like to say that they have to buy from the packers and that the packers have a great deal of influence on prices. There's a little buck-passing back and forth here.

But some confusion arises from the idea that price changes ought to be transmitted through the system instantaneously, which, of course, does not happen. There is also confusion about where price changes take place.

The idea that, in the long run, the consumer sets the price suggests to some people who have not studied the subject that price changes take place initially at the retail level, and then work back to producers. Price changes can take place almost anywhere in the marketing system, but generally the initial price changes do not take place at the retail level; they take place at earlier stages and then work through the system. But farmers often think that retail prices should be changed just as soon as a price changes at the farm level.

One thing that stands out in the statements we have heard is that we do have flexibility; adjustments do take place; and the balancing of supply and demand in a relatively free market requires fluctuations in prices. At times these fluctuations seem excessive, though probably more so at the producer end than at the consumer end of the food chain.

We have had some rather strong fluctuations in consumer prices recently, but farmers have been familiar with this sort of thing for many years, with some exceptions during the period when farm prices were pretty much determined by government programs. I certainly agree with Dr. Ahalt on the desirability of focusing policies on reducing the variability in farm prices and food costs, and that greater stability is a worthwhile goal. But the question it seems to me is: How much stability are we willing to pay for? This is particularly important if, as I think likely, progressive increments of stability become increasingly expensive.

In this connection, I'd like to turn to one of Dr. Brandow's observations. He said that recent experience has demonstrated both the large stocks that would be necessary to achieve year to year stability of prices and domestic utilization, and the limited capacity of private traders to carry stocks without marked depression in prices. Some people would conclude that, since the trade has a limited capacity to carry stocks, the government should assume this task. My conclusion is that the cost of carrying large stocks is excessive in relation to the probable benefits. Referring this morning to the prices at which Argentina is selling wheat, Gale Johnson said something to the same effect—namely, that the Argentines do not think paying the cost of storing grain would return worthwhile benefits.

Dr. Brandow brought out a number of well-known, but often overlooked, facts on the nature of agriculture. He pointed out that there is a wide range of differences in size and income among farm operators, and that many of the people who have very small agricultural sales have substantial income from nonfarm jobs. It was also pointed out this morning that the small farmer without the resources to produce much will not be greatly helped by price support programs that raise the prices of his small production a few percentage points. We need separate programs to deal with commercial agriculture and with the residual problem of agricultural poverty. As Brandow pointed out, this problem still exists to a degree, but not as much as in other years.

Finally, Dr. Brandow noted that economists are virtually unanimous in agreeing that much of the income benefit of farm programs becomes capitalized in land values. This is not exactly a new idea, but it is gaining greater acceptance. The first research that I can recall on this subject was published in the late 1940s with reference to the tobacco program. I can remember making this point about the capitalization of benefits in a great many meetings during the 1950s and early 1960s. When I first started making it, most of the people in the audience disagreed, or pretended not to hear me, or minimized it. But there is not much disagreement about capitalization anymore.

As landowners, farmers are not completely opposed to the capitalization of program benefits; in fact, they kind of like it. One of my associates made this point with reference to the capitalized value of peanut allotments. "You don't understand," he said, "this is a part of our portfolio." Well, I did understand—that's why it's difficult to change the peanut program.

Regardless of how beneficial capital gains—or the capitalization of program benefits—may be to the person who owns land when the capitalization takes place, it is unsound farm policy to ignore the effects of government programs on land values.

The capitalization of these benefits constitutes a windfall for those who own land when the capitalization takes place, but it raises production costs for subsequent owners. The long-run effect of this process is to make it more difficult for producers of the affected products to compete both in domestic and in foreign markets. And that is my real concern with the capitalization of program benefits. This is an important issue in the current discussion of proposals to base future loan rates and target prices on the cost of production, including annual adjustments for changes in land values. A better alternative would be to continue the present escalator clause, which basically adjusts target prices for changes in nonland costs with a possible further adjustment for changes in average yields.

In conclusion, I would like to say something in defense of administrative discretion. Agricultural policy has to deal with alternatives. Earl Butz, when he was an assistant secretary of agriculture twenty-some years ago, said that sometimes we have to choose between five or six alternatives that are all bad. If farm policy requires a choice between a law that fixes loan rates, target prices, or price relationships rigidly on a basis that is fairly certain to lead to problems and create a greal deal of trouble on the one hand, and secretarial discretion on the other, I personally would prefer secretarial discretion.

When the secretary of agriculture is given discretion, I hope we will have a wise secretary, and that he will use this discretion wisely. But even if he does not, and politics are a factor in the exercise of secretarial discretion just as they are in the passage of laws, it is still easier for the secretary to change his mind and to change a bad program when he has discretionary authority than to change something written into the law.

COMMENTARY

Julia C. Bloch

My assignment was to comment particularly on Mr. Ahalt's paper. Since the previous two discussants have very ably commented on the other papers, I will stick to my assignment. I approach it with a great deal of apprehension, because I may be the only nonspecialist, noneconomist, nonacademician in this room. Perhaps this will serve a useful purpose.

I plan to raise some issues, with regard to Mr. Ahalt's paper, from two perspectives: first, from the perspective of an average consumer (and I stress *average* because I have absolutely no experience in consumer advocacy); and second, from the perspective of someone very sensitive to the multidimensional aspects of food and agricultural policy, having been on the receiving end of a great deal of different kinds of interest group pressures. I have four points to raise with regard to Mr. Ahalt's paper.

(1) Mr. Ahalt does an excellent job in laying out the quantitative dimensions of food consumption, price, and expenditure trends (and, I might say that this is true of all of the papers presented in this session). Those dimensions, however, tell me that American food consumption patterns are affected by weather conditions, government decisions about agricultural policy, economic conditions, export demands, and demographic factors. What we eat is also very much affected by what is available in the marketplace, and also by what is promoted formally through advertising and informally through availability in institutional settings, such as supermarkets, restaurants, schools, and so forth. From a consumer perspective, therefore, I would like to hear some discussion of the processes that control food availability in the marketplace, in addition, some discussion of the impact of food promotional practices on consumption, prices, and expenditure patterns and trends.

(2) Mr. Ahalt's paper, and the others too, suggest that Americans have enjoyed a wonderful diet, that diet has improved since World War II, and that we consumers have survived the economic storm of 1972 to 1975 without having to downgrade that diet drastically. As a staff member of the Select Committee on Nutrition and Human Needs, I question that inference. There is a growing consensus among scientists and medical specialists that Americans have a very unhealthy diet, that our increasing consumption of fats, sugar, salt, and alcoholic beverages represent public health hazards. I would like to hear some discussion of the role of nutrition and health in food and agricultural policy. And related to that, of course, is the whole question of product safety.

(3) Mr. Ahalt's paper presents some interesting aggregate figures about consumption, price, and expenditure trends, but, since I am not an economist, aggregate figures don't mean much to me. How do we

translate those figures into meaningful configurations for policy considerations? For example, it is estimated that the average American family spends approximately 16 percent of its disposable income for food. That's not bad, compared with worldwide figures, but does that mean that the average family of four, earning a median income of $10,000, spends 16 percent of its disposable income on food, or does that mean that a family of four, earning $20,000 a year, spends that proportion of its income on food? It makes a big difference, and I don't have the expertise to know which is meant. Related to that, I would like to hear some discussion of how the economic storm of 1972–1975 affected the poor. Did it really not effect their consumption patterns, their nutritional levels?

(4) Mr. Ahalt concluded that it would be worthwhile to reduce the variability in farm prices and food costs. From a consumer's perspective, of course, that would be very good. I would like to take it a step further, however, and ask this question: Is that all that should be done? Someone else had already asked how that was to be done. What I mean is, what about policies aimed at reducing costs? I have heard a lot, for example, about direct farmer-to-consumer marketing. I don't know much about it, but we might look at it for discussion purposes.

Also, what about policies aimed at consumer education? Mr. Hamilton said that consumers have a choice, but it is certainly a very confusing choice. What about policies aimed at providing the consumers with accurate and sufficient information to make an informed choice?

I hope that the issues I raised help to galvanize the expertise in this room to focus on how best to integrate knowledge about agricultural production, knowledge about industrial operations, knowledge about consumer interests, knowledge about promotional practices. How can we integrate all the multidimensional aspects that should go into food and agricultural policy into a coherent whole? It seems to me that unless we integrate and balance interests of all these competing factors, we will not achieve a successful or a workable food and agricultural policy.

PART THREE

WORLD FOOD MARKETS, FOREIGN POLICY, AND DOMESTIC AGRICULTURAL POLICY

WORLD FOOD PRODUCTION AND INTERNATIONAL TRADE
IMPLICATIONS OF MARKET PROSPECTS FOR THE AGRICULTURAL SECTOR AND THE TRADE BALANCE

G. Edward Schuh

My paper is divided into two main parts. The first part is largely descriptive. In it I will discuss: (1) past trends in food output for world agriculture, (2) a set of projections for the developing-market economies for 1985, and (3) the importance of agricultural trade both to the U.S. agricultural sector and to the economy as a whole. The second part of my paper is more analytical. In it I will attempt to analyze the factors likely to affect our market prospects for the future, to include (1) what other countries and international agencies do about world agriculture, (2) the significance of the decline in the rate of productivity growth in our own agriculture, (3) the significance of the changed environment in which monetary and fiscal policy now operate, and (4) the role of our own domestic agricultural policy. I will then conclude with a brief summing up.

Background

One purpose of this part of the paper is to make an assessment of the trade prospects for U.S. agriculture. An important aspect of this is to understand what past trends in world output have been, and what the prospects are for the future. The first two sections of this part of the paper are directed to a brief presentation of data that will provide perspective on these issues. The third section will attempt to show the growing importance of trade in agricultural products both to U.S. agriculture and to the economy as a whole.

Trends in World Output. One way to gain perspective on past trends in the world food situation is by means of a comparison of the performance of the low-income or developing countries with that of the developed countries.[1] It is probably not sufficiently well recognized that food production has been expanding over the last two decades at exactly the same rate in these two groups of countries. In the period from 1952 to 1962, the growth rate in both sets of countries was 3.1 percent per year. And in the period from 1962 to 1972, it was 2.7 percent in both sets of countries.

The difference between the two groups of countries is in their respective population growth rates. The developed countries had a population growth rate of 1.3 percent in the earlier period, with the result that per capita production increased at a rate of 1.8 percent. In the developing countries, population was increasing at a rate of 2.4 percent per year—almost double that of the advanced countries—with the result that per capita production increased at a rate of only 0.7 percent, only slightly over a third as great as for the advanced countries.

The consequence of the same decline in growth rates in food output between the 1950s and the 1960s was quite different for the two groups of countries. For the advanced countries, the growth rate of population declined by about 25 percent, from 1.3 to 1.0 percent per year. As a result, the growth rate in per capita food production declined only from 1.8 to 1.7 percent. In the developing or low-income countries, on the other hand, population growth rates remained the same. Consequently, the growth rate in per capita production declined by almost 60 percent, from 0.7 to 0.3 percent. The growth rate in per capita production clearly widened between the two groups of countries from the earlier decade to the more recent decade.

During the decade of the 1960s and the 1970s the centrally planned economies became more important in international markets. Hence, data on their agricultural sectors are important as well. In the period 1962–1972, food production in the Soviet Union and Eastern Europe increased at a rate of 3.5 percent per year, while in the low-income centrally planned economies (including China) it increased at a rate of 2.6 percent. Given the difference in their respective population growth rates, food production per capita grew at a rate of 2.5 percent per year in the developed centrally planned economies, while it grew at a rate of only 0.7 percent in the low-income centrally planned economies.

The period 1972–1975 saw a period of unusual shocks to the world agricultural economy, as shortfalls in production of a rather large scale were compounded by monetary disturbances associated with the devaluation in the dollar and the shift to floating exchange rates among the industrialized countries. Distortions and rigidities in domestic

---

[1] These data are taken from D. Gale Johnson, *World Food Problems and Prospects* (Washington, D.C.: American Enterprise Institute, 1975).

agricultural policies that did not allow prices in international markets to be reflected in the domestic economies of many countries further aggravated the problem. These disturbances put unusual stress on international grain markets and focused attention on the problems of world agriculture.

The last two years have seen a distinct improvement in the world food situation. Despite the huge shortfall in production experienced by the Soviet Union in 1975, world food production increased 2.3 percent in that year, largely on the basis of a large increase in output in the United States and in the Far East. Preliminary estimates for 1976 indicate another increase of between 2 and 3 percent on the basis of a large increase in U.S.S.R. grain production and more modest increases on a generalized scale around the world except for drought problems in Western Europe. Wheat supplies available for shipment in 1976–1977 in major exporting countries are at record levels, but import requirements are the lowest in many years.

Projections to 1985. A number of conflicting concerns have dominated discussions of international trade in agricultural products in recent years. A longer-term concern has been that the Common Agricultural Policy of the EEC would close out or reduce the productive trade we developed with Western Europe after World War II. Although there were some short-term consequences from that policy, trade has gradually expanded again after the initial adjustment.

During the 1970s, the concerns with trade took on a different dimension. Rather than being concerned with lack of markets, the body politic and policy makers became concerned that foreign markets were too strong. Consequentiy, we had short-lived export controls of one form or another in 1973, in 1974, and in 1975.

There have been two aspects to the concern about foreign markets being too strong. The first is the instability that has arisen from the large fluctuations in the output of the Soviet Union—fluctuations that have been passed on to international markets. The second concern has been with the increasing dependence of the low-income countries on international grain markets. In this case the concern was that we would be swamped by a Malthusian specter that was haunting the Third World, and that our own living standards would be harmed by the need to supply food to a population that was multiplying in the low-income countries.

Data which provide a basis for the concern with the growing importance of the centrally planned economies and the developing countries in international grain markets are summarized in Table 1. In a very brief period of time, net grain exports from developed countries

Table 1

WORLD NET GRAIN EXPORTS AND IMPORTS

(in millions of metric tons)

Region	1969–70—1971–72 Average			1971–72—1973–74 Average		
	Ex-ports	Im-ports	Bal-ance	Ex-ports	Im-ports	Bal-ance
Developed countries	67.7	35.8	+31.9	91.0	36.9	+54.1
Centrally planned countries	3.9	10.7	−6.8	—	20.3	−20.3
Developing countries	6.4	25.5	−19.1	2.8	29.8	−27.0
Asia	3.2	14.1	−10.9	2.3	15.5	−13.2
N. Africa, Middle East	—	9.2	−9.2	—	11.6	−11.6
Africa	—	2.2	−2.2	0.5	2.3	−1.8
Latin America	3.2	—	+3.2	—	0.4	−0.4

Source: Derived from U.S. Department of Agriculture data.

increased from 31.9 to 54.1 million metric tons (70 percent). Net imports of the centrally planned economies, on the other hand, increased from 6.8 to 20.3 million tons (300 percent), while net imports for the developing countries increased from 19.1 to 27.0 metric tons (41 percent).

The International Food Policy Research Institute recently produced a set of projections to 1985 that have caused even more concern for the neo-Malthusians. Under high income growth assumptions and an extrapolation of growth rates for production that prevailed in the period 1960–1974, they project a net cereal deficit for the developing market economies of 82.5 million tons (65.6 million under a low-income growth assumption). Moreover, if the much lower growth rate in production of 1967–1974 were to prevail, the projected cereal deficits in 1985 would be about 200 million tons.

These data paint an even bleaker picture of the world food situation than had emerged from previous projections made by FAO, the USDA, and Iowa State University. What they suggest is a growing imbalance between the developed and developing countries, and a serious food problem in the low-income countries. The significance of these projections to world trade and to U.S. agriculture will be discussed in the second part of the paper. Before turning to that, however, it is useful to consider the changing importance of agricultural trade to U.S. agriculture and to the economy as a whole.

Table 2

IMPORT AND EXPORT COEFFICIENTS OF AGRICULTURAL AND NONAGRICULTURAL SECTORS AND TOTAL U.S. ECONOMY

(percent)

Year	Export Coefficients			Import Coefficients		
	Agri-culture	Non-agri-culture	Total econ-omy	Agri-culture	Non-agri-culture	Total econ-omy
1950–53	18.68	4.08	5.00	25.29	2.27	3.69
1955–57	26.39	4.29	5.24	26.38	2.48	3.51
1958–61	26.93	3.80	4.72	23.62	2.72	3.57
1962–65	32.67	3.82	4.83	22.60	2.93	3.61
1966–69	30.05	4.02	4.83	22.37	3.83	4.40
1970–74	38.38	5.13	6.28	22.01	5.87	6.43
1971	32.05	4.29	5.07	24.26	4.76	5.31
1972	32.64	4.30	5.16	22.45	5.32	5.84
1973	35.10	5.16	6.59	17.57	5.95	6.47
1974	51.75	6.83	8.50	24.11	8.17	8.76
1970–73	33.73	4.60	5.59	21.25	5.16	5.71

Source: Economic Research Service, U.S. Department of Agriculture, and U.S. Bureau of Census.

Changes in the Structure of U.S. Trade. There has been a growing economic interdependence among countries in the post–World War II period. Trade has expanded more rapidly than world gross output, with the result that individual countries have tended to become increasingly dependent on foreign trade both for markets and as a source of supply for important raw materials and other goods and services.[2]

Although less dependent on foreign trade than many countries, the United States has not been immune to the general trend, as seen in Table 2. The overall export coefficient increased by 25 percent between the periods 1950–1953 and 1970–1974, while the overall import coefficient increased by 74 percent. The commodity boom of 1973 and 1974, as well as the rise in oil prices due to the OPEC oil cartel, influenced the data in the latter period. But clearly, the basic trends were already in evidence in 1971 and 1972.

[2] This material is drawn from Antonio Brandao and G. Edward Schuh, "The Changing Structure of U.S. Trade: Implications for Agriculture" (Paper presented at the Annual Meetings of the American Agricultural Economics Association, Pennsylvania State University, August 1976).

U.S. agriculture, in particular, has become increasingly integrated with the world economy in at least three respects:

(1) Foreign markets have become quite important to our agricultural sector. As Table 2 shows, the export coefficient for agriculture doubled between the 1950–1953 and 1970–1974 periods. Although once again influenced by the data for 1974, when we sustained exports in the face of a large production shortfall at home, the export coefficient for agriculture had still increased by 80 percent if that unusual year is ignored.

Interestingly enough, the export coefficient for the nonagricultural sector increased by only 25 percent in the same period, and on a much smaller basis. Similarly, the import coefficient for agricultural products

Table 3

WORLD NET IMPORTS AND EXPORTS OF GRAIN, SELECTED PERIODS, 1934–1973

(annual averages)

	Net Imports (−) or Net Exports				
Country	1934– 38	1948– 52	1960– 62[a]	1969– 71[a]	1972– 73[a]
	(in millions of metric tons)				
Developed countries					
United States	0.5	14.0	32.8	39.8	73.6
Canada	4.8	6.6	9.7	14.8	14.8
South Africa	.3	.0	2.1	2.5	3.1
Oceania	2.8	3.7	6.6	10.6	8.9
Western Europe	−23.8	−22.5	−25.6	−21.4	−21.0
Japan	−1.9	−2.3	−5.3	−14.4	−18.5
Centrally planned countries					
U.S.S.R. & Eastern Europe	4.7	2.7	.5	−3.6	−14.2
China	−1.0	−.4	−3.6	−3.1	−6.3
Developing countries					
Latin America	9.0	2.1	.8	3.2	.6
N. Africa, Middle East	1.0	−.1	−4.6	−9.2	−13.7
Asia	2.4	−3.3	−5.6	−11.0	−14.8

Note: Grain includes wheat, milled rice, corn, rye, barley, oats, sorghum, and millet.
[a] Fiscal years.
Source: Economic Research Service, U.S. Department of Agriculture.

declined by almost 13 percent between the two base periods, while the import coefficient for the nonagricultural sector more than doubled, even ignoring the oil-based increases of 1973 and 1974.

(2) The second sense in which U.S. agriculture has become increasingly integrated with the world economy is through the tendency, over time, for countries to become more dependent on us as a source of grains. Given our present vantage point, it is easy to forget that, as recently as the mid-1930s, the importance of the United States in world grain trade was minimal (Table 3). Latin America was by far the largest net exporter at that time, followed by Canada, the U.S.S.R. and Eastern Europe, and Australia.

By the early 1970s, Latin America had become a net importer in many years, while the U.S.S.R. and Eastern Europe, North Africa and the Middle East, and Asia had all become large net importers. We, on the other hand, had become, by far, the dominant source of grain exports, supplying roughly 40 percent of the total.

(3) Perhaps the most important respect in which U.S. agriculture has become more strongly linked to the world economy is through our trade balance. Although little recognized in contemporary discussion of trade and trade problems, there has been a major shift in the structure of U.S. trade, with agriculture now making a major contribution to our trade balance.

Throughout the 1930s, the early 1940s, and the 1950s, the United States imported more agricultural products (in the form of coffee, cocoa, and other tropical products) than it exported. It was only in the 1960s that the trade balance for agricultural products became positive. And even in the first three years of that decade, *commercial* exports relative to total agricultural imports still ran a deficit on the trade account.

Table 4 documents the major change that has taken place in the structure of our trade. In 1971, we ran the first deficit on our current accounts in modern history, except for a tiny one in 1936. Associated with this was a large deficit in the trade account on nonagricultural products—a deficit that began to emerge in 1968, and for the first time since 1930.

The deficit in our trade balance of nonagricultural products grew rapidly from 1971 through 1974. But at the same time, the *surplus* on our agricultural trade account also grew. In 1973 that surplus was more than sufficient to offset an $8 billion trade deficit in nonagricultural products. In 1974, it was just $3 billion short of offsetting an almost $15 billion deficit in nonagricultural trade. And in 1975, of course, the $12.5 billion surplus in our agricultural trade contributed mightily to the record $10.2 billion surplus in our total trade accounts.

Table 4

U.S. AGRICULTURAL AND NONAGRICULTURAL EXPORTS, IMPORTS, AND TRADE BALANCES, SELECTED YEARS, 1950–1975

(in millions of dollars)

Year	Exports			Imports			Trade Balance		
	Total	Non-agri-culture	Agri-culture	Total	Non-agri-culture	Agri-culture	Total	Non-agri-culture	Agri-culture
1950–52	13,357	9,909	3,448	10,102	5,545	4,557	3,254	4,363	−1,109
1960–62	20,853	15,890	4,963	15,308	11,513	3,794	5,546	4,377	1,169
1970	42,590	35,331	7,259	39,756	33,986	5,770	2,834	1,345	1,489
1971	43,492	35,799	7,693	45,516	39,693	5,823	−2,024	−3,894	1,870
1972	48,876	39,475	9,401	55,282	48,815	6,467	−6,406	−9,340	2,934
1973	70,246	52,566	17,680	69,024	60,615	8,419	1,222	−8,039	9,261
1974	97,908	75,904	21,999	100,997	90,750	10,247	−3,084	−14,871	11,752
1975	107,247	85,353	21,894	96,952	87,624	9,328	10,295	−2,271	12,566a

a From *FATUS*, February 1976, p. 6.
Source: Economic Research Service, U.S. Department of Agriculture, and Council on International Economic Policy.

The year 1975 was unusual, however, because of the serious economic retraction both here and in other advanced countries. Our imports of nonagricultural products declined by $3.2 billion, despite the continued high price of oil, while our exports of nonagricultural products increased by almost $10 billion.

Nonagricultural exports were sustained primarily by a $7.8 billion increase in manufactured exports, composed primarily of increased machinery sales. These, in turn, were due to stepped-up spending of oil revenues by the OPEC countries on their construction and development projects, and the lag in shipments of some types of machinery against orders placed when foreign demand was stronger.

The important point, however, is that despite the U.S. economic recession, which brought with it the first decline in our imports since 1961, the trade balance in nonagricultural products still ran a deficit in 1975 of $2 billion. Agriculture, on the other hand, ran a surplus of over $12 billion, despite a rather sizable decline in commodity prices during the year. The change in structure of our trade appeared to prevail regardless of the unusual conditions of 1975.

This change in trade structure is of major significance to the U.S. economy. It puts a major constraint on our policy and should serve as a warning to those who want to intervene with our agricultural exports.

Some Issues as We Look Ahead

The analytical part of my paper was to be focused on the implications of market prospects for the agricultural sector and the trade balance. This implies an assessment of what the trade prospects will be, and an analysis of the consequences of those prospects for our economy.

Rather than to make a forecast of our market prospects, I have chosen instead to focus on a set of issues that I believe will be important in determining what those prospects will be. These issues are important in determining what the volume of trade is likely to be, and the stability of the markets that might emerge. Both of these factors are important in thinking about what kind of policy we should develop.

What Other Countries and International Agencies Do. In my view, the specter of a Malthusian world presented in discussions of the world food problem in recent years is vastly overdrawn. Although the continued rapid growth of population against a limited supply of land is a serious matter, we are not without recourse in attempting to deal with it. How the situation evolves will be largely determined by the policies countries follow vis-à-vis their agricultural sector, and the commitment of the international community to transfer resources to the developing economies on a reasonable scale and for the appropriate purposes.

The Malthusian specter emerges in part because we are prone to take a land-fundamentalist view in attempting to understand agricultural output and the growth in agricultural output over time. To take this view, however, is to ignore what we might learn from the development of our own agricultural sector, as well as that of countries such as Japan and Israel. In the case of the United States, our agricultural output has been expanding since the mid-1920s with very little increase in the stock of conventional or physical resources. To put some dimensions to it, from 1940 to 1970, for example, total measured physical inputs in agriculture increased only 4 percent, while output increased 58 percent. The bulk of the increase in output growth has come from a rise in productivity—a rise in productivity that was the result of a strong commitment to agricultural research and development and the rapid adoption of modern inputs by the agricultural sector.

In contrasting the past development of agriculture in the low-income developing countries with that of the developed countries, a number of important differences emerge. In the first place, output in the low-income countries has expanded in the post–World War II period largely because additional land was brought into production and because the agricultural labor force increased. Increases in productivity have played a much smaller role. In the advanced countries, however, land under cultivation has tended to remain static or decline, while the agricultural labor force has been reduced, in some cases dramatically. In these countries, the bulk of the increases in output have come from increases in productivity.

A simple comparison of grain yields between the two sets of countries tells most of the story. In the period 1934–1938, grain yields per hectare were the same in the low-income and advanced countries, approximately 1.15 metric tons. By 1952–1956, grain yields in the industrial countries had risen to 1.37 metric tons per hectare, an increase of almost 20 percent. Yields remained static in the low-income countries. By 1969–1970, grain yields were up to 2.14 metric tons per hectare in the advanced countries, an increase of 86 percent from 1934–1938. In the developing countries, however, yields by this date had risen to only 1.41 metric tons per hectare. This constituted an increase of 22 percent. Although yields finally started to move up in less developed countries, their rate of increase was still approximately only one-fourth the rate of increase in the advanced countries.

Another difference between the advanced and the low-income or developing countries is in their economic policy with respect to agriculture. The advanced countries have tended to protect and/or to subsidize their agricultural sectors, while the low-income countries tend to discriminate against theirs, both by failing to make the appropriate development investments and by discrimination through trade and price policy. Agriculture in the low-income countries has been taxed rather heavily through implicit taxes, and these policies have had rather large output effects.

As we look ahead, I suspect that we will see major changes in development policies. There is growing recognition, for example, of the importance of new production technology as the source of agricultural growth, on the part of both individual countries and international development agencies. World expenditures on agricultural research appear to have tripled from 1959 to 1974—from $1.3 billion to $3.8 billion in constant value terms. Moreover, an international system of agricultural research is emerging, based in part on some twelve well-financed international centers designed to strengthen our agricultural research capability on a world scale.

There is also growing recognition that the bias in development policy towards the industrial sector which prevailed throughout most of the post–World War II period was counterproductive. The crisis of the international commodity markets in the 1973–1975 period was an object lesson for many countries, since they were forced to pay very high prices for the imports they needed. More generally, there is growing recognition that the agricultural sector can no longer be ignored in devising development strategies, and that it forms the foundation for sustained economic development and industrial growth in the long run. In fact, the danger now may be that countries will turn to self-sufficiency as a major goal in their planning process and policy formulation.

The energy crisis is also likely to provide strong incentives for countries to strengthen their agriculture. The world breathed a sigh of relief when international capital markets were able to handle the petro-dollar recycling problem reasonably well in the short term, but, in my view, we are by no means out of the woods on this problem. Quite a number of countries have just about exhausted their borrowing possibilities, and a day of reckoning is rapidly approaching.

Adjustments to this problem are likely to take two forms. The first will be the loosening of fixed exchange rates as a means of ordering balance of payments. This can make countries such as Brazil much more competitive in industrial markets—and they are already competitive in products such as soybeans with an exchange rate that is overvalued some 20 percent.

In addition, many countries are likely to strengthen their agriculture either as a means of reducing their food imports or as a source of export earnings. For many countries an expansion in the exports of agricultural products may be seen as the only means of bringing their balance of payments back into balance.

In summary, there are a number of forces at work causing the low-income countries to take more positive steps to strengthen their agriculture. Moreover, we have learned much about how to develop agriculture, and the capability to develop new production technology for world agriculture is being strengthened. If countries and international agencies persist in these policies, there is no reason why agricultural output cannot be increased at a sufficiently rapid rate to keep up with a growing demand.

Some may view these developments with chagrin in terms of the export potential for U.S. agriculture. And if autarchic development becomes the order of the day, there could be serious problems. An important factor to keep in mind, however, is that rational development of the agricultural sector in most countries is likely to lead to a more rapid rate of general economic development in those countries and a rise in growth rates of their per capita income. Our future markets are likely to come from this source of demand rather than from periodic famines or supply-demand imbalances. The more likely problem will be the short-term shocks from devaluations designed to help bring external sectors into equilibrium.

The Leveling of Productivity Growth in U.S. Agriculture. Much of the competitive potential U.S. agriculture has had in international markets has been due to the technological superiority of our agricultural sector. The growth in productivity has been rapid and sustained, and though we discriminated against agriculture by means of an overvalued exchange rate,[3] the growth in productivity was such that we became increasingly important in international markets.

More recently, there has been a marked and little understood decline in the rate of measured productivity growth in agriculture. During the decade of the 1950s, productivity grew by 27 percent. In the decade of the 1960s it grew by only 11 percent, or at a rate only slightly more than a third as large as in the previous decade. This stagnation in productivity growth first emerged in the period following 1965, after a continued and sustained rise in the previous fifteen years. Productivity grew by some 10 percent in 1971, but has again stagnated since that date.

This decline in the growth rate of productivity is reflected in the growth rate in productivity for the primary factors of land and labor.

---

[3] See G. Edward Schuh, "The Exchange Rate and U.S. Agriculture," *American Journal of Agricultural Economics*, vol. 56, no. 1 (February 1974), pp. 1–13.

Table 5

GROWTH RATES IN PRODUCTIVITY OF U.S. LAND AND LABOR, SELECTED PERIODS, 1950–1975

(percent)

Period	Farm Output Per Unit of Total Labor	Crop Production Per Acre
1950–65	10.8	3.7
1965–71	6.9	2.0
1971–75	2.0	0.4

Source: Synthesized from data from Council of Economic Advisers, *Economic Report of the President, 1976.*

Data in Table 5 indicate a dramatic decline in the growth rates of both labor productivity and land productivity.

The reasons for this decline in productivity growth are beyond our present interests, despite their obvious relevance. One possibility is the passing of a technological "epoch" based on specific breakthroughs in plant breeding and a dramatic decline in the real price of fertilizers.[4] Another possibility is that the decline reflects the leveling out of support for agricultural research in this country, since constant-dollar expenditures on production research have been relatively stable since the mid-1960s. And of course, the earlier rapid growth rates in productivity may have been more apparent than real, and in fact a reflection of measurement errors in assessing productivity growth.[5]

If the stagnation in productivity growth continues into the future, the prognosis for our trade in agricultural products can be quite serious. Other countries are far below their technological potential. If they do indeed turn to modernizing and strengthening their agriculture, they can become much stronger competitors in international markets. Our ability to compete will then depend on whether we can or will revitalize our own agricultural research system.

The Changed Environment of Monetary and Fiscal Policy. The shift to a system of floating exchange rates, along with the emergence of an increasingly well-developed international capital market, has both changed

---

[4] For more detail on these issues, see G. Edward Schuh, "The New Macroeconomics of Agriculture," *American Journal of Agricultural Economics*, vol. 58, no. 5 (December 1976), pp. 802–11.

[5] Ibid.

the way that domestic monetary and fiscal policy impacts on the agricultural sector and increased the significance of such policy to agriculture.[6] These changes are likely to submit agriculture to a greater degree of instability than it has experienced in the past. In effect, agriculture will be forced to bear a greater share of the adjustment to monetary and fiscal policy than previously, while at the same time experiencing a greater amount of instability due to fluctuations in foreign demand.

During most of the post–World War II period, U.S. agriculture has been relatively isolated from short-term economic disturbances. The system of fixed exchange rates and the set of agricultural policies we evolved "protected" the agricultural sector from such disturbances. Foreign markets grew slowly over time; fluctuations in domestic demand were fairly limited; and agricultural prices were kept relatively stable (although trending downward) because of the price support program and the setting aside of land. When output fluctuated at home or abroad because of weather or other disturbances, the reserves in government hands could be used to offset it in the short run, and in the longer run land could be released back to production.

We are no longer in that situation. Our reserves in government hands have disappeared, and set-aside land has been released back to production. More importantly, with the present system of floating exchange rates in the presence of a reasonably well-developed international capital market, the adjustment to changes in monetary and fiscal policy will be largely through adjustments in the trade sectors (exports and import-competing sectors). Consequently, we can expect to have an agriculture subject to rather unstable demand, with the bulk of that instability due to fluctuations in foreign demand.

We can see this change in circumstances in the following way. The consequence of a well-developed international capital market is that the interest rate is no longer a completely endogenous variable subject to the control of domestic monetary and fiscal authorities. Rather, it takes on a high degree of exogeneity—depending on the relative importance of the country in international capital markets. When monetary authorities attempt to stimulate the economy by means of an expansion in the quantity of money, this expansion will put downward pressure on the rate of interest, other things being equal. However, to the extent that capital is mobile, there will be a capital outflow as a consequence of this policy—an outflow that will continue until domestic and international interest rates are equalized. The consequence of the capital

---

[6] The issues discussed in this section are discussed in more detail in G. Edward Schuh, "Income and Stability Implications of Monetary, Fiscal, Trade, and Economic Control Policies" (Paper presented at the Farm and Food Policy Symposium, sponsored by GPC-5, Kansas City, Missouri, February 22–24, 1977).

outflow is to bid up the price of foreign currency—that is, the value of the domestic currency would decline in international markets. The decline in the value of the domestic currency would make imports more expensive, while providing a stimulus to exports. The demand for domestic output would consequently increase, and adjustments in the trade sectors would be the means whereby the authorities would attain their stabilization objective.

Restrictive policies, of course, would have the opposite effect. Tight monetary policies would attract a capital inflow, thereby causing the exchange rate to rise. This in turn would dampen the foreign demand for exports while lowering the domestic price of imports. Adjustment would again be borne in large part by the trade sectors.

The consequence of this changed economic environment is that agriculture will be subject to more instability from domestic monetary and fiscal policy than it has been in the past, with the immediate impact of those policies reflected in a fluctuating foreign demand for U.S. agricultural output. An obvious corollary, of course, is that the monetary disturbances can come from abroad, with fluctuations in foreign demand arising from factors rather far removed from the immediate supply/demand balance for agricultural products. If we continue with our present system of flexible exchange rates and an increasingly well-integrated international capital market, we can expect U.S. agriculture to be subject to a great deal more instability in the future than it has had in the past, with fluctuations in foreign demand being an important source of that instability.

Domestic Agricultural Policy. There is much that I might discuss under the rubric of domestic agricultural policy. But I have chosen to focus on only two sets of issues: (1) the emergence of cost of production pricing, and (2) the notion that we should attempt to set the prices of our export commodities in international markets on the grounds that we have a dominant position in international markets.

Cost of production pricing is an important theme in a number of bills now before Congress. Such policies have a great deal of potential for mischief. They neglect that the prices of inputs such as land are demand determined or determined by the price of the product. Such policies can cause a gradual escalation of the price of agricultural products over time. This will have important domestic implications. Equally important, it can cause the rapid loss of our advantage in international markets. We can quickly be led back to strong government intervention in U.S. agriculture.

Clearly, U.S. farmers may need some form of income protection in the future, especially if they are subject to greater instability than in

167

the past. The proper means to provide that protection is through policies more directly tied to income itself and the factor markets. Income production provided through the product market leads to all kinds of deleterious consequences, as we should have learned from the past.

The secretary of agriculture has recently proposed that we make an agreement with Canada whereby we would jointly fix the price of wheat in order to avoid undercutting each other. At least by implication, back of his statement was the notion that we could fix the price of wheat just as the OPEC countries have fixed the price of oil.

A policy such as this has often been suggested by those who recognize the large share of world exports we supply. But our share of export supply can be a very misleading indicator of our power in those markets. What it misses is that most importers of agricultural products are only marginally importers. Because of that, their price elasticity of demand is relatively high, since they have ample domestic substitutes. This is a very different situation from that of the OPEC countries with petroleum because many countries have no other readily available sources of oil.

The pursuit of such a policy will provide further incentives to other countries to pursue autarchic development policies. That is counter to our long-run interests, for agricultural exports are important to us. Such policies will also badly damage our negotiating position in the multilateral trade negotiations, where we have argued for freer markets.

Some Concluding Comments

The last ten years have seen rapid and unexpected changes in the economic conditions facing U.S. agriculture. As we look ahead, the nature of our markets and how we relate to the rest of the world will probably be determined more by the actions of governments, both here and abroad, than by underlying market forces or the rate at which aggregate agricultural output increases relative to population growth and demand. The foreign market for our agricultural output can be steady and ample, or it can be very unstable and impose large shocks on our domestic agriculture. That will be largely determined by the economic policies that governments devise and implement.

Perhaps one of the most important things we should keep in mind is that food and agriculture policy now has to be interpreted and understood in a broad and ample context. The days when we could focus only on domestic food and agriculture policy are gone. The system of exchange rates, the nature of the international capital markets, the relative emphasis on monetary and fiscal policy all have an influence. To neglect them may be to neglect most of what is important.

FOOD AND FOREIGN AFFAIRS
THE ROLE OF AGRICULTURAL TRADE POLICY IN INTERNATIONAL COMMERCE AND DOMESTIC RELATIONS

Clayton K. Yeutter

Introduction

Until that now famous series of Russian grain sales took place in 1972, agricultural policy in the United States had begun to lose its potency. It had its challenges in the drought and depression years of the 1930s, and again during World War II, but in both of those cases the concern was whether enough could be produced for domestic needs. In the earlier of those decades, there was an additional preoccupation with the economic survival of farming communities. Farm families had to be strong in every sense of the word to live through the 1930s.

In the 1950s and early 1960s, a new problem emerged—recurrent surpluses. Those "ever normal granaries" of the FDR era became ever normally full and overflowing two decades later. Farm incomes plummeted, not because farmers produced too little, but because they produced too much. The situation did have its bright spots though, at least to some people; "cheap food" became a way of life in the U.S. Consumers experienced the pleasure of having more and more money left in their pocketbooks after doing their weekly grocery shopping. This occurred not simply because husbands (and the working wives) brought home a bigger pay check, but also because a smaller percentage of that pay check went for food. By the early 1970s, the percentage had dropped below 16, even though people were eating out more than ever before. American families contentedly went about spending more money for other things.

Consumers in importing countries also benefited from the surpluses (most of which were held in the United States and Canada). Exporters discovered that it cost money to store surpluses, and that one could afford to move them on the world market even if it meant shaving prices in some manner. This led, for example, to "food aid" programs in which a nation would either give away its surpluses, or sell them through the use of long-term credit with exceptionally low interest rates. With food aid programs (P.L. 480 for the U.S.), exporters could reduce their surpluses and feel like humanitarians at the same time.

The exporting nations soon learned, however, that their surpluses were too large to be fully absorbed by food aid; in other words, they could not even give all that grain away in the developing world. This then led to use of the export subsidy, still one of the most invidious of all trade practices. One can compete in any market if one's federal treasury is large enough. These subsidies proved to be costly indeed (though perhaps less costly than storage), but they moved a lot of food to importing nations at bargain basement prices. U.S. consumers were happy because food costs remained low, and taxpayer costs, though high, were tolerated because progress seemed to be made in reducing the surpluses. Exports increased dramatically, not just because of subsidies, but because of a growth in worldwide demand for food products and an ever widening competitive advantage for the American farmer.

Then in 1972 the Soviet Union triggered a never-to-be-forgotten series of events by entering the world food market in a massive way. Food prices in the United States skyrocketed, or at least consumers thought they did. Though the percentage of income expended for food never did rise beyond a mean of 18 percent, even that 2 percent jump seemed devastating to housewives accustomed to paying the same amount at the checkout counter every week of the year. Consumer advocate groups looked for villains in the picture, and almost everyone in the production and marketing process was castigated before the issue quieted down.

U.S. agricultural exports also skyrocketed, and this led to a strengthening of the dollar and a vast improvement in both the balance and the terms of trade (helped, admittedly, by the dollar devaluations of this period). Consumers benefited significantly from this, but few recognized those benefits. They, in fact, argued vehemently for the imposition of export controls, and the government complied, though only on a few occasions and for very short periods of time. The use of export controls shattered the image of the United States as a dependable supplier of food, and it will pay dearly for that in years to come.

American farmers entered a period of unprecedented prosperity. Farm incomes leaped, and the implement dealers, auto salesmen, and travel agents of small town America also had the finest derivative income years of their lives. Rural America, which had been in the economic doldrums, was revitalized as never before. Farmers, however, quickly capitalized their increased incomes into land, and farm real estate prices soared. Though this made net worth statements a lot more impressive than previously, it also reduced the nation's agricultural competitive advantage on the world scene—a troublesome omen for the future.

In 1973 and 1974, everyone became an expert on world hunger, and the media devoted hundreds of radio and TV hours and thousands of print lines to this topic. The twentieth century Malthusians had a field day; they hawked their doomsday philosophy on almost a full-time basis. Amid all the rhetoric, the most relevant response came from farmers around the world; they reacted to the excellent prices by expanding production, a basic economic principle which had nearly been forgotten in the Malthusian shuffle. As a result, the economy is now back to more comfortable carryover levels, and it is a propitious time for objectively examining agricultural trade policy in the United States and elsewhere.

Let us turn first to the developing countries, to whom this issue is often a matter of life or death.

Developing Countries

Production Disincentives. Trade policy has both its production and marketing aspects. In developing countries, the former is often more important than the latter. Unfortunately, in attempting to follow the cheap food policies of the developed world, too many developing countries have actually discouraged agricultural production. This may be politically wise in the short run, but in the long run it is a devastating mistake. This became painfully evident to food-importing, less developed countries (LDCs) in the post–1972 period, when their terms of trade deteriorated dramatically.

Of even greater significance is that industrial productivity in any nation simply cannot advance, and levels of living cannot improve, until manpower can be released from its agricultural sector. This calls for enormous increases in agricultural efficiency, an unlikely result when government is providing production disincentives.

Import Restrictions. Some developing countries have gone to the other extreme in production policy by opting to protect their domestic agricultural producers through the use of import restrictions (often as an accompaniment to high support levels). In many instances the economic objective is a laudable one in that it provides a production stimulus. Unfortunately, it is not a policy that is likely to lead to *efficient* production. Increased self-sufficiency is an understandable goal, particularly for countries that are experiencing balance-of-payments problems— Brazil is the classic example today—but the same argument can be made for all LDCs suffering through the present energy crisis. One must be concerned, however, lest import restrictions—taken for legitimate reasons—be retained when those reasons no longer apply. This has often occurred, to the chagrin of the offending nation's trading partners, and to the economic disadvantage of the world as a whole. Such violations of the spirit, if not the rules, of the General Agreement on Tariffs and Trade (GATT) call for a more careful and continual appraisal of such restrictions under the GATT, and for timely termination thereof.

The import regimes of some developing countries have been so protective that their domestic industries have become complacent, lethargic, and inefficient. This has reduced (or eliminated) their international competitiveness, thereby worsening the nation's terms of trade —the exact opposite of what was intended. To their great credit, the governments of a number of LDCs (Argentina and Colombia, for example) have recently recognized this incongruity and have had the political courage to do something about it by opening their borders to increased competition. Such action inevitably incurs the enmity of the protected domestic industries, but the government may actually have done them a great favor. An economically troubled firm or industry cannot survive indefinitely on the domestic scene, let alone in fierce international competition. If the firm or industry is forced to meet import competition head on (the assumption being that the import competition is fair), it may modernize, alter its management structure, and take other steps that will be in its own long-term interest.

Export Subsidies. A frequent rationale for LDC protectionism, and for the use of export subsidies, is that of developing infant industries. The idea, of course, is that in the absence of protection LDC industries will never be able to achieve the economies of scale essential to compete with developed countries. I am prepared to accept that argument—up to a point. Developing countries deserve a chance to improve their competitiveness, but there comes a time when an "infant industry" is no longer an infant. If the governmental protections and incentives are successful, the industry "grows up," and at that point it no longer needs or merits special privileges in international trade.

Some LDCs have suggested, in the Multilateral Trade Negotiations (MTN) in Geneva, that GATT rules should permit them to subsidize exports with impunity. That is simply an economically (and politically) unacceptable proposal. It has also been suggested that "safeguard" actions by developed countries should exempt all imports from LDCs. That too is an unacceptable suggestion, for the same reasons. Assisting the LDCs and their industries and firms to be competitive is one thing; to ask their developed competitors to battle them on a permanently disadvantageous basis is quite another thing.

Preferences. Agricultural products are a major export item, often *the* major export item, for many developing countries. Others have the resource base to become exporters once they get their economies on track. Thus, it is understandable that the LDCs delineate enhanced access to markets in developed countries as one of their principal objectives in the economic sphere. Though that objective extends to both agricultural and industrial goods, the former offer the greatest immediate potential for many LDCs.

The United States and most other developed countries have granted temporary tariff preferences to many developing countries on hundreds of items. The U.S. system, for example, encompasses about 2,800 items involving nearly $3 billion of LDC imports. (Most, however, are industrial items). More importantly, we import nearly $25 billion worth of these same goods from our fellow developed countries. Duty-free treatment for LDCs should afford them an opportunity to capture a sizable segment of that market.

"Special and Differential" Treatment. One disadvantage of preference systems, from the developing country's viewpoint, is that they are temporary. The U.S. system has a ten-year life, but it includes provisions for the earlier removal of countries and products from its benefits under certain circumstances. In other words, the system is by no means comparable to permanent benefits that can be provided LDCs in the Multilateral Trade Negotiations. For this reason, many LDCs see the MTN as the forum with the most potential for enhancing their market opportunities in the developed world.

In the Tokyo Declaration of 1973, which launched the current, seventh post-war MTN, the developed countries agreed to provide "special and differential treatment" for their LDC counterparts as the negotiations unfolded. A great deal of effort has been expended since then in attempting to delimit areas where special and differential treatment—which by definition constitutes a departure from the most-favored-nation principle—would be appropriate and desirable. The United States has expressed a willingness to consider such treatment in most of the MTN negotiating groups and has outlined its ideas on the subject in a number of papers that have been submitted in Geneva. I am optimistic that LDCs will gain significant market opportunities for their agricultural products before the MTN concludes.

Commodity Agreements. Nearly all developing countries have a constant concern with their balance-of-payments situation. With limited foreign exchange reserves, they are extremely vulnerable to price fluctuations in both export and import goods. Raw materials prices have traditionally fluctuated, sometimes violently, on world markets. In agriculture, this is often due to supply being a function of unpredictable weather conditions. With virtually all LDCs being either food importers or exporters, they continually suffer through the foreign exchange impact of erratic commodity prices. What is the answer? There are many possible solutions to this problem, but the one typically offered by developing countries is an international commodity agreement with buffer stocks.

One cannot summarily reject this solution for it has a lot of political appeal, at least at present; and it cannot be rejected on economic grounds, for a commodity agreement *may* be able to inject a certain degree of stability in the world market of a given product. With a strong commitment by exporters to honor price ceilings, an equally strong commitment by importers to honor price floors, price bands that are wide enough to permit the market to work most of the time, provisions for new suppliers to enter the market, a large enough buffer stock to be influential when the margins are reached, and no readily available substitutes, a commodity agreement has a fair chance for success. Rarely, however, are *all* exporter and importer nations willing to accept the cost, the discipline, and the commitment essential to make such an agreement work. Therefore, without even considering the philosophical aspects of international commodity agreements, one must conclude that the practical realities of economic life are such as to doom most such agreements to failure. In fact, a careful cost-benefit analysis will preclude most of them from even being initiated.

Many LDCs, however, view commodity agreements as a mechanism for raising the price of raw materials they export. In other words, they see some budding "OPECs" in the offing. But this is unrealistic; it is most unlikely that *any* commodity agreement that would achieve this purpose can be successfully negotiated. For this to occur, one would have to assume: (1) that importer participants in such an agreement will be inept negotiators, or (2) that developed country importers will deliberately accede to the use of commodity agreements as a new foreign aid mechanism. Neither would seem to be a reasonable assumption. Furthermore, if a commodity agreement were "successful" in raising prices, that success would likely be short-lived. Since developing countries are the primary importers of many commodities, they would be the ones to suffer most from the price rise. It would be rational to assume they would object (though one must wonder about this assumption in light of the compliant acceptance of OPEC). Beyond that, however, commodity price increases will unquestionably stimulate the development and use of substitutes. This alone will make most, if not all, price enhancing commodity agreements viable for only a short period of time.

The objective—shared by developed and developing countries alike—of affording LDCs a greater opportunity to expand exports, and perhaps a more attractive net income for those exports, is a valid one. It is also highly desirable in humanitarian terms, and for maintenance of peace in the world. But surely there are better ways to do this than through the use of international commodity agreements (at least as they have traditionally been designed).

Developed Countries

Production Incentives. As I indicated earlier, one of the paradoxes of agricultural policy is that many LDCs apply production *disincentives* to agriculture—even though their food needs are enormous, and even though this policy undoubtedly impedes their general economic development. The reverse of this paradox applies in many developed countries. They continue to apply production *incentives* to agriculture—even though the cost is enormous and the resultant surpluses can be sold internationally only through the use of export subsidies (to say nothing of the import restrictions that are necessary to keep the system functioning). In other words, many developed countries deliberately maintain an agricultural production plant that is uncompetitive internationally. They do this, allegedly at least, for social reasons. The argument made is that their respective countries are better off by keeping a substantial segment of the population in rural areas, rather than to have them migrate to the cities. (Though some migration is nonetheless occurring, the rate is quite low.)

It is not my intent to challenge the social policy of these developed nations. Nor is it my prerogative to do so; they have a sovereign right to choose whatever social policy they wish. I have traveled many of those countries, and I too appreciate the beauty of their countrysides and the quaintness of their small farms, inefficient as they may be. But as an economist I do object—and I believe other nations have a right to object—to the distortions that those social policies cause in the arena of international trade.

Unfortunately, from an economist's viewpoint, many developed nations have chosen to implement their rural social policies through the use of high support levels on agricultural products. This policy is probably the most distortive of trade (and perhaps the least cost-effective) that they could possibly have chosen. Both the European community and Japan have found, for example, that to provide reasonable incomes for their small agricultural producers, support levels must be set far above world market prices.

Export Subsidies. The upshot of this is that almost everyone is unhappy. Surpluses generated by high support levels must be sold on the world market through the use of export subsidies. This is not likely to please the more efficient farmers of the United States, Canada, Australia, New Zealand, Argentina, and other exporting nations who find their own exports undercut by the subsidies. Trade policy experts call this the "third country" subsidy problem, and it is an issue for which the present GATT rules are totally inadequate. (Because of this, the United States now has authority to deal with such trade practices under domestic law—Section 301 of the Trade Act of 1974—and about a dozen complaints have already been filed.)

Export subsidies can, of course, also be used to penetrate markets that would ordinarily be served by domestic producers. The European community, for example, has long subsidized its cheese exports to the United States. This not only undercuts exports by Australia and New Zealand (the third country subsidy problem), but also takes part of the U.S. market away from American dairy farmers. The most effective response to such subsidies is the application of countervailing duties (that is, a duty equal to the subsidy, which effectively neutralizes it), but subsidizing exporters contend that countervailing is inappropriate unless "injury" is shown. (I would counter this contention by asserting that injury is inherent in the use of direct export subsidies. After all, the purpose of such a subsidy is to penetrate a market that would not otherwise be penetrable.)

If export subsidies undercut world market prices, importers benefit from this unanticipated developed country generosity. So long as they are not attempting to develop their own production of the product in question, the price cutting is a foreign exchange bonanza for them. Nevertheless, they are concerned about the long-run implications of subsidy practices.

If developed countries use export subsidies to rid themselves of agricultural surpluses, they can use such subsidies to rid themselves of other surpluses too. Some of these will inevitably undercut exports from the developing world. Competing with the treasuries of the developed countries is not an enticing thought for LDCs with balance-of-payments problems, but perhaps their major concern is that developed countries typically use subsidies on products in which LDCs are no longer competitive. These are labor-intensive products, both agricultural and industrial, where developing countries now have either an absolute or comparative advantage. The contention of the LDCs, and a legitimate one, is that developed countries should be phasing out these industries, or at a minimum should be phasing out their uncompetitive firms. By no means should they be expanding production of such goods through the use of subsidies at a time when the LDCs are trying to find a meaningful niche in the international trading world.

Within subsidizing developed countries, economic joy is hardly universal either. Producers are obviously pleased by the support from their governments, particularly when it is partially hidden in higher domestic food costs and thus is not readily identifiable as a government subsidy. But taxpayers are not at all pleased by the costs they can see (storage and export subsidies for example), and they are uneasy about those they cannot see (the indirect impact of higher support levels on food costs). Thus, U.S. taxpayers objected vigorously to the million dollars per day spent to store American grain surpluses a few years ago, and also to the export subsidies used prior to and including the initial Soviet grain sales. The consumers of Western Europe, with food prices far higher than America's, must wonder about the wisdom of subsidizing beef sales to the Soviet Union when beef is not exactly a bargain in the supermarkets of Brussels, Bonn, or Paris.

A better way to avoid and/or deal with agricultural surpluses can surely be found.

Quantitative Restrictions. Quantitative restrictions—quotas or QRs—are one of the major impediments to the rational conduct of international trade. Whereas subsidies are the principal distortion on the export side, QRs fill a similar distortive role on the import side. No matter how competitive one may be, it is extremely difficult to penetrate a market walled in by a quantitative restriction. The variable levy, which increases as the world market price of a product falls, is no less onerous than the traditional QR. Voluntary restraint agreements, none of which are truly voluntary, are an improvement in degree, but not in kind. For purposes of this discussion both can be considered as quantitative restrictions.

As described earlier, developing countries have been able to rationalize at least some of their QRs under the GATT rules, usually on balance-of-payments grounds. Developed countries (including the United States), on the other hand, have struggled futilely to justify their quantitative restrictions, most of which are agricultural. Some which might have been appropriate when initiated (under safeguard rules, for instance) are no longer defensible and should have been eliminated years ago. Others are palpably illegal, and are being retained in circumvention of the GATT. Finding a solution to this problem will improve world agricultural trade immensely and is one of the priority objectives of the Tokyo Round of trade negotiations.

Standards. Standards should be trade-neutral, and both buyer and seller should benefit from their use. But that does not always occur. Japan, for example, some months ago rejected a shipment of U.S. citrus because the fruit had been sprayed with a particular chemical, yet that chemical had been approved for use by Codex Alimentarius, an international standards making body of which Japan is a member. This exemplifies the need to negotiate a procedural standards code in the MTN.

Administrative Guidance. There are times when nontariff barriers are extremely difficult to discover and characterize. A number of such barriers, applicable to both agricultural and nonagricultural goods, can loosely be described under the heading "administrative guidance." Customs procedures frequently fall into this category. Clearances are often inordinately delayed, and if the imported product is perishable, it may never reach the ultimate consumer.

This kind of barrier can also develop when a government official passes word to the private sector that import levels of a given product are becoming worrisome. The following month, orders from those private firms begin to decline. This can be just as effective as a quota, though it may never appear in the form of a law or regulation.

Other Distortions. I have concentrated my attention in this paper only on those practices I consider to be the most distortive to world agricultural trade. Many others could be mentioned, particularly in the nontariff barrier area, for nations have become innovative in protecting their domestic industries from competition.

I have not even mentioned tariffs. Though they can be disruptive too, and though the United States should further reduce tariffs in the MTN, competitive firms and industries can overcome many tariffs. Nontariff measures, on the other hand, can often stop a competitive firm or industry in its tracks.

Recommendations

It is indeed an imperfect world, and the imperfections in agricultural trade are some of the most imaginative of all. But let us not be pessimists. Those imperfections notwithstanding, American agricultural exports have nearly quadrupled in the past decade, not a bad record, even though a few rocks have been thrown in the path. Beyond that, consumers around the world want a better diet, and if that calls for importing agricultural products, they want to import.

Where does that leave the United States, in early 1977, as we move into the final phases of the Tokyo Round of trade negotiations, and as renewal of our own farm legislation is debated? I offer the following views for consideration.

(1) The United States must maintain its international competitiveness, so that it can deal from equity and from strength at the negotiating table. This calls for concerted action in many areas: agricultural research and extension programs; the development of new agricultural technology; stimuli for capital investment in agriculture; sound monetary and fiscal policies generally; and farm legislation that will not jeopardize the competitiveness that already exists. Government policies can help to maintain and enhance the efficiency of U.S. agriculture. Unfortunately, the large bureaucracy sometimes harms, while trying to help. I hope we can avoid that outcome in the future.

(2) If we are competitive, we ought not apologize for it, and we ought to use it to our advantage. This is not to suggest that we use food as a "weapon," the favorite term of the media these days; but it is a recognition of leverage, and the opportunity to use it for the benefit of U.S. farmers and for the nation as a whole. If we are not careful, we can give away that leverage in a variety of ways.[1]

(3) We should proudly defend our basic agricultural policies. With an agricultural production and marketing plant that is the envy of the world, we ought to try to convince others to move in our policy direction, rather than vice versa. Of course, conditions are different, and we cannot expect the rest of the world to do everything our way. In many cases, it would be inappropriate for them to do so. But neither is it appropriate to reject categorically our market-oriented, free enterprise system. Many elements of our system can serve other nations well, perhaps more effectively than what they now have. Futures markets, for example, have scarcely been used in many agricultural trading nations.

(4) We should unhesitatingly challenge the trade distortive actions of other nations, particularly those in the developed world. It does not make sense to have a double standard for trade policy (agricultural or industrial) among the developed nations. Though the energy crisis has had a greater impact on some than on others, most economies of the developed world are basically healthy; and to the extent that they have economic woes, trade distortions are not the proper means for responding to those woes. We have authority to deal with these trade practices both under the GATT and under Section 301 of the Trade Act of 1974. We should exercise that authority when the occasion demands. This

---

[1] The negotiation of an international grain reserve is an example of this. A grain reserve is like an insurance policy, the cost of which should be borne by the policy holder. In that case, grain importing nations should bear most of the cost, and not the exporting nations, as has happened in the past. It also means that we should not unilaterally create a "domestic grain reserve." Were we to do so, we would sacrifice all our leverage in this area, and the rest of the world would quickly lose interest in an international reserve.

is not economic saber rattling; it is simply the insistence that international trade be carried out in a fair, sensible, and rational way.

For many years we failed to respond in such situations, leading other nations to believe that they could use subsidies, dumping actions, import restrictions, and other means without experiencing anything more than a protest from Uncle Sam. And when the United States did respond to such indefensible practices (as we have recently), we were painted as the villain, as "protectionist." It is time that that perception be corrected once and for all.

(5) We should encourage all trading nations to be open, candid, reasonable, and rational in the development of their trade policies. This suggests that nations follow some basic public policy principles:

- notifying the GATT of trade actions contemplated or taken, a courtesy that is often not extended;
- consulting with nations that might be affected before, rather than after, actions are taken;
- using open, public procedures in the decision making process so that anyone with interest—nations, firms, individuals—may have an input; and
- keeping any restrictions temporary and no more onerous than absolutely necessary.

If these principles were routinely followed, international trade in agricultural products would be much more rational than it is today.

(6) If our agricultural policies are right, we should strongly enunciate them at the negotiating table. Other nations often expect the United States to compromise, or to "give up something." It is up to us to make a negotiating round or a conference a success. We are often chided for being too "theological" on trade issues, meaning we are unwilling to accept the other nation's position. But if the principle is sound, let's not abandon it. It just may be that once in a while the rest of the world is out of step, and we are in step. If we are confident that such is the case, we ought to have the political courage to say so and to stick with it.

(7) We must make progress on reducing agricultural trade barriers in the multilateral trade negotiations. With tariffs, subsidies, import quotas, export quotas, variable levies, voluntary restraint agreements, and other restrictions still proliferating, this is hardly the time to agree to disagree and come home. Previous rounds of negotiations, including the Kennedy Round a decade ago, have made considerable progress on the industrial side, but little in agriculture. This time we should stay in Geneva until we hammer out a set of agreements that will advance the cause of world trade in both sectors. This will benefit not only U.S.

farmers, but consumers around the world as well. In addition, it provides an ideal opportunity for many nations to change agricultural policies that they know are outmoded.

Perhaps the two major agricultural issues that must be dealt with in the Tokyo Round are export subsidies, and quantitative restrictions, that is, variable levies and quotas. Unless progress can be made in these two key areas, particularly among the developed nations, the Tokyo Round will be construed by the U.S. agricultural community (and by agricultural and other trade policy officials of many other nations as well) as being no more successful than the Kennedy Round. This, in turn, will lead to strong demands for unilateral action against the trade distortive practices of others. It would be better if all agreed in Geneva, first, not to impose new programs in these areas, and, second, to place sound constraints on existing programs, with a further agreement that they be phased out over an agreed adjustment period.

(8) Importing nations should be encouraged to take steps to provide for their own food security, rather than to depend on the surpluses of exporters for that security. Some of those steps are appropriate for the public sector, others for the private sector, and some could readily involve both. They involve such actions as: constructing additional storage for both raw and processed food products; buying or leasing storage in the United States and other exporting nations; the use of futures markets in the United States or elsewhere; and long-term contractual commitments.[2]

(9) We must provide for an expansion of international trade with the developing nations of the world. In many cases, this means enhancing their agricultural exports: at times, those exports will penetrate the U.S. market, in competition with our own producers; at other times, they will penetrate third country markets, in competition with our exporters. Nevertheless, this need should be accommodated in a reasonable and meaningful way. Rhetoric is not enough, and tokenism is not enough; when we say we prefer trade to aid, we have to mean it. If these nations are to become an integral part of the world economy we cannot reduce foreign aid, for the many reasons that are traditionally espoused, and then stymie "special and differential treatment" in the trade area too. That would be a hypocritical result, for which we would be duly and properly chastized in world public opinion.

(10) We should sell aggressively in world markets. Even if trade

---

[2] It is somewhat ironic that the Soviet Union, a nonmarket economy nation, has done a much better job of protecting itself against the instability of price fluctuations than have the market economy nations of the Western world. The Soviets are already aggressively pursuing most elements of the course that I have just outlined.

barriers are reduced or eliminated, we cannot expect buyers to come pounding on our door. There is much to be done in enhancing our reputation for producing a quality product, honoring our contractual obligations, being a dependable seller, and servicing the needs of our customers. In addition, there are a multitude of markets to be opened, in new places and for new products. Observe, for example, the many ways in which soybean products are being used in the Far East; many of the more recent developments are attributable to work by our soybean industry. Observe, in contrast, the few tasty, corn-fed T-bone steaks that are available, even in the best restaurants and hotels, throughout the world. Similar comparisons could be made with lots of other products. We have truly just begun to market U.S. agricultural products.

Conclusion

There are many uncertainties in the future of international trade in agriculture, uncertainties in domestic agricultural policies, uncertainties in the evolution of consumer movements, uncertainties on the political front, uncertainties in bilateral and multilateral trade negotiations. But the stakes are too high not to forge ahead.

One can always find reasons not to move toward freer agricultural trade, and it is even easier to rationalize moves toward greater protectionism. But neither the United States nor any other major producer can afford to go that route. Food is too important to the physical and economic well-being of the world, and it will become even more so as time passes. Furthermore, trade restrictions are too onerous, and the GATT rules for agricultural commerce are simply inadequate. This is not the time to be hesitant and indecisive; let us not back away from the challenges.

Apocryphally, a management consultant once advised his client not to view his difficulties as problems or obstacles, but rather as challenges and opportunities; to which the harassed manager responded: "Well, then I sure have a lot of insurmountable opportunities!"

I believe we *can* handle our agricultural trade challenges, simply because the rewards for doing so are enormous—a better quality of life for producers and consumers alike, worldwide. Surely this is not an "insurmountable opportunity."

COMMENTARIES

.

Jimmye S. Hillman

I want to compliment both Schuh and Yeutter in presenting very fine papers. Ed Schuh's paper came just as I was going to the airport, but I had a couple more weeks with Clayton Yeutter's, so his will probably get both barrels instead of one!

There are certain parallelisms in the papers in that they set up a type of developing-developed dichotomy. And in the case of Schuh, he brings in, or wiggles in, the Third World at a couple of places. Both point out that the policies in the LDCs have discouraged agricultural growth, development, and productivity. Both point out that there have been policies towards self-sufficiency which are denigrated by Schuh but not quite as much by Yeutter. Both point out the necessity of a strong trade, and healthy world agriculture, and especially their importance to the United States in the coming decades.

Except in those similarities, they take rather divergent approaches. At the crossroads, Yeutter goes off into commercial and agricultural policies, whereas Schuh goes into production and market structure analysis.

Before briefly discussion the papers, I would like to point out the danger of dichotomizing and of getting into an "I-thou" relationship with the developing-developed world. Anyone familiar with the great theologian Martin Buber knows what I am talking about.

But the "I-thou" relationship between a developing and a developed country sometimes permits an evasion of the principles Yeutter was so avid about about in his comments (and I agree with his avidness). The dichotomizing tends to let us skip over those principles. We could soon find ourselves involved with further classifications, for example, third world, fourth world, and fifth world; GATT and UNCTAD; and from that to the North-South, to the Lomé Convention, to FAO and IWC; and other types of dichotomizing and administrative classification, preferences and nonpreferences, and so forth. We might escape principles relative to production, growth, and distribution, and even the protectionist argument by all of this dichotomizing, which, to my way of thinking, is political classification.

Remember that political classification also means administrative classification. Preferences bring a bureaucracy and a potential for further dichotomization, because each person sets up his own type of world. There is, indeed, a danger that GATT will be swallowed up by UNCTAD, and I agree definitely with Yeutter's point of view on that.

In regard to Ed Schuh's paper, his title is a little like Marshall McLuhan's "the medium is the message." I got the medium; I don't know whether I got the message. The tone of the paper runs first to ominousness, then to sort of an assurance. In the first part of the paper, he points out the ominousness of the slowdown in productivity and of all of the other characteristics of developing countries, and of the slowdown of productivity in U.S. agriculture. And, of course, the data are arranged to show that slowdown in the productivity and growth rates. And then he says that, after all, the Malthusian specter is sort of far-fetched anyway.

Then he brings in the instability argument, with respect to Soviet purchases and production. It should be pointed out that this instability is not just a recent phenomenon—it has happened four times since World War II. He points out also the increasing dependence of the low-income countries on grain imports. He finds, as I say, the Malthusian specter vastly overdrawn, but he admits, at the same time, that there is potential in the developing countries to increase agricultural productivity.

I find little to quibble with in the paper—the overall presentation, the productivity issues, the trade structure issues. He develops and presents the monetary problems very well; I agree with his background analysis. The data that are presented are sound, and the instability rationale is well-drawn. Negligence of agriculture in the developing world, I think, is rightly pointed out. The so-called intervention through price-fixing is well-taken, too, as is the danger of too much self-sufficiency pointed out by him and by Yeutter in the developing world.

But the opposite side of that coin could easily be brought out. The opposite side of the coin is how much self-sufficiency is enough? How can export earnings be increased through agricultural exports, and how much should we encourage that? I will make another point or two about that.

The paper could have been improved by noting a couple of things. First, the real potential for production of food and export in the developing countries was not developed quite as much as it should have been. Perhaps that was not the purpose of the paper, but I would like to see that developed more. Second, what is the potential in the related temperate-climate world—in countries like Argentina that have the capability for production and export?

I just had another thought in this context. Perhaps I should have thought about it many years ago, as Gale Johnson did. After all, maybe the EEC does have a selected comparative advantage in agriculture. In a famous paper right after World War II, Austin Robinson argued that Britain had a comparative advantage in agriculture—what with its outmoded industrial plant and the noncompetitive nature of its industry. The self-sufficiency argument in Britain was presented very well by Robinson. In our zeal, maybe we should take a look at the EEC's position in that regard.

To add to El Schuh's expertise on monetary flexibility, I would add a point I learned with John Condliffe at Berkley in the 1940s. The gold point theory and the balancing mechanism of the Bank of England during the nineteenth century—and, in fact, up to 1925 when Britain went off the gold standard, but particularly, before World War I—did a wonderful job of what is now being done by floating exchange rates. There were indeed some violent eruptions in trade. There was protection, there was intervention, as in Germany and France, during the latter part of the nineteenth century. Our "free trade policy" was not as free as, and was more interventionist than, we would like to admit; and it was a tariff policy as opposed to the practices of intervention that most countries have been following since World War II. The Bank of England, and the short-run interest rate balance versus the long-range balance, and other factors, really did a beautiful job insofar as balancing was concerned. It was a lot better than the "snake in the tunnel," and the green pounds and green money, and the funny money we have today to try to make sense out of EEC monetary policy—within the community, and without the community, and between the community and other parts of the world.

I would like to have seen Ed Schuh define productivity a little more. This was not the place for that, perhaps, but maybe we can go into it in the discussion. Productivity and the definition thereof is really a hairy argument. The structural problems, which Schuh mentions as having begun for the United States in 1968, began much earlier, monetarily and otherwise. In fact, when Triffin wrote his famous paper in 1958 relative to the cross-over with respect to the U.S. trade and monetary position in the world, even it was a little late. Certainly it had begun as early as 1958 and was pretty well defined and accepted by that time.

The leveling off of productivity worries me. We have been looking at that in Arizona, for example, with respect to leveling off of cotton yields. In fact, lower yields may be a market phenomenon. There is no doubt that we can get better yields, but at what price? I would like to see the issue discussed in that context. If we discuss productivity only in the yield context, we will miss the boat entirely.

Yeutter's paper is divided three ways: dichotomy, shifts in policies, and a wrap-up. I will take them one at a time. It sets up the dichotomy between the developed and developing countries with respect to import restrictions, export subsidies, and several other matters. Then, the shifts in commercial policies are attacked with respect to the developed countries, pointing out preferences—especially the significance of the preferences which were "ground into" the Tokyo Agreement and our own U.S. Trade Act of 1974. And it rightly points out the difficult problems which might be engendered by accepting commodity agreements as an all-in-all with respect to trade policy.

One point I would like to make is that the variable levy, which the Europeans do not admit is a quantitative restriction, is, indeed, a quantitative restriction. I hope to come out with a little tract of 100 pages or so on NTBs very soon. In it I will prove "theoretically" that the variable levy is a quota, and acts like one. Indeed, it is a quantitative restriction.

NTBs are given their right place in the Yeutter paper. Standards are a very important part of the NTBs. The Codus Alimentarius, for example, operated especially out of the European context of food standards, and food distribution is more and more important as a potential restriction.

I cannot say enough about administrative laws. They are the subject for a paper in themselves. We have gone from tariff restrictions to non-tariff quantitative barriers, administrative law, delays, threats, under-the-table kicks on the shins, et cetera. As an illustration, Yeutter's paper has one administrator saying his country may have had enough American wheat. We in the United States do the same thing—we impose unwritten regulations on foreign exporters.

The ten points Yeutter mentions in conclusion really consist of only about four or five. Competition must be maintained, and everyone must challenge trade distortions; but what would we give up, and what would the other bargaining countries give up? This question contains three or four of his points. What does the United States give up—Section 22, peanuts, sugar, the beef quota, milk, or what? Also, what would we give up in bargaining with Canada and Mexico with respect to our own trade policies with them? And Yeutter points out the problems in developing countries of food security and expanded trade.

We must realize—and this may sound a little like pontification—that there are parts of the world which have legitimate objectives in addition to, and often in conflict with, the efficiency concept or the cheap food concept; in our case, it is our export policy. In the EEC, regional policy is very, very important. Switzerland has a law requiring 30 percent of the budget to be spent in some sense on rural development—to keep the mountains green and that sort of thing.

In regard to agricultural adjustment, FAO has conducted a major effort on certain agricultural adjustment themes. Good or bad, the organization is worried about agricultural adjustments, and I think we must realize that. Don Paarlberg has spent some time in those forums. Most important for us if there are indeed policies in conflict with the efficiency of export policy, is the costs of those policies. Can we "smoke them out," measure them, quantify them, put them in some economic context, and find out their real costs to the developed countries and developing countries? Trade and agricultural policies, in the final analysis, are but an extension of domestic policies. Our trade policy is very much an extension of our domestic policy.

My final point harks back to the self-sufficiency theme. How can we stop discouraging agriculture, without increasing self-sufficiency? The developing countries have discouraged agriculture, and we tell them to become more self-sufficient and more efficient. At the same time we are concerned that their products will compete with U.S. exports. How do we deal with that?

The natural consequence is for developing countries to become developed, and many of them do indeed become developed. Like us, however, they want it both ways. Mexico wants to be a leader in the UNCTAD—in fact, the former president wanted to be the director general of the United Nations—and yet, Mexico wants to be regarded as a developed country as well. It wants it both ways—both GATT and UNCTAD. That is difficult to obtain!

R. J. Hildreth

Reflections on these papers led me to think about some points made by T. W. Schultz in the Leonard K. Elmhirst Memorial Lecture, given at the 1976 meeting of the International Association of Agricultural Economists. Schultz sees an increasing opposition to economics in social and political thought, a debasement of economics by governments, and an unwillingness or inability by economists to challenge this adverse drift. He holds that opposition to economics is not confined to either high- or low-income countries, nor is it restricted to a particular type of government. He states that most of the high priests of national and international politics, whether they speak for the first, the second, or the third world, are at heart contemptuous of economics. He goes on to state the hard reality of costs of producing goods and services are not abolished, either by national or by international politics and herein lies, not only the hope, but the necessity of economics.

Most economists join Yeutter in supporting the idea of free trade, other things being equal. However, distortions and protectionism do exist. Pressures within countries lead politicians to rationalize moves toward greater protectionism. So negotiating teams, including those from the United States, come to the trade negotiation table with a knowledge of the benefits of free trade, especially in the long run, but facing the political and social realities in their countries. As Yeutter suggests, bargaining at trade negotiation tables takes place in a quid pro quo framework. Country A will remove barriers if other countries will remove certain other barriers. The Kennedy Round led to few reductions in the area of agriculture.

A suggestion: perhaps what is needed is to find some nonzero-sum games to play. So far in agriculture, the negotiators appear to have found mainly zero-sum games to play, and, as a result, few restrictions have been removed.

Policies other than trade have an impact on trade negotiations. For example, arguments for the number of imperfections stem from the desirability of development in poorer countries. There may exist in international relations the kind of argument that Milton Friedman puts forth in the domestic area. Friedman argues that the trouble with being poor is not having enough money, and, if the government wants to do something about poverty, it should give people money rather than adopt programs that lead to economic inefficiency.

The Carter administration may be following Mr. Friedman's advice, because there is some indication that it plans to help the less developed countries through international finance agencies such as the World Bank, rather than through general debt relief or commodity programs. If Congress goes along with this approach, the position for freer trade of the new U.S. negotiators at the Tokyo Round should be strengthened.

Schuh points out that floating exchange rates and international capital movements affect the volume and price of exports. These phenomena, as well as trade policy, have significant effects. Perhaps an eleventh point to add to Yeutter's "suggestions" would be for the U.S. negotiators to read Schuh's paper. We have not had floating exchange rates and large international capital movements for very long, and we know little about their effects.

Schuh at a recent Great Plains meeting suggested that should Brazil devaluate its currency—and there is some logic for Brazil to devaluate its currency—significant effects on the volumes of U.S. exports of soybeans, cotton, and corn would be felt. Just as it is difficult to negotiate individual sovereign nation agricultural policy at the table, so also is it difficult to negotiate exchange rates.

The leveling out of growth in U.S. agricultural productivity is a theme that was discussed yesterday and that comes back today in Schuh's paper. We do not know whether our productivity is leveling out—there are many data problems. But, I would like to share with you a casual observation on cotton yields. I recently participated in a southern state extension conference. I sat with county agents and cotton specialists in a half-day meeting. There has been decline in the average cotton yield in the last few years in the Delta, and no one knows what to do. The practices that gave them higher yields in former years do not give the same yields now. Factors such as weather, herbicide damage, soil structure, and others were discussed. The question is what to tell those farmers who want to increase yields. If there is a continued decline in yields, productivity will decline.

As a last point, not for your edification but your enjoyment, I would like to give you a bit of poetry by Kenneth Boulding:

> Economists have long portrayed
> The excellent effects of Trade,
> And frown upon the wayward nation
> That seeks to live in isolation.
> And though their arguments declare
> That Trade should not be free as Air,
> Yet broad considerations led 'em
> To have a prejudice for Freedom.

Philip H. Trezise

I read Ed Schuh's paper with considerable interest and profit. His emphasis on the importance of agricultural trade in our total trade, I suppose, is not needed for this audience, but it may be important to other audiences, including the new administration and the U.S. Congress. While the data are not new, it has been put together in a way that emphasizes the very significant place of exports of agricultural goods in our total exports.

I am less taken with the distinction Schuh has drawn between a balance in agricultural trade and a balance in nonagricultural trade. That kind of sectoral approach to the trade balance can justify trade restrictions if pursued very far.

I was also struck with the comments on the neo-Malthusian doctrines, which have acquired a following in this country and abroad in recent years. Schuh deals quite effectively with the food outlook for the medium-term future, and provides ground for comfort. Then, if his hopeful expectations for changes in agricultural policy in the developing countries are accepted, one could rest rather easily, for he offers the prospect that output will increase much more rapidly than population, and that we will get a leg up on the next century. By that time, it may be hoped that the rate of growth of population will have begun to tail off as well. For those of us who worry about the next century, if any of us do, the future may be a good deal more promising than is often assumed.

There are two points in the paper I would like to comment on somewhat more critically: one is a question of the decline in the rate of growth of productivity in American agriculture. It seems to me that one must not put too much emphasis on data for such a short period as he cites.

The period when the rate of growth of productivity seems to have fallen off sharply, according to his table, was a period in which we were bringing back into production acreage that had been retired. That presumably was the acreage that had been set aside on economic grounds. One should not be surprised that yields do not grow very fast when some considerable amount of less desirable acreage is returned to cultivation. That is one small corrective comment, if you will.

More generally, the period taken for judgment is rather short. The level of U.S. productivity in American agriculture, particularly in the feed grains, is so remarkably above that of our competitors that the catch-up period is likely to be a very long one. However, as Mr. Hildreth has suggested, this is an area where there may be a good deal of ignorance, and we may have much to learn.

Finally, Dr. Schuh discussed the impact of national monetary and fiscal policies on our trade account. He takes a rather alarmist view of the prospect that, under floating rates, our agricultural trade will be subject to greater fluctuations than were experienced in the days of fixed exchange rates.

Once again, I am at a disadvantage, since Ed Schuh has apparently written a longer paper in which this point is developed at length. I may be doing him some injustice when I express some skepticism about this concern.

For my sins, last winter, I spent a good deal of time reading the academic literature on the formation of exchange rates. The generally accepted view is that exchange rates in the short run are made in asset markets, and then the correction comes in the trade account. Well, this is all interesting stuff, but I wonder how much of a change it is from the days of when we had nominally fixed exchange rates.

Under fixed rates, there have to be adjustments. If monetary policy in the United States, as our allies and friends asserted for many years, was unduly free and easy, and if U.S. capital flowed in excessively large amounts to countries that were seeking to maintain higher interest rates and were more concerned with price levels than we were, then there had to be adjustment at some point or another.

Either a country had to take measures to offset capital flows, within possible limits anyway, or it had to act on general economic policy and general levels of output and demand. In one way or another, the trade accounts had to be affected.

So a change from fixed rates to floating rates obviously does not alter the requirement for adjustment. The adjustment must take place, and some of it must take place in trade accounts, if the swings are wide enough.

Apart from that, Dr. Schuh seems to suggest (maybe this is my reading of his comments, rather than what he intended) that changes in exchange rates—deriving from changes, basically, in monetary policies—will contribute more to larger fluctuations in trade than other factors will. I don't think that is true. We are still in a world in which changes in supply, because of weather or changes due to government policies or other events directly related to agriculture, will be the principal source of fluctuations in agricultural trade, as they have been in the past. The exchange rate question, relatively, is of very small consequence.

Somebody mentioned that Brazil might take over a much larger part of the world's soybean market if it were to devalue. Of course, the Brazilian exchange rate crawls anyway. It crawls downward steadily, because Brazil inflates steadily. If the exchange rate reflects changes in domestic prices, then the continuing devaluation of the Brazilian currency is not likely to be a major force for promoting Brazil's soybean exports.

Beyond that, of course, supply elasticities in Brazil and elsewhere are limited. Even if a temporary boost in exports were to be achieved by a devaluation, it does not follow that this would destroy or damage our export markets in any serious way, at least given present or probable volumes of output.

Turning to Clayton Yeutter's paper, it is difficult to disagree with most of it. On a point or two, I would perhaps challenge him. What I missed in his paper and in his presentation was a little more specific and graspable notion of how we would have gone about negotiating an agricultural package in the Tokyo Round, if the election turned out differently and he had remained in his post as a deputy trade representative.

If I heard him correctly, he said that the package should be one of encompassing industrial and agricultural concessions in some balanced way, and that we must achieve this. I would like to achieve it too, but I am bound to say that this is an old story, and we have not succeeded in the past in tying industry and agriculture together in the trade negotiations. I am afraid that we will be disillusioned if we persist this time. As desirable as having the linkage might be, I am skeptical that we will get it.

If I understand what is going on in Geneva, we are still blocked on the procedural point of fitting in agriculture. We have papered over the differences, but we cannot do that forever. If we are serious about improving the conditions of trade and agriculture—and I think we should be (on that score I am a loyalist from way back)—we have to do it in essentially an agricultural package.

Jimmye Hillman rattled off some horrendous items that we might have to put into the negotiation. If we have to put in dairy products, Section 22, marketing orders, and peanuts, they will be hard to accept, naturally. And I don't know how far we can go, as a nation, or what our negotiators can do, having Congressional pressures on them and pressures from myriad advisory groups.

The outcome is likely to be a package that does something for the agriculture of both sides, in which the negotiators proceed with a rather sophisticated understanding of the limitations that the other side is operating under. I will say a few more words about what might be in the package, but first, let me say something about Clayton Yeutter's remarks on social policy as a factor in agricultural policy, particularly in Western Europe but also in Japan. That's one way of characterizing it, but another way is to say that the political life of these countries, for better or worse, is closely linked to agricultural policy. The voting pattern in Japan and the position of the governing conservative party indicate that the limits within which a Japanese negotiator can act in dealing with rice policy, which is the heart of the Japanese agricultural policy, are very, very narrow. And they are narrow simply because the majority of seats the conservative party enjoys in the Diet are dependent upon votes in the rural sector.

That sort of thing will not change very much. To a somewhat lesser degree, the European countries are caught in the same situation—in which the political structure is heavily influenced by agricultural policy. People are indeed kept on the land deliberately, as Clayton Yeutter suggested, but not just from a liking for some green spots in the landscape, even though the intellectuals will talk about that. The more pertinent point is that politicians like to have areas where voting patterns can be depended upon. And, curiously enough, the left parties do not find this a bad thing either. One would suppose that in countries like France and Germany political pressures to get people out of agriculture might be strong, but they are not. That is a reality our negotiators will have to deal with.

I think our agricultural package will have to follow the community's general doctrine to look for a measure of organized marketing in grains. We may get some limits on the extent to which the community subsidizes its sales of its surpluses. We might, as Gale Johnson and I once suggested, get a partial freeze on price supports.

In this connection, it is interesting that the most recent proposal of the commission to the community's council effectively calls for a freeze on, or indeed a reduction in, price supports. As I remember it, it calls for about a 3 percent increase in prices, which is well below the rate of inflation.

But we had better have a modest idea of what we can do about price supports abroad. To say we should get rid of the variable levy, as both Clayton Yeutter and, I think, Jimmye Hillman implied, is a losing ticket. There will be some kind of protection, and the variable levy is a convenient device. Of course, it has the effect of a quota, and it is an extremely effective protective device. We had one once on sugar. If there is going to be protection, perhaps a variable levy is no worse than a quantitative quota. If we can deal with the support price, we will have dealt reasonably, it seems to me, with the problem of the levy. These are guesses, because I am not close to what has been done, and I certainly do not know how much room for maneuver our negotiators will have.

On a couple of other matters, I quite agree with Clayton Yeutter that we have some problems with the drive for commodity agreements, and if we followed the UNCTAD demands, we would do a good deal of damage to ourselves and to everybody else, to no benefit for anybody. There may be a few commodity agreements that are negotiable and workable, but I think that the commodity approach will not amount to much. There may be two or three additional commodity agreements with a stabilization objective in them. I do not believe we will get commodity agreements that aim to boost prices above what market forces would be, simply because the consumer nations will be unable to agree on them.

The political limitations on the United States and the other consuming countries are very real, and the benefits to the producing countries, many of which are a mixture of developed and developing, are unclear. Although we may try to arrive at agreements on sugar and a few other products, I would not expect very much progress in this area.

We will have to say that we will not sign up for a common fund for commodities. Whatever the repercussions from that may be, we could not join a common fund, and neither could most of our developed country trading partners.

I will make one final comment about the Soviet wheat deal, which Clayton Yeutter spoke of with more commendation than I think it deserves. I understand—or at least, I believe I understand—why we had to enter into the grain arrangement with the Soviets. The reasons strike me as compelling, and it was desirable to get out of a situation that was quite intolerable.

But, Yeutter says that the world market has absorbed 6 million more tons of grain this year because of the Soviet deal. If that is true, it means that the Soviets are building stocks. I do not know if they are or not, but I do not think it can be asserted as a matter of truth that we sold 6 million tons of grain more than would have been the case without the Soviet agreement. The difficulty with the deal is specifically that. We provided something of a commitment not to impose export controls under normal circumstances, so the Soviets got something. But it is hard to see what we got that we would not have obtained anyway. We did get around Mr. Meany and the longshoremen, which may have been necessary, but I do not see that we got much else.

That leads me to the more general proposition that a series of bilateral arrangements like this may be defensible in individual circumstances, but they are not the way we ought to proceed in our agricultural trade.

The exchange of letters with Japan does no great harm, but the letters give an impression of commitment that may not be warranted. These nominal commitments could lead to embarrassing situations.

One final point: Yeutter offered some thoughts on what we might do about aggressive selling. It sounded remarkably to me like barter agreements (if I misunderstood him, I apologize). I was taught that barter is not a very good way to conduct trade, once money has been invented.

PART
FOUR

POLICY ALTERNATIVES
AND IMPLICATIONS

A MARKET-ORIENTED AGRICULTURAL POLICY AND ITS IMPLICATIONS FOR THE FARM BILL

Don Paarlberg

My subject is "a market-oriented farm policy." What do I mean by a market-oriented farm policy? Since I am a professor, I will begin by defining my terms.

A market-oriented farm policy is enterprise agriculture, with the market functioning in accordance with advances in marketing institutions of the last half century. In contrast to proposals that would substitute public for private action, I propose an active but not a dominant role for government. This role, as I see it, is to improve the functioning of the enterprise system, to place a floor over the pit of disaster, and to help the individual equip himself better for his task as a decision maker.

Many earnest believers in a market-oriented agriculture allow themselves to be backed into a corner and forced to defend not a market-oriented agriculture but a caricature of it. They are forced into advocating a market-oriented agriculture not as it is or as it could be— but as it once was or as its adversaries contend it would be. I do not intend to fall into this trap. My support for a market-oriented agriculture does not include a defense of those abuses which sometimes occur in markets, for example, manipulation, misrepresentation, gross ignorance, and wild gyrations. These abuses happen in part because government fails to safeguard the responsible functioning of the competitive market.

The conservative cliché has it that any government action is contrary to a market-oriented agriculture. This need not be true. Wise government action can improve the functioning of the market.

I include the following as government actions helpful to a market-oriented agriculture:

(1) market supervision, as performed by the Commodity Futures Trading Commission,
(2) maintenance of competition, as overseen by the Department of Justice and the Federal Trade Commission,

(3) supervision of grades and standards,

(4) accurate price reporting,

(5) good outlook information,

(6) marketing orders, wisely administered at appropriate levels,

(7) loan levels which permit prices to fluctuate freely most of the time,

(8) target prices at relatively low levels, which might involve a payout every four or five years,

(9) carry-over of the major grains, of a sufficient amount to avoid scraping the bins between crops, and to avoid piling up excessive supplies of these stocks,

(10) overseas food aid, through Public Law 480, in quantities similar to those recently experienced,

(11) domestic food aid at levels substantially lower than recently in effect, and

(12) standby authority for an acreage set-aside program, to be used with reluctance and with moderation if supplies should become clearly excessive.

I have told you what I think a market-oriented farm policy includes. Now let me tell you what I think it excludes:

(1) loan levels so high that they run the very great risk of overstimulating production, pricing us out of markets, piling up excessive supplies and forcing us back into government production controls;

(2) target prices so high that they impose heavy costs on the treasury and induce a cost conscious government to restrict production in order to cut losses;

(3) the disaster payment, which provides crop insurance with no premiums; and

(4) the peanut program, an anachronism in today's farm policy world. (However, there are times when I think this program may be worth all it costs, just to keep before the public a living example of what happens when the government intrudes into the pricing and production of farm commodities.)

Market orientation, as I describe it, means somewhat less government involvement than we have had in the last few years.

If my position provides less contrast with the views offered by Dr. Schnittker than is desired by the people at this meeting, that is not a fault of his or mine. It could be attributed to those who drew up the program.

The Removal of Restrictions

We got into legislation for farm commodities more than forty years ago, during the Great Depression. The diagnosis, correct at that time, was that American farmers could not make a profit at the prevailing world prices. Our costs were too high and our prices were too low. The prescription was to raise the level of farm prices for the major crops. This objective was pursued by restricting production.

Thus we deliberately boosted domestic price levels above prices prevailing in the world market. Initially, this undertaking was helpful to the desperate farm economy. But results, pursued for forty years, were these:

(1) We priced ourselves out of the world markets and denied ourselves the market growth that might have been ours.

(2) Our artificially-boosted prices speeded up the advance of technology and increased yields, making necessary deep acreage cuts. In 1972 we held 62 million acres out of production, 18 percent of our cropland.

(3) Acreage limitations were painful, and mandatory restrictions proved unacceptable for most crops. Because of this, we began paying farmers for nonproduction. In 1972 these payments totaled $3.5 billion.

(4) The disinclination to accept tight supply controls resulted in piling up large carry-over stocks, which hung over the market, the market became stable, especially at the support level. The price floor tended to become the ceiling.

(5) Such farm benefits as the system generated tended to accrue to the producers on a per-bushel or a per-bale basis, thus conferring its greatest help to the large producers whose incomes were already above the average farm and nonfarm level.

This system caused much dissatisfaction. But we had become very dependent on it. It was clear to most, if not to all, that abandonment of the program would result in excessive supplies, sharply reduced prices, depressed farm incomes, and a severe drop in land values. We were afraid to dismount from the tiger. The diagnosis of forty years ago— that American farmers could not compete in the export markets at world prices—had become self-fulfilling.

This was the situation when Congress passed the Agricultural Act of 1973. The act embodied what has come to be known as "market orientation." It was passed with support from both political parties and with the concurrence of the executive branch.

The President signed this act into law. Scarcely was the ink dry before a series of phenomenal and unforeseen events occurred. Poor crops in the world, plus a worldwide inflationary upsurge, carried farm prices far above the loan and target levels. The secretary of agriculture used the authority given him by Congress to suspend acreage controls. Thus our agricultural policy became market-oriented.

Without intending to do so, and without major confrontation, and with relatively little pain, we were escalated out of a policy we had pursued for forty years.

Consider for a moment how good has been the experience associated with the removal of restrictions. (Note that I say "associated with" rather than "caused by." The distinction is relevant; there were multiple causes for the events of recent years.)

(1) Farm incomes during the four years of market orientation averaged, in real terms, 24 percent above the level of the four years preceding.

(2) Agricultural exports during these four years averaged, in tonnage, 46 percent above the previous four years. These exports helped generate the foreign exchange with which to pay for our oil imports and helped keep the dollar strong.

(3) Taxpayers have been relieved of the burden of paying for nonproduction.

(4) Consumers welcomed full production, which they rightly associated with an abundant supply of food.

(5) Business firms welcomed the larger volume associated with current policies.

(6) Laboring people favored the additional jobs that come from full resources use.

Of course, the policy change did not occur for certain crops: peanuts, tobacco, or long-staple cotton. And it occurred only partially for rice. But it did occur for the major crops.

Most people are now convinced that we can compete in world markets with the major crops. Our endowment in soil, climate, and topography is the world's best. Our farm people are unexcelled in the level of their technology and in their managerial skill. Our institutions—credit, education, research, transportation, and marketing—are the envy of virtually all our foreign visitors.

This new feeling, that we can compete, can also become self-fulfilling. This can lead to actions that bring about the postulate. Such is the power of an idea.

Reverting to the Old Policy. This is the setting within which the Agriculture Act of 1977 comes up for consideration.

The critical question, as I see it, is whether we continue with a market-oriented policy or whether we revert to artificially high prices, burdensome surpluses, and production controls. As you can judge from my comments, I think it is important that we continue the course upon which we have ventured.

I think it is unlikely that we would deliberately return to the policies from which we have now escaped. Consider the good experience we have had in agriculture under the new policy. Consider that in the recent presidential campaign, neither candidate advocated production controls.

If we revert to the policies we have just escaped, it is likely that we will do so unintentionally. We escaped from them unintentionally; we might again embrace them the same way.

This is how it might occur:

(1) Out of desire to help farmers, we might get the loan levels and the target prices too high.

(2) We might thus price ourselves out of the world markets and again pile up surpluses.

(3) To minimize such a pileup and to avoid the costly payments associated wtih excessively high target prices, we might again feel impelled to restrict output.

We would then come full cycle and, without wishing to do so, return to the programs from which we have escaped. Being at heart an optimist, I think we will not slip back into these outmoded programs.

A Hypothetical Cabinet Meeting

These are the days of simulation. I present to you a simulated conversation in the cabinet room, where the top people of the new administration are gathered to work out a position on farm legislation. Naturally, I am not knowledgeable about what goes on in such meetings. So this simulation is purely hypothetical. It goes as follows:

PRESIDENT CARTER: Bob, tell us about this farm bill they're hammering out up on the hill.

SECRETARY BERGLAND: Well, they seem to be moving toward a considerable increase in the target levels for wheat, corn, and cotton. It looks as if they want to increase the loan levels, too. The commodity people are in town, pushing for these increases. In most other areas they are staying fairly close to the law now on the books.

PRESIDENT CARTER: Are they going to do anything about peanuts?

SECRETARY BERGLAND: Peanuts have gone underground.

PRESIDENT CARTER: Bert, have you costed out the bill they're working on?

OMB DIRECTOR LANCE: It's hard to tell. Depends on the export markets. It depends on the size of the crop too. At the loans and targets they're talking about, it could run into billions. Mr. President, we have to remember your promise to balance the budget by the end of this administration. The last thing we need is a five-year farm bill with a multibillion price tag on it.

SECRETARY VANCE: Mr. President, if they get those loans too high, we'll be priced out of the export market. There would be pressure to go to export subsidies. That would antagonize our trading partners and scuttle the trade negotiations in Geneva.

SECRETARY BLUMENTHAL: Mr. President, if we price our farm products out of the export market, our trade balance will worsen and the dollar will be in trouble. The trade balance is bad enough already. Agriculture is our best earner of foreign exchange. Twenty-three billion dollars last year.

CEA CHAIRMAN SCHULTZE: Mr. President, if we go along with a sharp increase in loan levels we will be inflating food prices. We promised to hold down inflation, you remember.

PRESIDENT CARTER: Hmmmm. Hamilton, what did we promise the farmers during the campaign?

HAMILTON JORDAN: Agriculture wasn't really an issue. As I recall, you said something about relating the loans and targets to the cost of production, Mr. President.

PRESIDENT CARTER: So I did, so I did. Bob, does anyone know what the cost of production is?

SECRETARY BERGLAND: Our economists figure it six different ways, Mr. President. You can take your pick, from high to low.

PRESIDENT CARTER: Hmmmm. Let's take the low option. Bob, how many farmers are there?

SECRETARY BERGLAND: They are 4 percent of the population, Mr. President, and declining.

PRESIDENT CARTER: Bob, how much can we increase the loans and targets before we run into the problems that Charley and Cy and the others are worried about?

SECRETARY BERGLAND: My economists tell me there is a little room to raise the feed grains, and maybe cotton. Wheat is close to trouble even at present loan levels.

PRESIDENT CARTER: Hmmm. Well, Bob, you and Charley get your analysts together and see how much you can inch up these loans and targets without getting us into trouble. Then sit down with Herman Talmadge and Tom Foley and negotiate this out. Give them a little increase but not too much. Tell them they will have to claim victory on the basis of the small gains. State and Treasury can help with their contacts on the Hill. If we can get a reasonable bill out of Congress, we can sign it and everybody will look good. Let's play this one kind of low key.

Now let's turn to some of the tougher issues. How are we coming along with jobs and taxes and energy?

Conclusion

Beginning with the Agricultural Act of 1970 there has been some de-escalation of farm policy arguments. The reasons for this are not wholly clear. Maybe the public grew weary of an issue that had been on the agenda for an entire generation. Maybe most of the original advocates finally died off. Anyway, the spotlight shifted somewhat away from farm policy. It then became easier for negotiations to take place.

If one is in the glare of the spotlight, one's strongest effort is required. Defeat, even partial defeat, is a disaster. But when the spotlight shifts away, negotiation can occur. This is what happened. The Congress has produced better farm legislation since this issue was put on the back burner.

There are a few old battlers, with a few warmed-over speeches they could deliver and some diatribes they could repeat, who would like a revival of the old issues. The debate of the farm bill could provide the occasion for their use.

But we should be wary of these. We have been wise or fortunate, or both, in escaping from the program of the past. If we will set aside confrontation policies, there is reason to believe we can hold these gains. To draw up again the battle lines of the past will produce nothing but losers. If we treat the issue in low key fashion, almost everyone will gain.

POLICY AND PROGRAMS
FOR AGRICULTURE

John Schnittker

In an address to the American Agricultural Economics Association nearly eleven years ago, I described the agricultural policies developed in the early 1960s, especially the Agricultural Act of 1965, as the beginning of a market-oriented policy. The policy and program characteristics I cited then included some of those which Dr. Paarlberg has now included under his description of a market-oriented agriculture in a paper presented at the conference. These included:

- limited stocks and limited governmental activity in farm markets;
- prices usually above moderate support levels;
- very limited use of export subsidies and expanding trade;
- payments to farmers in lieu of frequent market intervention.

Those policies were enacted under fire; they have endured and have been improved by the 1970 and 1973 acts. I believe, and I hope, they will endure into the 1980s. My support for an active federal role in a market-oriented agricultural policy reaches back some fifteen years. I trust you will understand why I do not support the kind of federal role which helped discredit farmers and farm policy in the 1950s, built large surpluses, made the government a principal market for farm products, and increased budgetary costs except when crops failed here or around the world.

I hesitate to pose as a historian, but Don Paarlberg is in error when he says that the 1973 act began the turn to market orientation. In fact, the acts of the mid-1960s did this, ending the old "high–rigid" price support system and mandatory acreage allotments. Substantial improvements were made in 1970 and 1973. The 1973 act simply happened to coincide with the start of an era of world grain shortages, the effects of which brought increased market action and appeared to bring farm prosperity.

In defining his concept of a market-oriented agriculture, Dr. Paarlberg has left a broad area for federal participation. Once more, he and I are pitted against each other in a debate where the differences are rather narrow (but still important) and where we both deplore (or at least abstain from) the rhetoric of the most ardent advocates of limited, or expanded, federal roles in food and agriculture. After a brief digression, I will define the differences between us as sharply as I can.

I am extremely sorry to hear major farm organizations propose price support levels which, if adopted this year, would probably require either extensive use of export subsidies or occasional withdrawal of the United States from export markets. As an occasional educator on farm and food issues, I am embarrassed that "cost of production," including full land costs, is often cited as the principal criterion for setting price-support loan levels and target-price levels for the late 1970s and 1980s. This approach neglects the impact of such action on our exports and on the federal budget. I am surprised that, after several years of real prosperity, some farm groups are asking Congress and the administration to allocate as much as $5 to $6 billion per year, mostly to producers of grains and cotton.

On the other hand, I am pleased that we have put behind us the shrill rhetoric which, until a few months ago, had American farmers and the public believing that:

- Farm policies adopted in the United States since 1972 had permanently removed the government from agriculture.
- The recent prosperity of U.S. farmers was really the effect of a brilliant policy enacted by the Department of Agriculture under Secretary Butz.
- Grain crop failures of 1972 and 1976 in major regions of the world were of little importance to that result.

It is wrong to claim a new and irreversible direction in farm policy over the last five years. It is equally wrong to ask the Congress to perpetuate recent high farm prices and incomes by means of government intervention when the world grain situation has once again shifted from scarcity to surplus.

Most importantly, claiming too much credit for policy distorts public expectations of what the supposed "new" policy can do. With a simple extension of the 1973 act this year:

- Farm incomes in 1978 or 1979 may fall again.
- Export levels may decline, and surpluses rise as wheat and rice did during the last two years.
- Government expenditures may increase sharply.

It is understandable that those in office claim some credit for whatever happens, no matter what the real causes are. Officials must take the blame for events and actions over which they have no control, so they must claim credit where they can. But there are limits.

Some observers of the farm scene will be shocked by Dr. Paarlberg's long list of permissible federal actions in a market-oriented agricultural economy. Many persons who have testified in recent weeks for more government help via high price and income supports will surely cross me off the list of advocates of an active federal role after I state my case. Perhaps one paper entitled "An Active Federal Role in Market-oriented Food and Agricultural Policies" would have been enough on this final program.

There is danger of excessive rhetoric on both sides of the argument, which rebuilds the illusion that there is a great gulf between the positions of practical persons who lean toward less intervention and those who support more intervention. On the one side, the opening bid of farm groups which favor greater intervention is unrealistic. Federal payments which provide a large part of net farm income to farmers are no longer acceptable to the public. The extremists on the other side of the debate speak occasionally as if they would end every farm program except research and education. In fact, events have caused them to intervene when they had promised to abstain, and they generally support continuation of laws similar to those which have been in effect for many years.

In this situation, both sides, when pressed, endorse the idea that substantial use of the market should guide the allocation of resources and income distribution among farmers. In the U.S. farm policy debate, there are virtually no proponents of federal policies who would set aside market functions most of the time and make government a principal market for agricultural commodities, the principal determinant of agricultural export prices, or the actual instrument of such exports.

What do I mean by "an active federal role"? I adopt much of Dr. Paarlberg's list as my own, with limited exceptions and some important additions, as follows:

(1) A change in rhetoric is as important as a change in policy. The true approach to an active federal role requires an admission that there are certain roles, carefully defined, to be played by the government. Denials that the government would decide to limit farm exports, for example, have never been credible. The bipartisan position reached in this issue during the 1976 political campaign is an important achievement. There is no need for harsh rhetoric on this score when the next serious shortage occurs. The rhetoric of the present administration should be carefully modulated to avoid unnecessarily arousing concern on the part of some farmers and the food sector regarding intended intervention in grain or sugar markets this year.

(2) The levels of domestic food-aid expenditure have little to do either with a market-oriented agriculture or with an active federal role in agricultural policy. Those who wish to reduce food assistance expenditures do so for reasons unrelated to questions of agricultural policy.

(3) The federal role in establishing adequate carry-overs or food

reserves of major grains is probably the point on which Dr. Paarlberg and I—as well as groups that lean to more versus those that favor less government intervention in food policy—differ most. The public debate over grain reserves in this country during the past two or three years has been confusing. On the one hand, some administration spokesmen have assured the nations of the world that the United States would co-operate in arrangements for food reserves; on the other hand, others argued that the United States would never again carry large stocks of agricultural products.

Proponents of increased food aid and a better food security system typically suggested that some new and complex public intervention would be required in agricultural markets if the government were to establish a grain reserve to meet multiple objectives. Both sides overstated their case. The United States will take part in world reserves policy, and the United States will carry large stocks on occasion.

- Even as Secretary Butz scorned the logic of grain reserves, the Commodity Credit Corporation under his direction was becoming the caretaker, financier, and owner of rice and wheat from 1975 and 1976 crops. This does not amount to the establishment of a "reserves policy," but it has presented us with a reserve.
- Even as reserves and food aid proponents pressed for the establishment of reserve mechanisms and policies, the actual reserve was being established accidentally, because of large crops. To establish a "reserves policy," with most of the grain held by farmers with federal assistance via storage costs and loans, we could: (1) announce that 1976 price support loans will be continued so that farmers can hold the surplus wheat, and (2) determine and announce that any grain the government acquires will be sold only when prices have risen well above support levels, and that extending price-support loans may also be terminated under the same price conditions.

(4) Establishment of minimum trading prices in order to limit price declines for wheat and possibly other commodities in world trade is also an appropriate federal role and is closely related to grain reserves, whose key objective would be to limit price increases. Agreement and participation of many nations is required if the extreme lows and highs are to be removed equitably from grain markets. Agreements among only a few nations on minimum price level policies regarding establishment and use of reserves will limit the effect of both policies, leaving the nonparticipants to benefit from the costs incurred by a few countries. At the same time, inability to get all major grain importers and exporters to participate should not become an excuse for postponing action.

Federal Legislation

What is a proper "active federal role," consistent with our laws and the new administration's policies, for legislation in 1977?

(1) Loan levels geared to direct cost of production are generally appropriate and moderate. Wheat, corn, rice, and cotton intervention prices at or near $2.25 and $1.85 per bushel, $6.00 per hundred pounds, and $.38 per pound respectively, at the farm will protect farmers in 1978 from severe losses while not guaranteeing them a profit. They will probably not interfere with exports.

(2) Target prices no more than 10 percent above the loan levels suggested above would provide farmers with a material income supplement to cover a portion of land costs when market prices fall to or near loan levels. Target prices can be continued if the burden they place on the treasury is manageable and does not threaten higher priority programs. But it should be understood that the principal recipients of such payments would be the largest and most prosperous farmers. The annual maximum budgetary exposure would be slightly under $2 billion for feed grains—wheat, cotton, rice, and peanuts—with target levels 10 percent above established loan market price levels. This compares with $5 billion or more in some bills now being considered by Congress.

(3) Acreage set-aside features should be continued and should be used if reserves threaten to become burdensome surpluses.

(4) Efforts to negotiate a greater degree of stability into world markets should be pursued vigorously, but with a healthy respect for the limitations of such actions and for the lessons of past failures to raise average prices above long-term equilibrium levels.

Those are the principal elements of a broad policy embodying an active federal role in farm and food affairs. Price support intervention and expenditures for commodities other than grains should be proportional. Reserves would be held largely by farmers, so farmers could reap some of the gains when prices rose after poor crops, but their flow into markets should be regulated by government, not farmers. Food prices would rise somewhat when crops decline, but double-digit food inflation would be unlikely except following severe crop failures.

Food aid supplies would seldom have to compete with commercial sales. Exports would not be embargoed and would seldom be limited, since the grain reserve would serve commercial export markets, too. Market prices would fluctuate within a wide range to please the many risk takers among farmers, users, and speculators, and to facilitate hedging. But price fluctuations would not be as wide as in recent years. Farmers and consumers could plan ahead with greater assurance than in recent years.

COMMENTARIES

Hyde H. Murray

Let me say first of all that it is really great to be on this marvelous panel, with these distinguished agricultural economists. I, a mere lawyer, find myself overwhelmed by agricultural knowledge. The only economic law that I usually deal with is the law of supply and demand, and we try to repeal it, or at least postpone its effective date, regularly. Having said those nice things, let me now try to be as disagreeable as possible in regard to both of these papers.

I disagree with Don Paarlberg in two areas. First, his perception of history is a little bit off. The watershed occurred, not in 1973, but in 1962, when the Kennedy administration's proposal to establish a giant public utility type of agriculture was rejected, with passion and heat, in the House of Representatives. That rejection made Secretary Freeman and the Kennedy administration turn to other techniques in reaching accommodation on farm policy, and it marked the end of a formal administration proposal.

From that time, agriculture policy became a joint venture between Congress and the administration. A landmark, then, was 1965, when the present "voluntary" programs were enacted. Next came a one-year program in 1968; the 1970 act and the 1973 act which amended that 1965 change in those old granddaddies, the Agriculture Act of 1949 and the Agricultural Adjustment Act of 1938.

But, aside from that minor historical difference, my major difference with Don Paarlberg is over this ailing individual—what was her name? Margaret Orientation, that was it, little Margaret Orientation. I hate to tell you this, but I think she is dead. I think she died last fall, but people keep saying it's not so, that she is still alive and well some place here in Washington.

Of course, I am a pessimist, where Don Paarlberg is an optimist, about the continuation of this kind of an economic policy. Maybe I am overdramatic, or maybe I am exaggerating, or maybe I am pessimistic, but as an observer of Washington rhetoric for a long time, I try to listen to words and watch deeds with great care.

Margaret Orientation has a warm rhetorical memory, and her presence is praised by people in high positions throughout our city. But then, in this city, these people use words like *stabilize* when they mean *dump*, and when they mean *cartel*, they say *dialogue*. When Congress wants to go on a recess, it says it's a "district work period." When we talk about reserves, we do not talk about price controls to keep prices down; we talk about "cost expansion." Usually that means "reform," as it did when the purchase requirement on food stamps was eliminated. *Naughty* and *nice* become *good* and *bad* (or *evil*), and *right* or *wrong*. They get mixed up in Washington.

When I say Margaret Orientation is probably dead in farm policy, I am asked what evidence I have, or why I say such a thing, or where is the corpus delicti.

I can say maybe she isn't dead. Somebody said that she was seen in the hall of the Administration Building at the U.S. Department of Agriculture with Mrs. Bergland's husband, and that the secretary is fond of this concept.

But I can say one thing. Margaret Orientation was not in the House Agriculture Committee when it marked up the budget recommendations to the House Budget Committee.

For openers the Carter budget on agriculture was $2.2 billion over the Ford budget, and that did not include 1977. The Carter budget added $720 million for food stamps in 1977, and then another $880 million for 1978; and thus started with a $2.2 billion increase in USDA expenditures for FY 1978.

And then the Agriculture Committee broke down into a task force, made up of the senior members of the committee. We call them the "Senior 16"—the chairmen of the ten subcommittees, plus the chairman of the big committee, plus five Republicans, to preserve the good old rule "two to one plus one." In the course of three days, this group added from $2.2 billion to $4.4 billion more than what the Carter budget had added to the Ford budget. And the big difference, of course, was in the commodity programs. They were contingent on whether there would be a 1977 boost in loans, up to a maximum that would shock even John Schnittker.

The budget process was interesting. The committee voted, first, on a proposition to fund price support programs for milk at 100 percent of parity. That would cost $1.2 billion by itself, and it was rejected handily. Coming on its heels was a proposal to raise the dairy price support to 85 percent of parity. That only costs $650 million dollars, and it was shouted through with enormous enthusiasm. There was $650 million to raise the price of milk, at a time when the White House was talking about lowering it to 75 percent of parity.

Another key vote came when a freshman member from Kansas

moved to opt for the high range of all price supports and all target prices for the 1977 and 1978 crops, ranges which would easily put us into the export subsidy business. With no sweat and no question, we would go into the export subsidy business. That failed by a one-vote margin—15 to 16. And that one vote was cast by the chairman of the committee. The senior members of the committee—the old-timers—had lived through the 1973 act, which we praise as a bipartisan landmark. But only a third of the Agriculture Committee was around when that 1973 act was passed. So the Bob Poages and the Tom Foleys and the Bill Wamplers were almost outvoted.

Another amendment came from Congressman Nolan of Minnesota. He made a good speech, saying that two years ago Congress passed a farm bill, with target prices, a soybean loan, and all that good stuff; but Jerry Ford vetoed it, and Congress could not override the veto. Now, however, we have a Democratic president and Democratic Congress, so Congressman Nolan proposed to take that same farm bill, update it for inflation, pass it, and provide enough money for it.

Somebody at the Congressional Budget Office had figured out how much money it would cost—$3.2 billion—so Congressman Nolan offered an amendment to provide funding for that. It failed, on a voice vote.

We had amendments to increase food stamps another $300 million above the Carter budget, and that failed.

We had another amendment by the Rural Caucus, which came in at $16.4 billion. They skinnied it down to about $500 million, but they will keep at the $16.4 billion in loan authorizations and off-budget items when they go to the Appropriations Committee. They will have a White House conference on rural development, and they will pledge the full faith and credit of the United States to amounts of money approaching the total USDA budget at the present time.

Somebody said, "Well, so it's only money." Nobody seemed to be too worried about that anymore.

Somebody said he saw Margaret Orientation proposing a sugar quota that would sharply restrict the entry of foreign countries into our sugar market on either a country-by-country, or a total basis. Market orientation and sugar protectionism—how do they go together?

Somebody saw Margaret Orientation peddling a new price support program for a commodity that is not supported now—to wit, sugar. If this commodity is supported through a loan system, it will not work unless it applies to corn; or the corn sweetener industry will exploit it.

Somebody said Margaret Orientation was in Canada, trying to start a hotel. And I said, "No, stupid, that's a cartel."

Somebody said that Margaret Orientation was advocating grain reserve in the hands of farmers, but somebody looked at the farmers' hands, and they were firmly clasped around Uncle Sam's.

The point that I make is that we live in a town dominated by what I call social democrats.

I assume that everybody in this room is a democrat, with a little *d*. Some may say they are not Democrats, but Republicans, or Communists, or Whigs, or Independents, or something else. But those of us living in contemporary America are democrats, with a little *d*. Because, as Olof Palme, the outgoing premier of Sweden, observed, democracy evolves. Democracy was not just made up by Abraham Lincoln, or Thomas Jefferson, or George Washington—something we just continue to live by forever and ever. It changes as time goes on.

Our country started with political democracy. The idea of the right to vote, to assemble, to meet together, to speak one's mind, and to have a free expression of views, as well as our other civil liberties, are grounded in our Constitution, and all democrats—little *d*s—accept them.

As time went on, we moved to a concept of "welfare democracy," where the government has assumed certain responsibilities for age, infirmity, and other disabilities. Don Paarlberg, like almost everybody in the political spectrum, accepts a food stamp program as a desirable thing, per se. There may be quarrels about how it is run, or about where the stamps should go, but the program is accepted. The same is true of social security and of unemployment compensation.

Such programs are the wave of the future, and the wave of the future is where we are. The future comes fast for us. The future will decide whether we turn to capitalism, as part of a continuing form of democracy, or—I suppose—either to communism or social democracy.

Olof Palme says that social democracy is the wave of the future, that it is the answer for North America and Europe, and that most European parliamentarians are social democrats. They are the predominant party in West Germany, Great Britain, Sweden, and the other countries of Scandinavia, and they seem to be in ascendancy in America.

Social democracy, they say, rejects capitalism, because capitalism is based on greed, and we should grow food for people, not for profit. Profit is a bad thing—it should be spurned. We should not try to acquire profit. Scarce resources have to be allocated in a more just way than according to the intelligence, or the work, or the eagerness, or ability of certain persons. Capitalism is going out of style. It does not seem to be popular as a working dogma, certainly not in this town. At the same time, all of us here, no matter from what faction of the little *d* democratic spectrum, reject communism, because communism is atheistic: it rejects the notion of a supreme deity. That alone was enough to turn off the Arabs.

Communism accepts the notion of a dictatorship. It's a dictatorship of a small elite, of 3-5 percent in the Soviet Union, China, or any other Communist country. Only certain people can belong to the party, and they become the elite that run the nation as a dictatorship. They accept, advocate, and acknowledge that it is a dictatorship. That does not fit in with the philosophy of Thomas Jefferson or Alexander Hamilton, either one.

Also, communist countries tend to rotate around the foreign policy interests of the Soviet Union. Even the Communist countries are divided over whether the Russians should have a warm water port, as the old czars wanted.

Finally, the party in the Communist system is into everything—dancing schools and sports, as well as grain reserves and international negotiations with the U.S. government over wheat sales.

If communism is rejected, and capitalism is rejected, we move instead to social democracy. It has been my observation that social democracy, as we practice it in agriculture policy, has several common characteristics. Whatever the problem might be—world hunger, the energy shortage, drought—there are certain ways that social democrats tend to approach it.

And the first element of the approach is that there must be a federal solution for the problem. In fact, it is hard to find a wrong anywhere in America any more for which there is no federal solution. Last year, I thought there was one, but I was wrong. We came up with the federal chicken fighting law. It is now a crime to transport chicken fighting material in interstate commerce. Anyone daring to do such a terrible thing will be investigated by the U.S. Department of Agriculture, and the FBI, and other law enforcement agencies.

A second characteristic of contemporary social democracy is authoritarianism. It always favors a strong bill. Last year, during a scandal among grain inspectors in New Orleans, the district attorney down there put some of them in jail. When the news got back to Washington, the officials decided that there should be a federal law to take care of that problem, that federal inspectors should take over, not only at the ports, but in the interior, too. Nothing had been shown to be wrong there, but they were going to take over the interior anyway, so they would have a strong bill—a strong bill. Those in the House that wanted to let the states take care of the problem were for a weak bill, but the social democrats had to have a strong bill, an authoritarian bill, to be enforced.

The third characteristic of social democracy is a strong strain of self-righteousness, of doing the "good" thing, and of believing that the American people are "good." The fact is, of course, that they are good and bad, they are evil and virtuous, they are strong and weak, they are rich and poor, and they are noble and base—like all other human beings. But the proposals made by these social democrats are always "good," and anybody who is not for them cannot be "good."

And finally, the proposals of the social democrats are usually financially or fiscally extravagant and irrelevant. There seems to be no concern about ever paying for anything. After all, they say, it is only money.

In that framework, I disagree with John Schnittker. There will be no public outrage against large payments to farmers as long as no single one of them gets very much—as long as the large payments are in the billions in the aggregate, rather than in the hundred thousands to the individual senators. A $3 billion or $4 billion income supplement for wheat farmers can disappear easily, because there are not many big wheat farmers or corn farmers. But that is not true of cotton, and that is one reason why the cotton industry and the cotton growers prefer a market orientation to all those good things sought by other commodities producers.

There are scads of proponents of government intervention in Washington that are more than willing to run agricultural policy. They are in OSHA, in EPA, in the headquarters of the AFL-CIO, in the White House, in the State Department, and in a whole bunch of committees in Congress besides the agriculture committees. In fact, a whole lot of people think that farming is just too important for farmers, and they intervene, and have their say on policy.

One other point, there is no institution right now to enforce fiscal discipline. In time, maybe that will change. Maybe there will be a dialogue in the White House some day as Don Paarlberg described, but there is none now.

An administration has come into this town, taken the old deficit budget, and increased the deficit by $20 billion and the outlays and tax revenue loss by $30 billion in 1977. Then it took the 1978 budget and added $10 billion to it. And no sooner was the ink dry on the third concurrent resolution for the new budget control act than the House of Representatives took up a bill to fix the roof on the Kennedy Center, and waived all budget act points of order against it.

They said it was "needed." And after all, they were only $70 billion in the hole, so why not $70,004,700,000?

There is no budget restraint in this town at this time. Deficits of $57 billion in the coming year, and $70 billion in the current fiscal year can only fan inflation, as the government borrows or prints all that money. And there is no prospect of discipline. The Agriculture Committee—a conservative committee in the panorama of Congress these days—has increased the Ford budget for agriculture from $13.6

billion all the way up to $19 billion plus; increasing the Carter budget by 4.6 billion dollars.

In conclusion, the more I think about it, the more I think that little Margaret Orientation, age fifteen, who was born June 20, 1962, died November 2, 1976.

The watershed water is flowing to the left. As Congressman Sebelius said, if you want to be a big flea in this town, you want to travel with the tall dogs. The tall dogs are moving us toward social democracy for America.

Willard W. Cochrane

The present policy positions of Don Paarlberg and John Schnittker seemed very close together to me. Further, the gap between Don Paarlberg and myself, on American food and agriculture policy, has narrowed considerably in recent years. All three of us are reasonably serious students of economics—maybe not the world's leading theorists, but serious students of economics. As such, we recognize, first, that the market is an efficient allocator of productive resources and should be relied upon, wherever possible, to allocate those resources; and, second, that the market can produce great inequities. Because of that, there is a need, from time to time, to use the powers of government to deal with these inequities. All three of us recognize this.

The big issue is how much the government should be used. On this point, economists of good will can disagree, as we saw Don Paarlberg and John Schnittker disagree today. But their disagreement was not very wide.

Those two may serve as proxies for all of us. Gale Johnson and I do not argue nearly as strongly as we used to about policy. A rapprochement has been at work here for quite a while.

This same thing must be occurring in the farm organizations but not for the same reasons. The Farm Bureau and the Farmers' Union are not as far apart as they used to be, but I don't think the study of economics is doing it.

In my judgment, the grand policy statements of politicians, the sophisticated policy statements of economists, and the discussions on policy at conferences like this do not determine how much government intervention we will have in the food and agriculture sector. Let me emphasize this: *circumstances largely determine the amount of government intervention.* I believe that very firmly. Circumstances turn the policy trick. If there are a series of short crops around the world, sharply rising food prices will cause American consumers to scream for programs such as price controls, export embargoes, expanded food stamp plans, and on and on. If there are a series of bountiful crops around the world that cause farm prices to fall drastically, farmers will demand higher levels of support, income subsidy payments, production controls (voluntary, of course), and so on.

Perhaps it makes little difference whether the Democrats are in power, or the Republicans. The Democrats will gallop forward a little more rapidly than the Republicans in bringing this intervention about. But I was surprised at the speed with which Earl Butz dished out money and took over grains in 1971 and 1972. The Republicans, in that particular year, got into the game very quickly, when there was just a little surplus and an election was coming up. I would also point out that the Republicans do things for consumers. President Nixon brought about price controls to help consumers. He was willing to engage in this kind of social democracy, too. Even conservatives intervene in the market when *circumstances* dictate.

Circumstances determine whether we have a large or small amount of government intervention. We are a democracy, and we do not like to see anybody bleed too much. All of us are willing to permit, or encourage, the government to intervene to deal with circumstances judged to be undesirable or harmful.

It might be asked why these circumstances have such power to bring government into the food and agriculture sector. To me the answer is simple. It all goes back to the nature of the demand for food.

Although people's demands change over time, in any given life style consumers require and demand about the same quantities of the same kinds of food day after day. This is true for Indians, it is true for Americans, it is true for Japanese. Consumer food demands may change in twenty years, but in the short run, consumers require and demand about the same quantities of the same kinds of food day after day.

If there is a slight food shortage, those people and their representatives will scramble all over the place, trying to acquire supplies, and this scrambling will send food and farm product prices skyrocketing. We saw this in 1972–1973. World grain production, instead of increasing nearly 3 percent that year as it had, decreased about 2½ percent, and that was enough to send every government scrambling for supplies. Everybody has to have food, in about the same amounts, meaning that, in economic terms, the demand is highly inelastic. Food prices are sent skyrocketing.

If there is a small surplus, consumers do not start eating four meals a day. They might eat a little more, but they eat roughly the same amount.

The demand curve on the down side is the same as it is on the up side, extremely inelastic. So farm prices—but not necessarily food prices, for reasons that most of us know—gyrate in the extreme. A fine line separates shortage and surplus in the food and agriculture sector, and it is easy to move from one to the other. Because of the extreme price inelasticity of demand, any slight movement one way or another sends shivers up consumers' spines, and prices along with them; or it sends shivers down the spines of farmers, and sharply falling farm prices.

I think it has ever been thus, and I don't think this food price phenomenon will change in the future. This phenomenon has been with us for a long time, and the concept of aggregate demand for the individual consumer, or the individual family, or the individual nation, may be even more inelastic in the future than in the past. Throughout the world, the belief has become accepted that everybody is entitled to enough food. If anything, the demand for food is more inelastic now than it was in the past.

Government should recognize and understand this and do some effective forward planning to deal with this kind of feast or famine situation. But, for some reason, governments do not seem to understand this. Whether in this country or in India, governments visualize each surplus or shortage as though it were an isolated phenomenon. They do not seem to realize that this basic price elasticity phenomenon is always with us. A particular shortage may be due in one year to bad crop conditions in South Asia and the next time to bad weather on the plains of North America, and the next time it might be because China has come into the market and bought 10 percent more than it had in the past.

The reason for each surplus or shortage may be different, and it is next to impossible to predict when or how one of these supply variations will occur. But we do know that these things always are occurring, for one reason or another. The reason that the shortage or the surplus produces conditions that are considered intolerable to consumers or to farmers is this strongly inelastic demand for food.

It is important that our government and the governments of India, Brazil, and so forth, recognize that this food demand phenomena will continue to make the food and agriculture sector unstable—more unstable than society is willing to accept.

Hence, time and again governments are pulled into the food and agricultural sector to try to stabilize it. My criticism is not that governments are induced to intervene, but that they are forced to intervene in an ad hoc fashion to deal with ad hoc situations. The phenomena are not really ad hoc. We should have learned by this time that wide, sharp, and unpredictable farm price fluctuations are the norm. We should have been thinking about long-run, useful ways to dampen those price fluctuations, whether market-oriented or not.

PART FIVE

U.S. FARM POLICY: WHAT DIRECTION?

In the final session of the conference, a panel discussed the proposed changes in farm legislation. This discussion was videotaped for educational and commercial TV, and the edited transcript presented here was published separately as an AEI Round Table.

ROUND TABLE

JOHN CHARLES DALY, former ABC News chief and moderator of the Round Table: This Public Policy Forum, part of a series presented by the American Enterprise Institute, touches every American home and pocketbook and, in its broadest context, the stability of the international community.

One in twenty-five Americans lives on a farm; the rest of us buy the products from those farms and pay the taxes that finance agricultural governmental programs. The year 1977 is a benchmark in this complex, sometimes tortured, interrelationship. The legislation authorizing the complex of farm programs is a tangled web of efforts to resolve the agricultural crises of past decades. Much of this legislation expires this year. This year represents a new opportunity, then, for Congress and the people to find new initiative and, perhaps, solutions to such thorny problems as boom-bust prices, subsidies, quotas, tariffs, and ways to accommodate the basic planting and harvesting cycles of our farms to the sophistication of space-age technology in weather forecasting.

Congressman Foley, as chairman of the House Committee on Agriculture, what changes in farm legislation do you feel are particularly important to carry out in 1977?

THOMAS S. FOLEY, U.S. House of Representatives (Democrat, Washington): This is a benchmark year not only because the basic farm legislation—the so-called Agriculture and Consumer Protection Act which was passed in 1973—is expiring, but also because a number of other major agricultural bills expire this year as well, including the most important of the nutrition programs that the Department of Agriculture administers, the food stamp program.

The expiration dates of these bills are occurring as a new administration is coming into office, so a major agriculture program will be enacted for the first time under the Budget Act of 1974.

In answer to your question, the legislation will have to reflect the changed conditions of American agriculture and international trade. In recent months the boast made about the 1973 bill, that it provided for full production with protection, has seemed hollow to many American farmers. Prices, particularly of grains, have dropped dramatically.

The legislation will have to walk a rather narrow line between the wishes of those who would like to see greater expenditures in this area and the rather tight fiscal constraints that exist in the Congress. Some want to see higher price supports * for farmers. Others, on the farm and off, want to make sure that the price supports do not become so high that they interfere with our foreign trade or result in the takeover of stocks by the government. That would be resisted by most of the American agricultural community.

Briefly, I expect that the philosophy of the 1970–1973 bill, which was more market-oriented than previous programs, will be continued in the new bill. There probably will not be a return to the old style of marketing quotas and tight allotments, but the question of at what level to set target prices * and loan rates * will be critical.

MR. DALY: Congressman Findley, you are a member of the House Agricultural Committee, the sponsor of the Famine Prevention Program, a self-help program to improve food production in hungry nations, and the author of a book entitled *Federal Farm Fable* and two *Reader's Digest* articles entitled "Sugar—A Sticky Mess in Congress," and "Let's Plug the Billion Dollar Farm Drain." What do you consider the most important things that consumers have to lose or gain from 1977 farm legislation?

PAUL FINDLEY, U.S. House of Representatives (Republican, Illinois): This year, certainly, can be critical for the interests of consumers. The interests of the American people are, however, much more broadly at stake. We can make blunders. We can set loan rates and target prices too high. That would increase food prices, not inordinately perhaps, but, nevertheless, the trend would be upward.

But the greatest mischief that Congress might cause the American people would be in their capacity not as consumers but rather as taxpayers and as citizens.

The Ford administration gave to the Carter administration an agricultural plant that is in its healthiest condition in at least forty years. The challenge this year is to avoid making mistakes. The finest thing that could possibly happen for consumers, as well as for taxpayers and citizens with even broader interests, would be a simple extension of what we have now. The plant is going full speed, and government payments are down. The average farmer depends on the U.S. Treasury for only

---

* This term is one of those defined on page 236.

about 2 percent of his income, whereas before the Republican administration, this figure was as high as 27 percent.

People in the rural areas now have almost the same per capita income as city dwellers. Farm exports have tripled since 1972—and this is of vital interest to every citizen. We need the earning power of American agriculture in foreign markets. And, as Congressman Foley has stated, we have a narrow line to walk. Some test votes in the Committee on Agriculture indicate a strong tendency to raise loan rates to a level that could cause great difficulty in the marketing of farm products abroad. If that happens, we will have surpluses to contend with; we could easily stumble back into the same costly surplus condition which led to an inefficient agricultural plant.

MR. DALY: Dr. Schnittker, you recently suggested a limited one-year extension of the present farm price support bill to allow more time to construct some fundamental new legislation, as you put it. Now, what fundamental new legislation do you support?

JOHN A. SCHNITTKER, former undersecretary of agriculture: I am not so much concerned about fundamental new legislation as I am about the need to avoid making serious mistakes in new legislation. Much of what I think about the current year was summarized by Congressman Foley. We have a new administration and very little time, considering the budgetary process that Congress now goes through. Since we have an act on the books—the 1973 Farm Act—which has never really been tried, we should continue it. We should keep the price support levels relatively close to those established during the most recent year. This would give us another year to see whether some fundamental new legislation is needed. Such legislation might be in the areas of price stabilization and disaster prevention—areas untouched in farm programs. Some people tend to claim that all of the good effects of the period from 1973 to 1976—higher prices for farmers, good incomes, and high exports— were the result of the 1973 act. This is really a rewriting of history and is not even fair to the 1973 act.

MR. DALY: Dr. Yeutter, as one who has operated a 2,500-acre farm, taught agricultural economics, headed the Consumer and Marketing Service of the Department of Agriculture and served as an assistant secretary of agriculture, and who was President Ford's deputy special representative for trade negotiations, what new legislation would you like to see affecting international trade and relations?

CLAYTON K. YEUTTER, former assistant secretary of agriculture: There are really two elements in this international package: one is domestic farm legislation, basically the subject we are talking about tonight; the other is negotiations to reduce trade barriers around the world, so that we can penetrate new markets. One really has to work on both elements simultaneously.

With respect to farm policy, we want a domestic farm policy that, if possible, will facilitate the movement of U.S. agricultural products on the world scene, or at a minimum not hamper or impede the movement of these products.

Some years ago we permitted our support levels to go beyond world market prices, and they became uncompetitive. We were the residual supplier—we sold our products after everybody else in the exporting business had sold theirs. That is an oversimplification, but it is the essence of the situation. The only way we could be competitive then was through export subsidies.*

Some changes have been made through the years. U.S. farmers can now compete with anybody in the world. That being the case, we need an international environment in which we are permitted to compete. We want to avoid international regulatory schemes in which we will lose some of our competitive advantage at the negotiating table. We also want to avoid returning to the high price support levels that my colleagues here have mentioned.

There are other elements on the international scene, the use of credit from the Commodity Credit Corporation, and Public Law 480,† known as the Food for Peace program. We may need them for domestic foreign policy purposes, over and above humanitarian considerations, and certainly we should keep those tools available to the secretary of agriculture.

By and large, Congress should exercise restraint in legislating in this area, and allow the secretary of agriculture some discretion in the setting of loan rates so that he can make sure that we stay competitive. In other words, maybe Congress ought to keep its cotton-pickin' hands off loan rates. [Laughter.]

CONGRESSMAN FOLEY: Dr. Schnittker mentioned rewriting history. The original position of Secretary Butz and the Republican administration was not the program that became the 1973 act. The administration finally agreed to bipartisan congressional initiatives, but first, it wanted to phase out all the farm programs over a period of five years. What actually was adopted was a congressional concept, initiated by the Senate Committee on Agriculture and Forestry. The target price, for example, was generally credited to Milton Young, the Republican sena-

---

* This term is one of those defined on page 236.
† These terms are explained on page 238.

tor from North Dakota, as the beginning of a movement away from the more rigid allotments and market quotas of previous programs. But we had been moving in that direction over the years. It is sometimes said—I think, wrongly—that we now have a Republican farm program, which Democrats resisted. If the Democrats had resisted it, it could not have been enacted by the Congress in 1973, which was almost as heavily Democratic as it is today.

DR. YEUTTER: Farm policy is not very partisan any more. A great deal of the political conflict is gone, one reason being that farm policy has become such an internationally oriented endeavor. Almost everybody on both sides of the political aisle agrees that we want to maintain our export momentum. A sound international economic policy is really a nonpartisan effort.

CONGRESSMAN FINDLEY: Could I just add a little more bipartisan commentary? [Laughter.] I would like to salute the fine cooperation of the Democrats in the Congress in bringing about the 1973 act, and also to criticize my own party a bit for what happened to wheat loan rates last fall. The administration overreacted to the political climate of the time by raising wheat loan rates too high. As a consequence, wheat had difficulty moving aggressively into foreign markets, and that experience should be a warning that we should not raise loan rates even more.

Farm philosophy cuts across party lines. I find myself voting with Congressman Foley quite often, and I have noted quite a substantial change in the political and the philosophical outlook of Republicans on the House Agriculture Committee since I joined the committee. I suspect Chairman Foley has noted some changes on his side of the aisle.

One of the problems we face in this Congress is that so few members have any memory, as politicians, of the high price support, high surplus, high cost era immediately after the Korean War. I hope we can find a way to educate these new members in time to avoid disaster.

CONGRESSMAN FOLEY: About 60 percent of the House of Representatives was elected since 1970.

DR. SCHNITTKER: We may have had a bipartisan farm policy, with everything sweetness and light, but we had better have a major fight on farm policy this year or we will have a disaster.

CONGRESSMAN FINDLEY: I agree.

DR. SCHNITTKER: A series of proposals have been made in 1977 that are right out of the 1940s and 1950s, proposals to raise price supports to levels that are unsustainable in the world market. There are proposals to spend so much money on farm programs—mainly for the big farmers—

that the budget would be unbalanced, and other, higher-priority programs would be starved.

We have gotten off to a very bad start in the 1977 farm debate. I do not know whose fault it is. The Congress, in its wisdom, required the Department of Agriculture in the 1973 act to make some studies of cost of production. "Cost of production" has become the "parity" of 1977. We are on the way toward supporting farmers through the budget in big crop years, at full cost of production, starting a spiral of land costs which will go higher and higher. It will cost $5 or $6 billion in one year, and $6 or $7 billion in another year.

The fight in Congress will not be a partisan fight. It will be a fight between the people who look back and the people who look ahead in farm policy.

The panel here tonight represents those who look ahead. I wish we had somebody on the panel who was advocating high loan rates and high budgets, but we will have to represent them by proxy.

DR. YEUTTER: I share the view that we need to focus on these issues in 1977 because, amazingly enough, although target prices and loan rates have been in existence a long time, there is still confusion about what they are, how they work, and what they are supposed to do.

Income protection for farmers should come from target prices. They should give some minimum assurances on the income side.

Loan rates, on the other hand, should not be used to provide an assured income level. If we attempt to do that, we begin to get into the cost of production concepts that Dr. Schnittker talked about. One can always rationalize a high cost of production, if one wants to put a high enough value on land, and that leads to loan rates that are so high as to make us uncompetitive. We ought to stop talking about loan rates as income protection and concentrate on target prices as income protection.

A loan rate serves only two functions. One is to serve as a source of financing for farmers, who are able to borrow from the government at a lower rate of interest than from commercial sources. The other function is to provide an incentive to increase production when that is desirable. If carry-over levels are too low, the government can raise loan rates to stimulate additional production. But, I repeat, we should not use loan rates as a basic income protection device. Unfortunately, many proposals reaching Congress this year speak of using loan rates for precisely that purpose.

CONGRESSMAN FINDLEY: The attitude of the new President is an element of great importance. Jimmy Carter, from the Deep South, was involved in the production and marketing of peanuts, one of the historic "basic"

228

crops. He has called for a balanced budget by the end of his four-year term. He has also called for budgetary restraint this year. An interesting test of his commitment to budgetary management will be the farm bill. His recommendation in regard to peanuts, for example, called for a cut of about $30 million in fiscal year 1978. This would require some very substantial remodeling of the peanut program. So far, that remodeling is not in prospect. The President will have to use the weight of his office to obtain the support of his peanut constituency for the remodeling of the program, and I do not see that happening.

Sentiment already visible within the Agriculture Committee favors higher price supports—loan rates is simply another term for that—and that would result in higher budget outlays. There could be a doubling or a tripling of the outlay for commodity programs, in comparison with outlays last year under President Ford.

This would affect President Carter's objective of a balanced budget at the end of his term. For this reason, he will probably exercise a great deal of influence on the outcome of this battle, but will he accept high price supports, which guarantee high prices at the expense of the consumer and taxpayer, or will he surmount his historic base in the Deep South and force some changes?

MR. DALY: While we are on this issue of loan rates and price supports, let me pose a question which is raised by some of the philosophical statements of Secretary Bergland. Under the 1973 contract, a crop receives price supports for one year, and, if the market falls below the loan rate, then the government takes ownership. Secretary Bergland proposes a program of price support loans that would induce farmers to enter into long-term agreements to store their grain and to market the grain only in times of dwindling supplies and rising prices. What would be the effect of replacing the present one-year loans with this program? Would it, for instance, stabilize the loan payment structures at a lower level than we have had in recent years?

DR. SCHNITTKER: Actually, the program need not be much of a change from the earlier one. We have had one-year loans under the price support program for many years, and, occasionally, these loans have been extended for several years. Secretary Bergland has proposed that the authority be given to extend them to two or three years in one order, instead of year by year. The risk there is in giving the farmer the option of deciding when the loan would be terminated and when the grain would be called in.

This should be part of a reserve package, and a reserve, to be useful, must be available. Only the government can manage a reserve with a view to the public interest. Therefore, the government must have some control over the reserve, and it must be able to terminate whatever benefits cause the farmer to hold the grain, even to require the farmer to market it within a certain period to prevent prices from rising. This is not a great change.

CONGRESSMAN FOLEY: I would agree with Dr. Schnittker, but Secretary Bergland has also suggested that the authority either to raise the interest rates on loans or to reduce the time period would be needed under certain circumstances. Some flexibility is needed to keep the farmer from holding his crop unnecessarily for two or three years. In other words, there would be some incentives that could draw the grain into the market, if necessary.

DR. YEUTTER: Whether we adopt that program or continue the present system will not make a great deal of difference in domestic farm policy. The more fundamental issue is whether we should have any kind of formal grain reserve or food reserve program. If we should have such a program, should it be in government hands or private hands or some combination of the two? And, how would this program relate to what we do internationally?

We must be careful in 1977 not to become involved in a grain reserve program that would work against the best interests of the United States. Over the last several years there have been a number of such proposals, and there will undoubtedly be more in 1977. Congress should look at them with a jaundiced eye before embarking on something that might adversely affect international economic policy.

CONGRESSMAN FINDLEY: We cannot separate the foreign market from our discussion of domestic policy. Last year and the year before and the year before that, we sold in the range of $20–$22 billion of agricultural products abroad. We bought a lot of farm products, too, some $10 or $11 billion, but we had an immensely favorable balance of agricultural trade.

The mischief this Congress might do to our domestic farm programs could affect foreign markets. If price supports rise too high, we will have a buildup of surpluses. Farmers will then seek some kind of income protection. This would probably result in a set-aside or land diversion program. Our plant would become less efficient, and we would have less chance to compete in foreign markets. The U.S. dollar would be under even more severe attack than it has been.

DR. SCHNITTKER: To return to the question of leadership for a minute, there are three focal points for leadership: the presidency, the Senate, and the House. Two of them have a real chance for leadership, but the

Senate is permanently gerrymandered in favor of the farmers in the small states. It is difficult to conceive of real discipline on farm legislation in the Senate. Maybe it could happen if the Budget Committee puts up a fight. The White House, of course, needs to assert leadership, in order to defend the budget.

The House has been the eye of the needle on much legislation in recent years. In 1977 all House members will look at farm legislation. Urban members once felt they did not know enough about farm bills, so they looked the other way and voted for whatever they were asked to vote for. If this attitude prevails in 1977, it might result in bad legislation.

CONGRESSMAN FOLEY: Dr. Schnittker mentioned that reserve policy has to include some government levers to make it work. I do not think anybody is proposing to go back to large government-held stocks or reserves. Secretary Bergland has talked about extending the loan programs for farm-stored grain, or at least farmer-controlled grain—not for high CCC stocks. That point ought to be made clear.

People in urban America who are concerned about running out of food sometimes are unaware of our situation. On a talk show I heard, a participant said he did not favor exporting wheat to the Soviet Union or to any other country when we barely had enough wheat to go around. We have had two back-to-back crops of about 2.1 to 2.2 billion bushels; we use about 700 million bushels a year for all purposes domestically. As of May 31 this year, we will have between 1.1 billion and 1.2 billion bushels of wheat on hand, the largest carry-over since the early 1960s.

DR. YEUTTER: To supplement what Congressman Foley said on the reserves question, there are two aspects of reserves that must enter a policy discussion. One of them is food security. As Congressman Foley has indicated, that is not a problem here in the United States. Food security risks are those of importing nations. Japan has a food security risk because it produces very little. We do not have a food security risk because we are a major exporter. Therefore, from that standpoint, we have no motivation to have any kind of formalized grain reserve in the United States.

The other aspect is price stability. Some suggest that U.S. consumers, and other consumers around the world, would benefit from a reserve program that would stabilize markets a bit. Some suggest that a reserve would even benefit farmers because it would give them a little more assurance of income levels or price levels and a little less worry about inordinate fluctuations.

I am not at all sure that this additional stability is worth the cost. One would have to make a cost-benefit calculation to establish whether the storage costs and all the other elements of conducting a reserve program are justified by the price stability benefits. There is a difficult decision to be made on the price stability side; the decision on the food security side is an easy one.

If we want to consider international issues, then the question becomes a matter of whether an international grain reserve will contribute to peace in the world or to better relationships with other nations. That is a decision that the administration will have to make, based upon the cost-benefit tradeoffs.

But my primary point is that if we have a grain reserve we should negotiate it, and the importing nations should pick up their share of the tab. We should not unilaterally establish a food reserve and have the U.S. taxpayer pick up the tab for everybody else.

CONGRESSMAN FINDLEY: Congressman Foley is correct in saying that nobody is proposing larger reserves. I cannot name a single member of the House of Representatives or Senate who is trying to establish large government-held reserves. But a lot of them are clamoring for high price supports and high loan rates, and they do not seem to recognize that large government-held reserves and high price supports are the two sides of the same coin.

MR. DALY: Congressman Findley, past farm programs have been criticized because their benefits were said to have gone primarily to well-off farmers, with little help for the small or poor farmer. You were author of the law limiting federal farm payments to $20,000 per farmer. Does that action take care of that criticism or should more be done?

CONGRESSMAN FINDLEY: It is a recognition of the social aspect of farm legislation. Actually, the payments have not been made for several years, except for rice, thanks to a number of factors, including good leadership in the Congress and in the Ford administration. These payments have not been made, and therefore the payment limitation has not been effective. But there is no question that large commercial farmers in the past have been able to make adjustments in planted acreage to comply with the set-aside requirements of the basic program, and thus they became eligible for more payments than the small farmer.

In the past, farm programs have generally benefited the big operator more than the small operator. The only successful effort to meet this problem, in my memory, has been the payment limitation. Frankly, I think $20,000 is much too high, but that is the best compromise level we could achieve.

MR. DALY: There are those who say that since 1972 we have entered a new era of worldwide food shortages. Does anyone agree and, if so, what is to be done?

DR. SCHNITTKER: We have had extensive food shortages since 1972 and a real fear that the shortages could become even worse. We might have had serious famines in many countries if crops had failed as badly in 1976 as in 1975. We are certainly in a much different situation now than we were in the 1950s or 1960s, when the crops were much more stable and predictable.

One simply does not know whether the trend will continue. Personally, I am impressed with the climatologists' argument that the weather pattern of the world has changed slightly for the worse, as far as crop production is concerned, and that we have to expect slightly greater variation and more bad years in the next five or ten years than in the period before 1970. I do not expect famine or disaster, except perhaps locally in an occasional year. But a slower rate of growth and greater instability, yes.

CONGRESSMAN FOLEY: At the International Wheat Council in London we have been discussing the idea of setting up some kind of international food reserve in wheat. These discussions have been going on for some time, but not much progress has been made up to this point. There may be some attempts to expand these efforts. If we are moving into a period of changing climate, with more droughts and crop failures, we may need some cushion in the form of international stocks in the basic food grains. In recent years, however, we have had some very large replenishments of world stocks of wheat. The longer-term question is whether we can keep ahead of the population increase in the world.

Looking ahead a decade or so when 700 million people may be born in Asia alone, the question of whether the world, collectively, can produce the necessary food to feed the new population is still a real and open question.

I want to compliment Congressman Findley as the author of an act to stress development of the agricultural sector in food-deficient countries. We could make the mistake of providing too much food aid, too many concessional sales, which might smother the incentive of food-deficient countries to provide for their own agriculture.

We cannot feed the world ourselves; we cannot project more acreage in Iowa, Illinois, Kansas, Nebraska, and Washington to meet the projected population increases.

CONGRESSMAN FINDLEY: I am convinced that there is a critical world food problem and that it will become worse rather rapidly. It is true that the increase in production of food has been about equal to the increase in population, but the increase in production has not occurred in the areas of greatest population increase.

The Third World has experienced a steady increase in population, with a lowered death rate and an increased birth rate. These countries have not had the capacity to increase their food production at the same rate, nor have they had the purchasing power to buy food elsewhere. Financial incentives can result in a tremendous increase in food production in the world, but the Third World will need the means with which to buy the food or to grow it.

One encouraging development is the emphasis by Congress, with presidential support, on enabling the land grant universities to help Third World countries do a better job of teaching their farmers. This has great promise, not only in enabling the Third World to feed itself but also to build little by little a broader, more sturdy base from which they can start having a better life in other respects.

DR. YEUTTER: Congressman Foley mentioned production disincentives in some importing countries. That is a real problem in increasing food production around the world. Many nations not only fail to provide incentives for their farmers but also provide production disincentives, which allegedly help consumers and keep the price of food low.

CONGRESSMAN FINDLEY: Sometimes our P.L. 480 program is a disincentive to food production in some of those countries.

DR. YEUTTER: No question about it. Congressman Foley mentioned the discussions in London on food reserves. When one suggests that importing countries pay their share, they quickly lose interest in any kind of international food reserve. Whether anything will ultimately materialize, only time will tell. In the interim, the importing countries can protect themselves from this food security risk. They can put up additional storage in their own countries and store more grain than they are now storing. The Soviet Union is doing this to a considerable degree. The Japanese and others should do more.

These countries can buy from us on long-term contractual bases and thus give themselves additional security of supply. They can participate in our commodity markets here in the United States. They can do a number of things unilaterally to protect themselves, without getting involved in a grandiose international reserve scheme.

CONGRESSMAN FINDLEY: I was intrigued when the Farm Bureau recommended a year or so ago that a food reserve of dollars, not wheat, be established. The exporting industrialized countries would contribute to a fund to buy food where and as needed. That system would make more sense than piling up a reserve of wheat in some central point.

DR. SCHNITTKER: Congressman Foley called attention to the fact that wheat stocks increased sharply in the winter of 1977. In fact, by the middle of 1977, when the new harvests begin, the world will have about as much grain stored away as it had five years ago, just before the so-called Russian wheat deal or the first big crop failure in this recent era.

The world has built a food reserve quite accidentally. If we are to avoid frittering away those 40 or 50 million tons of increased stocks on cattle feed, if we are to avoid sending it off to Russia or someplace else the next time there is a short crop, if we are to have it when we need it for a food emergency in some poor country, or for price stability here at home, or to export for cash to maintain our own balance of payments, then we need a food reserve policy. This simply means a set of guidelines on how we will eventually use the grain that we have accidentally accumulated. The question of a food reserve is not really mysterious. While we have talked about a policy, we have built a reserve.

DR. YEUTTER: To comment a bit on Dr. Schnittker's remarks, I am not at all convinced that it is frittering away stocks to use them on livestock production. We must hope that others around the world can afford to feed livestock too. I do not think we would solve the world's food problems by suggesting that we diminish livestock production in the United States.

DR. SCHNITTKER: I would never suggest that.

MR. DALY: Secretary Bergland has expressed great interest in weather forecasting. He objects to devising an economic policy that is based, as he describes it, on average weather, and he sees a need to develop an economic model to adapt to changing weather conditions at home and abroad. In terms of long-term goals, is there any clear idea of what new legislation should encourage research and improved technology at home and overseas?

CONGRESSMAN FINDLEY: I think Bob Bergland is a great guy, and I encouraged President Carter to name him secretary of agriculture, but I hope he did not mean what he is quoted as having said. If he did, his admirable goal of a market-oriented agriculture would wind up as a "market-oriented" agriculture run by a GS-15 in the U.S. Department of Agriculture. It would be truly a government-managed system. Furthermore, it is foolish to try to gear farm production planning to the vagaries of weather.

MR. DALY: It is time to open the question and answer session. But first, let me ask a favor. Some of the terms used today would not be familiar to the city dweller. Definitions would be helpful. One of these is *loan rate*.

DR. SCHNITTKER: A loan rate is the actual price at which a commodity is supported. Wheat in 1977 is being supported at a level not lower than $2.25 per bushel at the farm. It is supported by means of a government loan to the farmer which helps him hold the wheat off the market until the price is at least $2.25 a bushel. Support and loan rates are interchangeable.

MR. DALY: *Target price* is another difficult term.

CONGRESSMAN FOLEY: A target price is set in an act, but it is subject to escalation in terms of certain inflation factors. It is designed to offer protection for the farmer. If the average price for a crop in the market falls below the target price, then cooperating farmers are paid the difference between the actual average market price and the target price. If the target price were $2.50 and the average market price for wheat were $2.25 during the marketing year, then cooperating farmers would be paid twenty-five cents a bushel, the difference between $2.25 and $2.50.

There are, however, payment limitations. For most crops the limitation is $20,000; for rice, $55,000. There are target price programs for wheat, feed grains, cotton, and rice.

MR. DALY: Since the international area is a particular interest of yours, Dr. Yeutter, will you take the last definition, *export subsidy?*

DR. YEUTTER: An export subsidy is a government payment to help the sellers of a given country to be competitive on the international market. Those sellers might be the government itself or they might be firms in private industry.

The terms *support levels*, *price supports*, and *loan rates* are used interchangeably. If those prices are at, say, $3.00 a bushel for wheat but the world market price is $2.50, the sellers of that country obviously will not do very well in the world market, at fifty cents above the prevailing price. But if that government grants a fifty-five cent per bushel subsidy, then they immediately become competitive because their price drops from $3.00 to $2.45—five cents a bushel under the prevailing market price. Noncompetitive sellers obviously like export subsidies, which enable them to compete in the world market.

CONGRESSMAN FINDLEY: Dr. Yeutter said it is a government export subsidy. I would like to stress the word *government*. There is no mysterious fund or source of money for price supports, for target price payments, or for export subsidies. The money comes out of the U.S. Treasury, out of the general revenues. Every U.S. taxpayer contributes to the fund from which these supports are paid.

MR. DALY: May we have the first question, please?

LUTHER WALLACE, University of California at Davis: Congressman Foley, we see a great many policies beyond the control of the Department of Agriculture—policies on health, transportation, taxes, energy— which bear on agriculture. Will your committee try to let the USDA know what is going to happen before it happens?

CONGRESSMAN FOLEY: We have tried to do that with one program, the Federal Insecticide, Fungicide, and Rodenticide Act, which is administered by the Environmental Protection Agency. That legislation required that notice of any proposed cancellation or suspension of a pesticide be provided in advance to the secretary of agriculture. He was given thirty days to make comments on the proposed action by the EPA. The legislation also required that the EPA administrator set up an independent board of scientific advisors, nominated from outside the agency, and they, too, would have an opportunity to make comments. This is an effort to give the Department of Agriculture the kind of advance notice and opportunity for comment that you mentioned.

LAWRENCE RENS, staff economist, Federal Trade Commission: I would like to direct my question to Dr. Yeutter. It is my understanding that the Department of Agriculture has released some 60 million acres for production since 1971–1972. Do you foresee any problem with this in the event that foreign demand drops off, and if you do, what kind of policy should be instituted?

DR. YEUTTER: The acres you mention had been held out of production in the old set-aside programs, soil bank programs, and conservation reserve programs. They have now come back into production, and that is very healthy for our economy and welcome news worldwide for people concerned about agricultural production levels.

As to what might happen if we have gone too far, that is another issue. The acres involved are not highly productive, and will not boost production all that much.

As mentioned earlier, we do have very high carry-over levels on many crops right now, and that poses a policy decision that the new administration may have to face, particularly if we continue to have good crops and if the levels keep climbing. The policy question is, Should we move some of that production onto the world market through the use of CCC credit, P.L. 480, and other devices that would give some impetus to the movement, or should we trim our production in order to bring those levels back?

One way to trim it would be to return to a set-aside program of the kind we had before. That tool ought to be in the secretary of agriculture's kit, and it is now. I hope he does not have to use it. I would much prefer to see that land continue in production, but at the same time we must recognize that the secretary and the administration have an obligation to maintain farm income at a reasonable level. Certainly the secretary of agriculture ought to be allowed some discretion in deciding whether to do that through a set-aside program, direct payments, CCC credit, or other means.

MR. DALY: For city dwellers, could P.L. 480 and CCC credit be defined?

DR. YEUTTER: P.L. 480 is familiar to most people as the Food for Peace program. It has two aspects. One is the grant aspect, under which we provide food on a donated basis to needy people around the world. The other, the loan aspect, is where we sell the food to them on long-term loans with very low rates of interest. P.L. 480 has been a useful device through the years to help feed hungry people around the world and at the same time to serve the secondary objective of helping to move some of our surpluses.

CCC credit is a nonsubsidized program in which we provide intermediate-term credit, up to three years, for buyers of U.S. agricultural products at a rate of interest that reflects the cost to the government of obtaining the money. This is an advantageous and attractive rate, and the three-year credit is also attractive. The program also helps us to compete in world markets.

CONGRESSMAN FOLEY: The nomenclature may confuse some people. P.L. 480 stands for Public Law 480 of the 84th Congress.

CONGRESSMAN FINDLEY: And CCC stands for Commodity Credit Corporation. It is a bank supported entirely by U.S. taxpayers to the tune of $15 billion in total assets.

LINWOOD TIPTON, Milk Industry Foundation: Congressman Foley and Congressman Findley, what kind of restraints do you anticipate on the loan rates, particularly this year, from the Budget Committee? Will that be a major factor, and how will it affect this year's legislation?

CONGRESSMAN FOLEY: As I mentioned earlier, this year, for the first time a major farm bill is being considered under the budget act, and, yes, the Committee on Agriculture must let the Budget Committee know what, in its judgment, the programs it might enact would cost in budget outlays and budget authority. The Budget Committee must make a judgment on the various functions of the budget in agriculture.

It is our experience over the three years the budget act has been in existence that it has teeth. For example, in 1975, the first year of the budget act, the Congress passed a bill that provided support for milk at 85 percent of parity. The President vetoed that 85 percent price support for milk, and it appeared that the Senate would override the President's veto. When the Budget Committee objected that the 85 percent level would put the agricultural function of the budget over level, fifty-one senators turned around and supported the President's veto. Many of them were for 85 percent of parity but they voted to support the budget act.

CONGRESSMAN FINDLEY: Could I just add a word of definition about what 85 percent of parity price support for milk means? It means that the government will guarantee the price at a level of 85 percent of the base period, which was back in the World War I era. I am not sure what the parity price of milk products is now, but it is about 80 percent. Undoubtedly this is a profitable level or the milk would not be produced. This means that at 85 percent of parity the government would be guaranteeing a profitable price of production to every dairy farmer in the country. The total production would be guaranteed by the U.S. taxpayer.

WILLARD W. COCHRANE, University of Minnesota: I was taught about forty years ago that tying price supports to cost of production was the worst thing to do, and I taught that for twenty years. But the newspapers in Minnesota suggest that Congress is thinking very seriously of tying price supports in a new act to cost of production. Congressman Foley and Congressman Findley, how close are we to legislation that would tie price supports to cost of production?

CONGRESSMAN FOLEY: Quite close. I said during the campaign and afterwards that I had grave reservations about using the concept of cost of production to determine loan rates.

There are many other factors that should be more prominent than cost of production figures. First, it is difficult to establish a cost of production. I do not think any three producers of the same commodity in the same country would agree on the actual cost of production for that commodity. But even if a formula could be devised, applying it to loan rates would involve two risks.

First, it starts to dominate the consideration of what the loan rates should be, forgetting for the moment about interference with the movement of the commodity in trade and a possible takeover of the commodity by the CCC.

Second, it will build in an implicit escalator in the setting of the loan rate. The impact of inflation on cost of production is easily determined under any formula. There will be an effort to make upward adjustments in price support when international circumstances and various other operational realities may indicate that that is not a wise decision.

I share your concern, but there is strong bipartisan support for it in the Committee on Agriculture and in Congress.

CONGRESSMAN FINDLEY: There will be bipartisan opposition, too, symbolized by our presence here today. In a sense, we have been concerned for about forty years with guaranteeing the cost of production to farmers. That is how the parity concept got started. The base period back in World War I was chosen as the point of reference in deciding a fair price, mainly return on the cost of production, for the farmer.

We have had variations. There was talk in the 1950s about 90 percent of parity as the objective. In a sense, that meant 90 percent of the cost of production. But factors have changed over the years, and it was finally agreed that 90 percent of parity would be cost of production and a fair return. Now we have 85 percent in prospect for milk. Rice and peanuts are at about 75 percent of parity. We still cling to a cost of production yardstick in federal legislation. It is a dangerous game and we ought to stay out of it.

DR. YEUTTER: To add to that, I do not believe there are even *two* farmers in the United States who would agree on cost of production. If Congress uses a cost of production calculation in this farm bill, it will be immensely controversial, and there will be a continuing hassle over what cost of production ought to be. There is just no way to resolve what land costs should be put in a cost of production formula. If somebody insists that we do this, we should do it on the target price end rather than the loan rate end. I hope we do not even do it on target prices, because it is undesirable there, too. But at least this would be the lesser of two evils.

I would hope that we could find a less controversial way to establish just target price levels.

We have mentioned many times the danger of making ourselves uncompetitive around the world. As a trade negotiator, I would point out that in Geneva we have been telling others to get away from their high-support, export-subsidy policies, and we would look hypocritical if we start going down that same road ourselves.

DR. SCHNITTKER: There is a terminology problem here as well. High target prices, which mean high payments to farmers in some years, are actually backdoor export subsidies.

W. E. HAMILTON, American Farm Bureau Federation: We hear a great deal about the world food problem and hungry people. Some of this discussion suggests that we are facing a situation in which the world may not be able to feed its people because we do not have the capacity to produce. I suspect that the problem for the immediate future is not capacity to produce but the capacity of some people to buy. In other words, the problem of hungry people is the problem of people who do not have capacity to come into the market system and buy food which could be made available if they had that capacity. I wonder if members of the panel would comment on this view.

DR. YEUTTER: Purchasing power is a major element in this picture. In the relatively short-run—ten or twenty years or thereabouts, while population is under at least some semblance of control around the world—purchasing power will be more of a problem than the availability of food, barring some tremendous natural disaster.

Purchasing power is of great concern to us, both as humanitarians, wanting people to have an opportunity to eat a decent meal every day, and as exporters. We need purchasing power around the world to sell the products of U.S. farms. Purchasing power has been greatly hampered in the last three or four years by the worldwide recession and the oil crisis. The actions of the OPEC nations have been devastating, drastically reducing purchasing power for food. Some countries and people have had to choose between petroleum and food. As we pull out of this world-wide recession, as we are doing now, purchasing power should rise around the world, and everybody should benefit.

CONGRESSMAN FOLEY: In the long range we may find that the world's capacity to produce is outstripped by its population.

There are still some major growing areas of the world that could be brought into production, but expensive developmental programs would be needed. These areas include the Sudan and the Amazon Basin. In the short range, although food stocks have gone up dramatically, many people do not have the capacity to buy. The problem of international payments is very acute for the Third World.

MARVIN L. HAYENGA, General Foods Corporation: For many years prior to 1974, the domestic sugar industry was controlled under farm legislation. Since 1974, the sugar industry has not been carefully protected; there has been only a modest tariff on imports. The International Trade Commission has, however, indicated its intention to recommend a protective import quota on sugar imports. How do you believe the Congress will react to this recommendation? Is there a better policy alternative?

MR. DALY: As the author of "Sugar—A Sticky Mess in Congress," would you care to answer that, Congressman Findley?

CONGRESSMAN FINDLEY: Happily, sugar is not a sticky mess in Congress now. It was when I wrote that article back in 1966. Subsequent to that date, Congress had the good judgment to let the sugar act expire. I regret that the International Trade Commission recommended quotas and I hope that President Carter will see fit not to act upon that recommendation. It is true that some sugar producers are having difficulty under the present price situation, and I am sure some sugar producers always will, unless we go back to a system in which the government keeps the market price high enough so that even the inefficient can make money. The price of this, of course, would be higher cost to the consumer. I am amazed and delighted with the reaction of the market to the end of the sugar act. A lot of the users of sugar in this country have made contracts abroad; they have found that they can deal through marketplace channels. Their market system, in a sense, had atrophied during some thirty years under the sugar act, and now users are finally getting back into business. They found that getting out of the cage of government's control, they can fly after all. We should resist the temptation to reconstruct, in any degree, a sugar act similar to the one we had in the past.

CONGRESSMAN FOLEY: Happily enough, we have a disagreement. I think we do have a problem in the sugar area. We import about half of our sugar in the United States, and we produce about half. We may not have a domestic sugar producing industry very long unless we have some form of price supports or quotas on imports.

Secretary Bergland has mentioned the possibility of a very modest price support program on sugar, which would be backed by quotas to restrict imports to protect that price support. We are talking now about a price support of twelve or thirteen cents a pound.

It was not long ago that American consumers were paying forty-five and fifty and sixty cents a pound for sugar, and—

CONGRESSMAN FINDLEY: —and they were screaming.

CONGRESSMAN FOLEY: Yes, indeed. If we raise the price support too high, obviously not only would the consumers have a problem but also the high fructose corn sweetener industry would probably take away a lot of the industrial market.

But I do think some modest price support program—either through direct price supports, backed by quotas, or a tightening of the so-called world quota—is essential to protect our basic cane and sugar beet industry. If that does not happen soon, we will see it disappear.

CONGRESSMAN FINDLEY: Present law does give the domestic producers of sugar approximately two cents a pound protection against foreign imports; they are not left totally on their own.

CONGRESSMAN FOLEY: The one danger for the consumer is that if the production of sugar ends in the United States, we will become completely dependent on world markets. Those markets are increasingly tied to long-term contracting and preferential sugar agreements that other countries have established. The so-called free market can be a very short one, a volatile one. There could be wide swings in sugar prices, very low sugar prices one year, and very high prices a few years later. Consumers may wonder why they are paying forty-five or fifty cents again for sugar.

DR. YEUTTER: One thing that people who advocate restrictions on sugar imports have a tendency to forget is that they are illegal internationally under the General Agreement on Tariffs and Trade (GATT). We were one of the leaders, beginning back in the 1940s, in forming that agreement, which attempts to establish some sensible rules in the conduct of international trade.

Our quotas on sugar today are probably illegal under GATT, but nobody complains about them because they are not restrictive. If we pass legislation that imposes restrictions, whether they be quotas or some other form of restriction, we would likely find ourselves in violation of the GATT rules. And it is a little difficult for us to insist that other people follow the GATT rules when we do not want to follow them ourselves.

CONGRESSMAN FOLEY: The problem is, first of all, that other people do not follow the GATT rules. Almost every country is in some kind of technical violation of the GATT rules. Except for the last three years, the United States has had a sugar act which, according to Dr. Yeutter, was illegal under GATT until 1974 when the act expired. All during that period we had quotas on sugar imports.

CONGRESSMAN FINDLEY: That program was not illegal under the GATT because it was covered by a grandfather clause; it was in existence before GATT was initiated. That grandfather clause is now no longer applicable.

Simply because other people violate the GATT rules—and they do—is no justification for us to violate them too.

DR. SCHNITTKER: It is only fair that we have some kind of price stabilization program for sugar, unless we end the price stabilization programs for wheat, corn, cotton, rice, and everything else. But moderation is the point, and simplicity—legality too, but in moderation. [Laughter.]

Moderation and simplicity are far more important than legality, because violations under GATT rules are legion.

CONGRESSMAN FINDLEY: The American sugar producer has no idea today how efficiently he can produce sugar. For about thirty years he operated under the tightest government control ever inflicted upon the producer of any commodity. The producers have been out from under the act for a couple of years, and they are just beginning to test their wings. We should wait a few more years before deciding how high the price has to be to protect the efficient U.S. producer.

CONGRESSMAN FOLEY: Almost every country in GATT has some kind of sugar program or participates in one, in some way or another. It is drawing a rather tight legal bow to say that the United States cannot have a modest program of price support—and I agree with Dr. Schnittker that it should be modest—without violating GATT or creating an enormous reaction.

If we establish a program that is questionable legally, we will hear about it from the negotiators at GATT, but the United States should not be too inhibited in this area. Contrary to the position of Congressman Findley, if we wait a few more years, we may not have a domestic sugar industry.

DR. YEUTTER: If we are going to violate GATT rules by this new scheme, we should go into it with our eyes wide open and recognize that other countries will very likely put restrictions on U.S. agricultural products. We cannot complain too vociferously when they restrict our exports if we have just restricted theirs.

CONGRESSMAN FINDLEY: The broad objective of government policy should be to permit countries to produce whatever they can produce most efficiently. One of the problems caused by the sugar act was that it screened out the foreign countries that had a natural advantage in the production of sugar.

Paul Douglas, the late Senator from Illinois, once said we could probably grow bananas on Pikes Peak if the government would support the price of bananas high enough. We can grow enough sugar in this country to supply the entire U.S. requirements, but our policy should be to adjust our agricultural plant to produce the things we can produce best and import the things other countries produce best.

MR. DALY: If I dared, I'd say, "How sweet it is not." [Laughter.]
May we have the next question, please?

ELLEN HAAS, Community Nutrition Institute: Over the past eight years, consumers have learned the hard way that they have a great stake in agriculture and farm policy. Despite Dr. Yeutter's comment that we do not have a food security problem, consumers did learn when prices went skyrocketing that they were in a very insecure position and that there was no safeguard system or food reserve plan.

I would like to know how Congress can address this issue and balance the needs of consumers with those of farmers. Also, what kind of operating rules can be established that would not be a farm depressant, and can we have a grain reserve system written into our legislation this year?

CONGRESSMAN FOLEY: I do not think we will see that enacted. I do not know of anyone who proposes a formal reserve in the sense of a government-held stock purchased by the government.

Under the reserve concept as Dr. Schnittker defined it, we will be encouraging farm storage of grains probably with facilities loans, with some increase in the loan period, and with some incentives, as well as some reverse incentives to release grain under certain circumstances. In that sense, we may well get into a reserve policy.

We do have a great reserve of the basic food grains, wheat and rice. We have the largest stocks in the last fifteen or twenty years in both of those commodities. Some consumers still worry about the possibility of running out of commodities, but that is simply not a concern. The question is, as Dr. Schnittker said, how to manage this existing reserve or a very large carry-over.

CONGRESSMAN FINDLEY: Consumer concern is a real problem, though, because a growing percentage of U.S. citizens live in cities. They really do not understand the importance of agricultural sales abroad. When prices tend to rise, as they did recently, and consumers begin to clamor for export controls, they strike at the heart of the American export economy.

Farm exports are the best earners of foreign exchange. It would be very harmful, not just to farmers but to all citizens, if we were to turn the faucet on and off on export markets. If we do that, a country like Japan—which has to import about 85 percent of its food to survive— will hunt for dependable sources of supply. When they find alternative sources, our markets will dry up. The attitude of consumers should be of vital concern, not because we will run out of food at a reasonable price in this country, but an urban-oriented Congress might do something foolish, something that would hurt the entire country.

DR. YEUTTER: I really believe, Ms. Haas, that the secretary of agriculture has enough tools at his disposal to provide an acceptable level of food price stability for consumers. He could do the things that Congressman Foley outlined without a formalized grain reserve and large holdings of government stocks.

The better route is the one available now, rather than anything beyond it. Consumers are taxpayers, too. Certainly, an almost infinite degree of food price stability can be provided, but there is a cost to that. If we become involved in an extensive grain reserve program, with large government stocks, consumers will have to pay for it with higher taxes. It is in the best interests of consumers to achieve an acceptable level of price stability without incurring inordinate costs.

DR. SCHNITTKER: I am glad we got embargoes and reserves linked, finally, in the same discussion, because they are intimately related. In the last few years embargoes have been the most divisive single action affecting both the farmer and the consumer.

Nobody wants to embargo exports of grain and soybeans, and there would be no need to if we have a well-managed reserve. We came close to disaster on this issue during the presidential campaign in the fall of 1976. Both candidates said that we would never again embargo exports. The next morning, both pulled back and said that embargoes might be necessary in an emergency.

It is possible to talk to farmers about this issue these days without being shot off the platform. The point is that if we do not have any stocks at all, or if we have stocks and let them get away from us too quickly, then an embargo is a possibility. But if we do well with our stocks, we can avoid an embargo.

CONGRESSMAN FOLEY: Consumers tend to feel that when the interests of farmers go up, the interests of consumers go down and vice versa. There is a feeling that because we experienced very stable food prices from the end of World War II until the beginning of the 1970s, this stability should be a consumer right, that everything else might be going up in an inflationary cycle but somehow food is exempt from that. This is an unrealistic expectation.

We would hope to have lower levels of inflation and more stable prices than we have had in the past. Certainly we want nothing like the run-up in 1973 and 1974 to occur again. But consumers buy from the food markets a couple of times a week. There is no psychological insulation of the kind that we have on the purchase of a car, where payments may extend over twenty-four, thirty, or forty-eight months. One cannot really expect food prices to go down or stay the same when every other item of the national economy is going up by 3 to 6 percent.

CONGRESSMAN FINDLEY: For many years the U.S. government, through the Commodity Credit Corporation, a U.S.-owned corporation, was the primary merchandiser of grain. Happily, the government stockpiles have now disappeared. This has been good for all concerned, but it left a private sector that was unaccustomed to doing its own merchandising.

When the price of wheat went up, bakers warned that if we did not stop the export of wheat, there would be no hot dog buns and no birthday cakes. It astonished me that sensible, experienced people in industry could spout such nonsense. Since then, they have begun to use the futures market to provide for their needs, something they had not done before.

Japan and the Soviet Union, which have enormous needs for handling grain, are building additional storage facilities. When the U.S. government got out of the warehousing business, the slack was picked up elsewhere in the world food economy. As a result, it is not likely that the sort of crisis we had a few years ago will be repeated.

DR. YEUTTER: Certainly if the Soviet Union can learn how to use our capitalist economy and our private enterprise methods, our own businessmen ought to be able to do so, too. The government does not have to do everything for everybody in the U.S. society.

As Congressman Findley pointed out, the Soviet Union knows how to use our commodity markets, how to construct storage for additional grain, and how to use our circular sprinkler irrigation units to get more security of supply. They are protecting themselves in the world market in which they now live, and I would hope that we, who are supposedly accustomed to operating in a capitalistic society, will do so too.

RAY BAKER, Organization for Economic Cooperation and Development, Paris: Does the panel feel that a well-managed domestic reserve would enhance or diminish the probability of reaching an international grain reserve agreement?

DR. SCHNITTKER: I think it would definitely enhance it. The United States ought to do everything it can to get other countries, such as Japan, India, and the Soviet Union, to build reserves of their own, but somebody must lead. In recent years the United States has often had this role. If we provide both a reserve and a policy, we would have a better position in international negotiations, and we would encourage the rest of the world.

But we should not act as if we were the only country that has ever built reserves. India will have stored 10 million or perhaps even 15 million tons of grain at the end of the wheat harvest in April or May of 1977. Since it had a good crop last year, the Soviet Union has probably left more grain out on the collective and state farms this year as a kind of reserve. This is a very good time to get the reserve and a world reserve policy.

CONGRESSMAN FINDLEY: It is conceivable that we might have a very poor year, in which the production of food in this country would be short. We would not run out of food, but there might be a short carry-over, short enough to cause deep consumer concern. Generally, there are long-term signals when a development like that occurs. An existing law allows the secretary of agriculture to offer incentives to farmers to store their grain on their own farm. The secretary has considerable latitude when he receives a signal of a short carry-over in corn or beans, or whatever. He has the authority—and if he does not have it, I am ready to vote to give it to him—to take bid contracts from farmers to establish a sufficient reserve, in order to provide an adequate carry-over.

CONGRESSMAN FOLEY: I am not sure how much incentive there is to enter into an international grain agreement. Carry-overs in the United States and Canada, which account for about 70 to 75 percent of the exports of wheat in the world, could reach 2 billion bushels—with about 800 million in Canada and 1.2 billion in the United States. Under such circumstances there is little interest in entering into an international food reserve program, especially one that the importing countries would have to help finance. This is a fact of life. India, the Soviet Union, and some other countries are making strenuous efforts to develop their own stocks. The Soviet Union, for example, has indicated no interest at all in participating in the negotiations of the International Wheat Council.

DR. YEUTTER: Providing leadership in the world is one thing, but doing the job for the rest of the world is another. The rest of the world wants us to do it and pick up the tab. For reasons of food security and price stability, the importing nations have a greater interest in a reserve system than we do. Why should we operate an international grain reserve and provide what in essence is a Marshall Plan for the major importers? The Soviet Union, the countries of Western Europe, and Japan can afford to participate in an international grain reserve. If we have one, we ought to have participation by all major importers, and they ought to share the cost.

So far, these countries have indicated little interest in doing so, and, as Congressman Foley points out, they indicate even less interest as our carry-over levels go up. It has not been the United States that has held up those negotiations. In London we offered to participate in an international grain reserve. But the other countries have shown little enthusiasm for sharing.

DR. SCHNITTKER: Dr. Yeutter asked for reasons for a U.S. initiative in grain reserves. There are several very good ones: one, to do something about the grain reserve; two, to preserve our position in world export markets when crops are short, and earn foreign exchange; three, to have food for the food assistance programs when we need it; and four, to achieve domestic price stability.

These are all good reasons for a U.S. initiative. But the most important point is that it is not a question of having a reserve or not having one—it is here, and we need some kind of a procedure for managing it, or it will be dumped on the market, to the farmer's disadvantage, the first time the price rises a few cents.

DR. YEUTTER: I agree with all of that as a basic premise, but I would add that we should not give away the store. If we become involved in a formalized arrangement, it should be negotiated and not done unilaterally.

If we unilaterally establish the mechanism, there will be no international grain reserve. Representatives of other countries have told me that they will not participate. Why should they if we will do the job for them?

U.S. FARM POLICY: WHAT DIRECTION?

CONGRESSMAN FOLEY: We all agree that we do have a kind of reserve already in place, which has been built up in the large carry-over stocks. We all agree that if we enter into an international agreement, it ought to be one in which our importing colleagues participate.

GOODY SOLOMON, *Washington Star*: Dr. Schnittker, in your initial remarks, you said that one reason a one-year extension of current legislation was preferable to brand new legislation is that current proposals resemble those of the 1940s and 1950s, which gave the money mainly to big farmers. Would you please elaborate on that?

DR. SCHNITTKER: I referred to the proposals for high price supports and high target prices or federal payments. Since most corn, wheat, and cotton is produced on rather large farms, albeit family farms, most subsidy money or loan money would go to those large farmers. This is an unnecessary and bad policy, particularly because it would take money from other programs in a fixed budgetary situation.

CONGRESSMAN FINDLEY: The question is, Will the climate be any better in a year than it is today? I would like to see a five-year extension of the Agriculture Act of 1973, with a little remodeling on the food stamp program, but mainly leaving the commodity programs alone. Perhaps in the next twelve months we can make some educational effort, but I am not optimistic.

CONGRESSMAN FOLEY: Without trying to identify what a good or bad bill is, I think all of us would favor the extension of a good bill for more than one year. If we had a bill with some serious defects, it might, ironically, be more trouble if it lasted only a year because the House of Representatives is not usually at its finest shortly before an election. There is a danger that the worst features of a bad bill might be exacerbated in an election year.

MR. DALY: This concludes another public policy forum presented by the American Enterprise Institute for Public Policy Research. On behalf of AEI, our heartfelt thanks to the distinguished panelists, Dr. Schnittker, Congressman Foley, Congressman Findley, and Dr. Yeutter and, also, to our guests and experts in the audience for their participation.